I Walked with Heroes

GENERAL

CARLOS P. ROMULO

I Walked with Heroes

ILLUSTRATED WITH PHOTOGRAPHS

HOLT, RINEHART AND WINSTON

NEW YORK

87558–0111
Printed in the United States of America

For my grandchildren

CARLOS III
MIGUEL ANTONIO
VIRGINIA CARIDAD
RODRIGO LUIS
ALESSANDRIA TERESA

and all children—this book is
written with hopes of the time to
come, when no child shall lie down
in terror or waken to hunger, but
shall know himself as a being of
unique value in a safer and
kindlier world.

Acknowledgment

IT HAS been said that a man's life may be divided into four chapters: creation, realization, appreciation, and recollection. He begins by creating; what he creates becomes a reality. The reality is either appreciated or not; then comes the perspective of years, he looks back at his yesterdays—reminiscence, recollection.

I am grateful to Beth Day, of the *Reader's Digest*, who first suggested the idea of my writing these memoirs; and to Harry Shaw, formerly Editor in Chief of Henry Holt & Company, Inc., who came to me and urged me to begin indulging in recollection and to set my reminiscences in print. He wrote me several letters before I even started to consider the idea, and after two meetings with him at the Waldorf's Peacock Alley such was his persuasive power I finally gave in and consented to broach the subject to my literary agent, Harold Matson.

A word about Hal Matson: After eighteen years of close association with him I can say that as an author I have consistently followed his suggestions because I have found them unerringly sound. I have placed every worthwhile manuscript I have written in his hands and his judgment I never questioned and he has always been proved right. There are many honest men in our world, but none I would trust as blindly as I trust Hal.

I should have started with Evelyn Wells, than whom I never had a more loyal or devoted friend. I first met her in San Francisco in 1942, when I landed in that city from Bataan and was indeed a lost soul. Since then she has been my editorial guide, adviser, and able

I

and patient collaborator; she has stood by me all these years of my writing career as no single individual has, and I want to make of record my profound and abiding gratitude to her for all that she has given me, especially for her friendship that I will treasure always. Because of my heavy daily schedule these memoirs would never have seen the light of day had it not been for her constant urging, her encouragement and inspiration. When I say I walked with heroes I should add that I also worked with a heroine, a heroine in abnegation and selflessness, my dear friend Evelyn.

I count myself fortunate that in the publication of these memoirs I had a patient and understanding editor, Beulah Harris, whose competence won my admiration, and I want to make of record also my sincere appreciation for her valuable coöperation.

Miss Iluminada Panlilio, my tireless and efficient secretary, spent her entire summer vacation typing my manuscript; Mrs. Milagros Valderrama assisted her; Mr. Manuel A. Viray checked my historical data; my former secretaries Misses Helen M. Rumple, Marjorie da Costa, Marjorie Cooke, and particularly Anne Dragon, who had attended with me many international conferences, had kept a complete file of my correspondence and records from which I drew extensively for my facts. To each and every one of them my sincere thanks.

—C.P.R.

I Walked with Heroes

One

OTHER lives may find their happiest moments infiltrated with tragedy, and their proudest touched with comedy. This has almost invariably been true of mine. My proudest hour found me, the newly elected president of the United Nations, perched atop three thick New York City telephone books given me in lieu of a cushion that I might see and be seen by the delegates below the podium.

A small man from a small country had been awarded the privilege of speaking for his country in the world's highest court—the first Asian to be given that honor. "The barefoot boy of diplomacy" had come a long way from the quiet provincial town of Camiling.

Camiling lies in the hilly farm section of the province of Tarlac on the island of Luzon. When my wife and I take our grandchildren there they are puzzled by the smallness of my birthplace. "Why are there no tall buildings?" they ask me. "Why are the houses only one story high? Where are the sidewalks and why are the roads full of dust?"

Then I try to explain how Camiling has changed since I was a little boy. It has grown, its population now is thirty thousand, and it has a modern market and a motion picture theater on the Plaza. The church has been remodeled, but the old convent and the brick building where I started public school still face on that pretty little park, and it is much the same as it was on that day, almost sixty years ago, when I found Clemente hanging there.

In those days of our lost innocence, mine and Camiling's, there wasn't a bathtub or a telephone or a piece of machinery in our town. Now as I look up, always nervously, when a jet plane darts over the hills I realize how we have changed since this century began—myself, my town, and my world.

It has been said each man lives many lives. The oddity of mine is in their complete diversity. Each might have been lived in a different country and a different age. Not one emerged from another or resembles another.

Each time the change has come with shocking swiftness and as a complete surprise. Not once did I ask for it, nor was I prepared in any way.

Why these many changes—to me? And how did they come about? To understand, I must think my way back through these differing lives.

Again and again I have reached what seemed to be the point of no return. At each new start I resolved to do my best. Each time, just as I reached the plateau of achievement in my new role, the world would whirl under my feet and I would find myself adjusting to a new career and a new point of view.

In reviewing these shifts in fortune I am struck by the fact that I entered each new career thinking it would be my life's work and determined to make it a success, and each time I was just on the mark of achieving that success when the lightning struck.

For example, I was happy when I was a student, looking forward to a teaching career. I satisfied that ambition while still very young. I taught English at the University of the Philippines, was made head of the English Department, and later I was elected to the Board of Regents. I looked forward to a long, useful, and uneventful life as an educator, and to a ripe and revered old age as friend and guide to the young.

So what happened? I found myself a crusading editor and up to my neck in Philippine politics.

As a newspaperman I determined to be the best I could possibly be. I worked incredible hours. I became editor in chief of a newspaper chain. I had security, and the power and excitement only a newspaper top executive can know. All this I threw over to follow the political hazards cast by our great leader, Manuel L. Quezon.

Slowly I rebuilt my way to the command of another chain of newspapers. Reporter as well as publisher, I won the award that is every newspaperman's dream, the Pulitzer prize.

In my career and my personal life I was a happy man.

Manila held all I loved—my wife and four sons and our beautiful home, where we entertained friends from all over the world.

Pearl Harbor shattered the idyl. My family vanished behind the battle lines and for years I would not know if they were living or dead.

All I loved, all I had accomplished were gone. The Philippines was the captive of Japan. I was homeless, my family and my fortune lost.

I always say I did not enter the war; I was tossed in. One day I was a peaceful publisher and the next I was the most unmilitary soldier ever to don a United States uniform, made for him overnight.

The end of World War II found me a general, entitled to wear all the Philippine and American decorations the military authorities had seen fit to give me. Meantime I had turned lecturer, and crisscrossed the United States on speaking tours in an effort to bring the Filipino point of view to the American people.

There was the return at MacArthur's side to the Philippines, the almost incredible miracle of finding my family, and the pressing need, once the excitement was over, of starting the long way up again.

The Philippines and I were both nearing the half-century mark. My country was looking forward to the freedom for which we had fought and prayed for half a century. I could not afford freedom. I had, thank God, a family in need of my support.

As usual I was given no time to ponder this problem. As if by magic I was transformed into a diplomat.

Always I had regarded myself as one of the most forthright and undiplomatic of men. Many times I have heard myself wail, "Now what have I done?" when summoned before some august tribunal. Usually I had been brash enough to tell the truth when silence was wanted.

I was totally ignorant of the intricate art of diplomacy on any level. Nevertheless I was made Philippine Resident Commissioner, then Ambassador, and sent as the head of the Philippine delegation to the founding of the United Nations at San Francisco.

Four years later I was elected president of the General Assembly.

Those close to me know the reason for my pride in that honor. In speaking for the Philippines I was speaking also for all the other small nations that had been for so many centuries voiceless.

Like all my other careers this came to me with unexpected swiftness. Looking back I can see that the branches of my life were not so far apart from one another as they seemed. I did not change my identity when I left an old career for the new.

Together they form a pattern. Each experience stayed with me, growth over growth, to form the protective armor I wear today.

The mind and heart waste nothing. Each phase of life contributes to the whole man.

Under the layers of armor I am what I was in my earliest days, with all the flaws and weaknesses and ideals peculiar to man. If certain emotions seem stronger in me than in the average man it is because I have not lived an average life. Within, I tremble against injustice and with a passion for freedom. I felt those emotions first as a very young child. They have never left me. For freedom, for myself or others, I have always been willing to fight, and at times to die.

Call this egotism if you will, but it is every man's right to be subservient to no other man. In me the will toward freedom has prevailed over all the other emotions I have experienced to their fullest, having been son and lover, husband and father and grandfather, provider of security for those I love, and their defender in a threatening world.

It is not of the outer adventures of my many lifetimes I write now. I have told of them in other books. Instead, I hope to reveal the man who survives under the layers of armor and the changes that have shaped him while shaping his world. I have never written of this man before and no one knows all of him, not even I.

But I shall try to be honest about this curious, complex fellow, who is still student and teacher and soldier, reporter and editor and writer, and, lastly diplomat. And who, despite these many changes, remains in part the child Carlos, who was born just before this century began in the town of Camiling.

How could I fail to know change, born as I was at the start of this century, which in the long tomorrow may prove to be the most terrifying, revolutionary, and yet hopeful, of all the world's centuries?

Revolution, flaring up in France and America, had fired the Philippines with the determination to break free of Spain. I was born just as my country achieved that freedom, so in a sense I may say the Philippines and I have grown up together.

Our forces under Aguinaldo won their final victory and proclaimed the Philippines a free and independent republic in Malolos, Bulacan, on January 23, 1899, nine days after I was born. That republic lasted but ten days, and almost half a century would roll by before the Republic of the Philippines was reborn.

But for the first ten days of my life I was a free citizen in an independent country, and I like to remember that. Much of my adult life would be spent in the fight to regain that lost freedom. During that time we grew up, my country and I.

Despite war and threats of annihilation the Republic of the Philippines is on the map, and so, to my constant surprise, am I.

This then is the story of a man and his world.

It is the story of a nation many times reborn and of its people, who led by their heroes have had to fight their way into the realm of human dignity.

In the 1940's wherever I lectured in the United States Americans came by thousands to hear a Filipino—a man from the Orient—tell of the fight for democracy being waged in the Philippines. To me this history of the Philippines is the history of our new world, for the struggle is not confined to the Philippines; the whole world is massed together in a surge toward individual freedom. This movement, which has been gathering force over the first half of this century, owes much of its impetus to the Philippines.

Three years before I was born our greatest revolutionary leader, José Rizal, was executed by the Spanish for planting ideas in the Filipino mind that later were to arouse our people to fight for freedom. His murder fired the Islands with greater ardor, and open revolution began when a new leader, Andres Bonifacio, led the first action against Spain at the village of Balintawak, Bulacan province. That shrine with its monument, "The Cry of Balintawak," corresponds in the Philippines to America's Concord bridge.

My grandfather, father, and uncles took part in that revolution. My oldest brother remembers that during those war years Spanish friars disguised as servants lived with us. The friars must have felt at home in our casa with its many religious oil paintings brought to the Philippines by our Spanish ancestors. I knew nothing of all this, for I made my appearance on the scene as the fighting with Spain ended.

But my country's troubles were not over.

The Philippines was a very small mouse trapped between two

great lions. A shrinking Spain was fighting to the death to hold our islands. One year before, America had declared war against Spain. While the Filipinos fought, America flexed her muscles and watched with profound interest the struggle in the Pacific.

For an understanding of the way we won our freedom I recommend the reading of Margaret Leech's prize-winning biography, *In the Days of McKinley*.

All too often a fluke can make or unmake history. By chance, as the last Spanish forces capitulated on Luzon, Admiral Dewey was stationed with his fleet at Hong Kong, off China's coast only seven hundred miles away.

So it was that on the night of February 4, 1899, ten days after the Philippines had proclaimed itself a free nation, bands of war-weary Filipino soldiers found themselves fighting a new enemy outside Manila's historic walls.

The new enemy was America.

American soldiers, better equipped, trained, and fed, fresh in the field and spoiling for action, swung into the combat the Filipinos thought had ended. By morning it was over. The Americans had won. That day Emilio Aguinaldo issued a declaration of war against the United States.

The United States hastily ratified its treaty with Spain and rushed shiploads of soldiers to the Philippines.

The exhausted Filipinos fought on, taking to the hills and guerrilla warfare. Among the fighters in the hills around Camiling was my father. My first memories of him are of his secret visits to our home by night for clean clothing and food.

The protest ended in the spring of 1901, when Aguinaldo was captured by Brigadier General Frederick Funston, by trickery, we were told. The year 1902 brought final surrender.

Although there had been years of fighting and but ten days of independence, yet those ten days had seen the birth of the Filipino dream of freedom that would never die.

When final surrender came I was only three years old, but

already there were implanted in my small impressionable soul
the beginnings of a rebel.

The guns of war reverberated in our hills, but Camiling itself
was a peaceful town, quiet, off the beaten track, surrounded by
rice fields planted in rows, tier on tier against the skyline.

The houses were mostly nipa huts, with here and there a two-
story balconied casa. Our house was the Spanish type and so
was my grandfather's across the street. The two houses were
about four blocks from the Plaza, which was the center of the
town. They were alike except that ours was larger, for our
family was growing. They were soundly built of brick, with
tile roofs and long balconies, and within, the high-ceilinged
rooms were lined with Philippine hardwood. Their large windows gave a sense of airiness, coolness, comfort, and elegance,
so welcome in a tropical climate, and I was sorry when some
years ago my brother had our old home torn down and replaced
with a modern split-level farmhouse. Nothing can ever excel
the comfort and dignity of those old Spanish casas.

The furnishings had been brought to the Islands centuries before by my mother's people on the Spanish galleons that came
once a year to the Philippines and returned to Spain by way of
California and Mexico. The dark, carved, richly polished furniture—armchairs and consoles and tables—had also come from
the Old World. The crystal chandelier and the family altar with
its tall image of the Virgin holding her Son were from Spain.
So were most of the oil paintings, dark and old and as richly
colored as church windows. Some were family portraits, but
most of them were religious. My favorite was the large repro-
duction of "The Last Supper" that hung in our dining room.

Many of these valued family possessions were in my home in
Manila and were lost when that home was destroyed by the
Japanese.

Our house and grandfather's had lovely gardens. Ours went
all around the house, but my thrifty grandparents planted orna-

mental shrubs and trees only before their house, for in the rear were the big sheet-iron *camarins* where rice and corn were stored against an advance in price. Around the *camarins* my grandparents had planted fruit-bearing trees.

I was brought up to respect the land. We were not rich but we were comfortably well-off, and I learned early that all we had came to us from the land. Our tenants worked the family farms by the *kasama* (share) system, giving back part of the produce to the owners in old Spanish style.

Camiling was a typical Filipino town, with an overlay of the Orient, and its people were modest, sweet-tempered, and dignified whether rich or poor. Spanish was spoken along with our several dialects—Pangasinan, Ilocano, Tagalog, and Pampango.

In our home, by speech, manner, religion, and heritage, we were Malay and Spanish; in the home of my grandparents the heritage was pure Malayan. Also from my mother's side came the old family names we would in turn give our children: Peña, Sison, Cabrera.

We were an affectionate family, and our grandparents' home was like an extension of our own. Also close to our lives were the aunts and uncles and their families, who lived in other homes scattered about Camiling. There would be times as I grew that our town seemed like one large family group, for everyone seemed related to me in some fashion. I knew everyone, and everyone was kind to a small, trusting boy.

Priests from the church, nuns from the convent, shopkeepers, farmers in from the hills, all were my friends. The closer circle of intimacy was formed by parents and grandparents, sisters and brothers, cousins and uncles and aunts.

The world would expand as I grew and my own importance would lessen in my mind with the years, but I have never lost the sense of security that came of being the petted and privileged small member of a large, affectionate family group. Around us was the exciting life of Camiling, beyond, the unexplored and waiting world, and over us all was God.

Under such circumstances a small boy with a healthy amount of self-pride could know himself to be the exact center of his universe. Children know their importance and it is their right. To cut down any of their self-esteem is a crime against God.

I was fortunate. Among my most valued attributes is the capacity for happiness. I can marvel now that this quality developed during a time when all the older people around me were oppressed by fear. Under the stress of revolution, the constant threat of torture or death, our elders never permitted the children to suspect that all might not be well. Although I was aware that my father was in danger, at the same time I was conscious of the security of the family circle and Camiling, and that watching over us always was the familiar, mysterious, frightening but trustworthy presence of God.

God knew everybody, saw all we did, and my infantile mind held Him in awe. I knew exactly the way He looked, and He bore a distinct resemblance to my grandfather.

I remember little of Don Alberto Romulo, for he died when I was still young, but I recall a presence of great kindliness and dignity, which for some reason inspired in me a similar feeling of awe. I had no such reservations toward my father, who in appearance and manner was very like my grandfather. Both were typically Malayan in appearance, and father and son shared a dominant trait of gentle, almost knightly, courtesy.

But my father, Gregorio Romulo, had none of his father's severity. Father was good-natured, had a wide streak of fun, and knew how to play with children. At times he played with me as if he were himself a child, but then he would be serious and talk to me in older terms; still I would understand. I never had reason to fear him, but because I loved and respected him his word was law.

Toward my mother, Maria Peña Romulo, he was loving and respectful; she was the same toward him. The courtesy they showed each other was reflected in our family life. Love and formality ruled our home, and one did no harm to the other. In the intimacy of home we might relax in every way except respect.

In Spanish the familiar "you" is *tu*, the formal, *Usted*. Brothers, sisters, and servants, and a spouse, can be addressed by the informal *tu*. I used the formal address when I spoke to my father or mother, grandparents and godparents, uncles and aunts and older cousins, and even my older sister, Lourdes. I used the polite phrases that lend courtesy to Spanish and Filipino life, and when I left the house or returned to it I kissed the hands of my father and mother and any older person who chanced to be there. Returning from play, studies, or Mass I paid them this small honor gladly, because it showed my love.

In our home Spanish and Oriental traditions were combined, and both respect parental authority and age. Parents keep their position of authority in the home not through fear but through respect.

I believe it is a good thing to respect older people. My sons in many ways have been Americanized, educated in the United States, but in the home they still address their mother and me as *Usted*.

My grandsons, for reasons of their own, call me Captain Hook!

I have been lenient with my children, but there were certain ironclad rules, and one of these was respect for parental authority. There has been no need to emphasize this, for the rule was based on love. I do not think it did me any harm, nor has it harmed my sons. Each in turn grew into men I respect as well as love; each does his best, and the family as a group is of primary importance to all of them.

I make no pretense of knowing child psychology. I have always loved children, starting with my small brothers and sisters as they entered my life. But I believe that a child who has love and respect for his family and recognizes the over-all authority of God is a happy child, and a happy child makes a successful adult.

There are doubtless other systems, but I was content with this one, and my sons, in their turn, have never complained.

For my own father I had intense admiration. He was always handsomely groomed; his mustache, white as I remember it, was carefully trimmed, and even in the hottest weather, when other men wore only a white *camisa* or shirt, he wore not only his coat, but a vest, and carried a cane. Despite his great dignity he was rapid in speech and movement, characteristics I inherited from him.

He was openly affectionate, and when deeply moved, he would weep. It annoyed him that he could not hide his emotions, and he greatly admired my mother for her ability to control even her tears. Once when I was older he said to me: "There is this difference between the civilized man and the uncivilized: the cultured man can always control his emotions. Emotions are for private use."

He was not being fair to himself. He was cultured and the most civilized man I have ever known. And when grief came and we would see his tears, we loved him the more for them.

Our mother's emotions ran as deeply as his, but she covered hers with a dignity that at times seemed like coldness, although her family knew better. In temperament she was a complete reversal of what is considered "Spanish." The Filipinos are as a rule as emotional as the Latins, and my Malayan father was no exception to his race.

There was never any doubt in our home as to the real source of family authority. My mother ruled us with a velvet scepter. Small and soft-spoken, she reigned with the discipline of love. She had been a beauty when she was young, and she carried the authority of beauty until she was very old.

After MacArthur returned to the Philippines and I had been sent back to the United States to make my report to Congress on conditions in Manila, American soldiers liberated Camiling. Frank Hewlitt, interviewing my mother for the United Press, described her as a small woman, widowed, and "with the dignity of a Spanish queen."

I read that interview in Washington, and I realized that I had never seen her behave in a manner unworthy of a queen.

One of my favorite childhood memories of her is of the day our house caught on fire. Mother calmly called her six children about her, ushered her brood out of the house as sedately as if we were going to church, and stood us in line in the middle of the street. She counted us quickly, "One-two-three-four-five-six," warned us not to move, went calmly back into the burning house, and came out carrying boxes containing family documents. Putting these down beside us, she made a brisk recount, "One-two-three-four-five-six," warned us again not to stir, returned into the house, and came back with more valued possessions. She did this again and again until the fire was out, and each time she counted us in line like an army on parade.

We thought it typical of Mother's foresight and efficiency that she had the six of us divided equally as to sexes, a boy and a girl, a boy and a girl, a boy and a girl. In that way all had partners and nobody felt left out. With such a neat arrangement there could be no sibling rivalry. We played no favorites in our home and, looking back, I can find no instance of my favoring one brother or sister more than another. If I spent more time with Lourdes it was because she was closest to me in interests and years.

My mother dressed us alike according to sexes: the girls in short gingham frocks for every day and ruffled white for church, and the boys in tight short pants, white ruffled shirts, and small caps. All over America and in England small boys dressed like that as this century was beginning.

Whatever we did, we did as a group. The six of us left the house and returned to it together. We played, went on picnics on the banks of the Camiling River near our home, and visited relatives, always together. We started grammar school in closely knit relays. We six grew up together. We still find time to come together, and thank God for the privilege.

How lucky we are that there has been no break in our circle. Adult living enforced separate ways, but I believe my brothers and sisters and I are successful because we have all had happy personal lives, and in my mind that is the highest success. Before family content all other honors are as dust.

My oldest brother, Enrique, is a physician.

My sister Lourdes, the second child, married Carlos Kipping, son of an English engineer who helped lay down the tracks of the Manila-Dagupan railroad.

I am next in line, and have no quarrel with the life that has been mine.

My sister Soledad married a Justice of the Supreme Court, Cesar Bengzon.

Gilberto, like myself, became a teacher. He has a private school in Camiling and is the manager of the government's Charity Sweepstakes.

Josefina, the baby of the family, married Alfredo Eugenio, an engineer who did such good work before the war as Civil Defense Administrator of the Philippines.

We have, all six of us, led fairly well-balanced lives. The tragedies we have known have been the inevitable results of illness, death, or war. We have carried no inner grievances. The happiness we knew as children has remained steadfast, and in my mind it is owed, along with such content as we have achieved, to the affectionate, protective Catholic home in which we were allowed to stretch our expanding personalities to their fullest, but never to the extent of crowding another personality. Our parents drew for us a firm line in respect to our dignity and that of others, and the training would serve us well when we took our places in the outer world.

TWO

MY FORMAL education began while Camiling was still taking an active part in the protest against America. I could not have been more than three years old when my elders decided it was time I learned the alphabet.

The school I attended was the most exclusive in the town—I was the only pupil. Classes were held across the street in my grandmother's home, and she was both faculty and principal.

Young as I was, I had firm opinions concerning my natural rights. It seemed an infraction of liberty to be forced to study inside while the other children played out-of-doors. My older brother had suffered this course and was in public school. Sometimes my sister Lourdes accompanied me, but most of the time I went my laggard way alone.

At ten every morning I was forced from my home and across the street, urged on by cries from both houses. I made the crossing last as long as I dared. Scowling, I would enter the big cool room where my Grandmother was waiting, erect and formidable in a straight-backed Spanish chair. Doña Juana Besacruz Romulo was dignified and charming, and I dearly loved her. But how I hated those implements of torture: the "infant" books in Spanish, the pencils, and slate. In one hand she held like a scepter a long-handled, ivory back-scratcher such as all the Chinese stores sold in those days. I dreaded it! If I forgot and let my thoughts wander to the cries of play coming through the windows, down that scratcher snapped on my tender knuckles with the sting of a red ant.

But I knew how loving she could be when I tried to do well, and how precious was her praise!

19

Learning was easy for me, and I enjoyed my lessons when I could close my mind to the fun going on outside. I began my ABC's in Spanish at Grandmother's knee. When I recited without an error she was pleased and praised me in her soft, limpid Pangasinan. Sometimes my grandfather would stand in the doorway, looking tall and very old, and he also would show his pleasure that little Carlos was showing such aptitude for learning.

But my mind wandered from the letters and my body ached to be free. I was not amenable to routine and never would be. Later I would learn to submit to it because it saved time and trouble in the end, but that was a lesson I had not learned at the age of three.

With each morning that trip to Grandmother's became more undesirable. My bare toes clung to the warm velvety dust. I was Shakespeare's schoolboy, creeping at snail's pace, my eyes seeking any loophole that might offer a chance to escape.

I found it one morning when Grandmother's attention was distracted by men carrying farm produce into the sheet-iron *camarins*. The door of one of the storehouses stood open while the sacks of rice were carried inside. By keeping well to leeward of the workers I was able to dart unseen through that door.

It was dim and hot and dusty within. I hid behind the piled sacks of sweet-smelling grain and did my best not to sneeze. Then someone closed the door and I knew I was safe. I was also hot and dusty. But free.

The hours went by and the noonday sun beating down on the tin roof made the *camarin* almost unbearable. My throat was dry with thirst and dust and I had never been so miserable. I was also very happy.

Why did freedom, even in hiding, mean so much to me?

I could hear my name being called, the sound circling round the house and then the orchard. I snuggled deeper into my dusty lair.

Of course I was discovered after a few hours and dragged

out in disgrace, but I was still pleased with the disturbance I had caused and the missed hours of study.

After that I took to hiding in the orchard until the *camarin* was opened and then slipping inside. When that was discovered, orders were issued that anyone opening the *camarin* must stand guard at the door until it was safely locked again. From my hiding place in the orchard I could hear the men warning one another, "Watch out for little Carlos. Don't let him slip past!"

I found other hiding places. My favorite tree was a guava behind Grandmother's house. Its thick, leafy branches made of it a great green tent, much cooler and nicer than the sheds. Its branches spread into wonderful nesting places, and best of all they were heavy with ripe guavas, which were and are still one of my favorite fruits. Now I could rest in comfort and no longer suffer hunger or thirst.

This too was discovered, and each time I disappeared I would hear the summons, "Search the orchard!" I had to give up hiding in the tree.

All the ingenuity of an inventive child was taxed in finding my next hiding place. Behind the house, as with most of the houses in Camiling, was the open well. The large wooden bucket was lowered into this by a bamboo pole. I discovered I could use the bucket as a seat and lower myself into the well by sliding down the bamboo pole, hand over hand. It was dark and cold and earthy down there and certainly not comfortable, but I was charmed with my discovery, for who would think of looking for a child down a well! The sound of my name being called overhead made fine reverberations in my damp cave.

"Carlos! Carlitos! We know where you are!"

But they didn't know, and I had outwitted the grownups and was pleased with myself.

But the adult world was too clever for me. Soon a servant came to the well for water and I was hauled up like a damp kitten and delivered, unrepentant, into my grandmother's hands. Doña Juana had a grandson with a will as stubborn as her own.

After that, they no longer set guards over my hiding places; they watched me.

So, reluctantly, alternating with whacks from the ivory scratcher, I worked my way through the Spanish ABC's, the *Cartilla* (primer), and the *Caton* (maxims). And when I had done well my good grandmother taught me my infant prayers and the rudiments of our religion in the form of stories of the saints. She also told me the history and legends and folklore of the Philippines and its people—all in Spanish.

Dear Bae (our pet name for her). If I were a fairy godfather and could grant a wish to every child in the world I would wish for each one such a grandmother as mine. I believe in grandmothers for children. The part mine played in helping to shape my life is beyond calculation. I owe her much, and most of all for her enduring patience with one who must at times have been a most exasperating little boy.

I wish now I had listened with greater care and remembered more of all she told me, for in a wonderful way she wove the history of our family into the tapestry of the Philippines.

Actually, comparatively little is known about the origin of the Filipino race, but later, when I studied the anthropological and historical background of my country, I was amazed to remember how much my grandmother had known and how closely her stories, told to a child, adhered to history.

I was not a good listener. I wanted to be out and away. But much that she said stuck in my memory and is with me still. For she was relating to me the origin of that curious small rebel, myself, and history as it relates to his own being can be fascinating even to a very small child.

The Philippines, like the United States, is made up of many kinds of people. The Filipino is a curious creature, a conglomeration of many races and cultures. In direct descent he is the civilized product of the Malayan race.

My grandmother could not tell me from whence her Malayan ancestors came—and neither do the historians know the origin of these sea adventurers who arrived in the Philippines centuries before Christ was born—but she had heard they came from some island far away off the coast of Asia and that they crossed the always savage waters of the China Seas in paraos, small hand-carved boats.

I was impressed by this story. How brave those long-ago relatives had been to cross the unknown waters and start a new race in a strange country!

They were a cultured people, the Malayans, as civilized as any people living at that period in the world. Some were weavers of cloth, others skilled in the making of articles of glass and iron. Many were farmers and planted the rice that would become the basis of the Philippine economy.

But they were not the first people to occupy our seven thousand islands, any more than the Pilgrim Fathers were the first to live in America. Long before the Malayans came and long before recorded history, so my grandmother told me, the Negritos—who are our Philippine aborigines as the Indians are those of America—came to our islands from someplace, my grandmother believed, in Asia.

Anthropologists have found Neolithic implements in our islands, and the Negritos are believed to be the descendants of these early citizens of the Stone Age who may have found their way into the Philippines two million years ago.

Following the Malayan, other cultures filtered into our Islands.

Oriental unity is an historic fact. In the eighth or twelfth century there was the Srivijaya-Vishayan Empire, which is considered the earliest Malay state of considerable extent. Centered in Sumatra, it embraced Siam, Burma, the southern Peninsula, Borneo, western Java, Ceylon, the Moluccas, and the Philippines. This empire gave way in the thirteenth and fourteenth centuries to a greater one, centered in Java, called the Madjapahit Empire, which, by the end of the fourteenth century, had extended its influence over the whole territory of

Malaysia, including Sumatra and New Guinea. Both of these empires at times extended their influence as far north as the island of Formosa.

At some time during this period a direct tie existed with ancient India. Our native dialects contain many Sanskrit words, the beginnings of Aryan infiltration. I understand there are also traces of Sanskrit in the speech of certain modern American Indian tribes.

Our authentic records begin in the tenth century, when Chinese traders, sailing along our coasts, kept business records of their trading transactions with the Malays, which are still preserved in China. Records were also kept by Arab and Indian traders who made voyages to the Philippines about this time.

But even before this there is evidence of a definite infiltration of early Christianity!

A strong infusion of Hindu and Javanese blood followed, and in the fifteenth century Islam was introduced to the Malayans. There are still many believers in Mohammed in our islands.

The most important of these early centuries, to the Philippines and to me, was the sixteenth, for it was at this time, my grandmother told me, that our own family history began.

My ancestors were members of the civilized Malayan group found in the island of Mactan by the Spanish explorer Magellan when he landed there in 1521 carrying the cross. He fought a duel with swords with Lapulapu, the Malayan chief, and lost, and is buried on the island.

But before dying Magellan had introduced into the Philippines the Spanish blood, culture, and religion that were to play such a strong part in the future of the Filipino people. And it was the Spanish who named the Moslems, who had grouped together mainly on the Island of Mindanao, "the Moros (Moors)."

The early Spanish brought groups of religious orders from the Old World. Augustinians, Dominicans, Jesuits, and Fran-

ciscans crossed two oceans to bring the Christian faith to the
many-islanded country discovered by Magellan.

Then, as now, the Filipinos were gentle, friendly, and eager
to learn. Spanish speech infiltrated into the many dialects. Spanish blood mingled with blood from the Orient. Filipinos became proud of their Spanish blood, without relinquishing an
iota of their pride in the Malayan.

My grandmother had no Spanish blood, but she made me
proudly aware of the Spanish blood I had inherited from my
mother's side. And somewhere far back, she told me, Grandmother had a Chinese ancestor.

Is it a distorted childhood memory that I believe this ancestor
to have been Limahong, the great Chinese adventurer who har-
ried our coasts in the sixteenth century and was known as "The
Pirate"?

Piracy is a matter of whose privacy is molested. If Limahong
had been Spanish he would doubtless have been known as "the
Conqueror" and Hispanic history would have revered him.

At any rate, he was the leader of the Chinese adventurers who
in 1574 beached their small ships—which had both oars and
sails—in Lingayen Gulf (where four centuries later the Fil-
American forces would fight their delaying action against the
Japanese) and attacked the city of Manila, which had been
founded by the Spanish only three years before.

They failed to take the city, but Limahong and his crews of
Chinese Vikings did not return to Cathay. They settled along
the Lingayen Gulf and married into Malayan families, and
among them was perhaps the unknown forefather of my grandmother. Pirate or no, he was one of my earliest heroes.

By 1600 the Spanish held nearly all our islands. They had become our teachers, our religious instructors, and our conquerors. Some were our ancestors.

Meantime, in this same sixteenth century, a great deal more
was happening. The Island of Luzon had been Christianized,
whereupon groups of Moslems from the island of Mindanao

turned to piracy and made flying raids on our island. They were making surprise attacks on Manila as late as 1837.

Civilization brought the Philippines enemies from every side. Portugal was challenging Spain's hold on the archipelago. England realized a rich prize had escaped her hands. Sir Francis Drake and Thomas Cavendish—heroes in England, pirates to us—prowled and attacked our coastal towns, causing reproving shakes of the royal crown in Madrid. In 1762 a British expedition made a sneak attack on Manila and captured it.

"Did they keep it?" I asked, worried, for my childish sympathies were far more Spanish than British even though my father had only recently been involved in our revolt against Spain.

But my grandmother told me, no, Manila had been returned to Spain within two years following the terms of the Treaty of Paris.

And after that, she told me, in her beautiful, musical Pangasinan, there had been peace in the Philippines until the very end of the nineteenth century, when the Americans came.

That was where I came in. I knew about the Americans and my father's part in the fight against them. In the Spanish prayers taught me by my grandmother I had prayed that his life be spared and the hated Americans driven out of Camiling.

That was the only unwelcome chapter in the dramatic story of my country as told me by my grandmother, as I, only half-listening, half-remembering, realized the history of our country was also in a way the story of myself.

What a curious pattern was my ancestry in that foggy past. Later I would try to untangle the many races and rovings, the ambitions and explorations and greed and wars, the cultures and the religions that had merged in one small boy in the Luzon hinterlands. In my veins was the blood of the dedicated and the venturesome, the pious and those borne to these islands by greed. Malayan and Spanish, Aryan and Oriental, and far back

—and my secret favorite—that swashbuckling Chinese pirate.

When I learned to study maps I would look from the Philippines to east and west, south and north, and know the world had swept in from all sides to merge in the Philippines. We were the meeting place, the melting pot of the nations, the bridge upon which rested the four corners of that world.

It was lodged early in my childish mind that the Philippines stood in the exact center of the world, and the thought placed a strange burden on me. I was a Filipino—heir to a multicolored, glowing past. The memory of that background must never be permitted to tarnish. A Filipino was in a position of trust. He had to hold his head high and always show his best side to the world.

Somehow my grandmother drummed that point of view into my wondering mind. She made me aware of my value, not as her grandson and the child of my parents, but as a Filipino, the last word in a tremendous saga. The long adventuring and striving must not be wasted.

So along with my daily prayer that my country be set free I asked to be worthy of my country and its heroes.

It was somewhere in this early stage of my life that I learned that this respect for the Filipino per se was not shared by all people. I don't know how I found that out, but I have a long adhesive memory. As I grew older I found I could memorize an entire chapter after one reading, and I often reported complete speeches without jotting down a note. In fact, that talent was to have a share in shaping my life. I also seem to be able to reach further back into memory than the average person, for much that I am recalling now took place before I was three.

I remember, as distinctly as if I were that child again, lying in my bed at night and hearing the creak of the kitchen door and my mother and father whispering together. Then I knew my anonymous soldier-father had crept into his home again after days spent fighting the American soldiers in our hills.

My hearing was as acute as my memory. My parents never knew how much I learned from their whisperings.

I learned to fear for my father's life and the presence of his enemies. I learned who they were. They were the "bad men," the American soldiers who were bivouacked in the Plaza, not four blocks away from our home.

I hated those blue-eyed foreign devils, with a child's helpless hatred.

I would hear my father's final whisper to my mother, "Don't let the boys go near the Plaza."

So of course I had to go there.

As one probes an aching tooth, so I found myself drawn to the little park where the enemy sat around their camp-fires, cleaning the guns that might any day take my father's life from us; cooking, eating, joking, singing, as if they were men and not monsters. They sang sad lonely songs for their homeland, and although I did not know the meaning of the words their sadness almost melted my heart. "Farewell, my Bluebell," was one, I found out much later, and "Just Before the Battle, Mother."

They seemed as unhappy at finding themselves strangers in a strange land as we were at having them here.

But they had other, hateful songs, and while I could not understand these either I knew they were tuneful insults to my people. Some of these intruders in our country were quite obviously looking down on the Filipinos as members of an inferior race.

It was my first suspicion of race hatred and I found it difficult to bear. How dared these crude, rough-speaking strangers look down on us!

I would return to a household gentled by centuries of civilized living, and curl up in a comfortable chair to puzzle my way through this mystery. I reached the conclusion that these Americans, who represented the America I hated, dared look down on my parents and their good, sober, industrious neighbors, and label them outlaws, simply because we were not free.

Because the Philippines was not a free country children were taught to smuggle food and ammunition to their fathers hiding in the woods; wives met their husbands under cover of darkness, good men hid in the hills and crept home by stealth, like guilty animals; and women stood by their doors in icy contempt while American soldiers violated the privacy of their homes searching for men and guns.

All this—because we were not free.

Then, as I have told on other occasions, two terrible events happened in rapid succession. I went to the Plaza one morning and found the body of our neighbor Clemente hanging on the gallows the Americans had built in our little park. He was a good family man and the father of several of my playmates. Shortly after I learned from a whispered midnight conversation between my parents that my good, kind grandfather, the head of our family, had been captured by American soldiers and given the "water cure" when he refused to tell where my father was hiding.

I had no idea what the water cure was, and it was years before I learned it was a form of torture revived by these twentieth-century American soldiers from the Spanish Inquisition. Water was forced into the victim's stomach by means of a funnel or tube, so that the tortured one sometimes ruptured, often died.

By the time I learned this I also had learned that such acts in the Philippines were limited to a few sadistic soldiers of the type that can be found in any army or any neighborhood. But when I was three I had no such facts to comfort me. I blamed America and our not being free.

My grandfather came back to us, somehow older and gentler and saddened, and he did not live very long after that. What had been done to him was never discussed before the children and I could not tell anyone that I knew. Since I could not talk the matter out it festered in my mind and added to the fear I felt for my father and to my hatred of the Americans.

Why did these horrors serve to draw me back to the Plaza?

Wide-eyed and wondering I watched the soldiers eating and singing around their campfires, and in my innocence wondered why God did not strike them dead.

Then, as I have told so many times and as General Mac-Arthur has related, an American sergeant whose name I never knew lured a half-dozen small Filipino youngsters to his side. He gave us the American fruit we had never tasted—apples— and read to us from a wonderful little book called Baldwin's *Primer.* Did he have small boys at home and was he lonely for them?

This must have been the truth of it, for he and other soldiers drew us against our will into their adult military circle. They knew how small boys love to be treated—as men among men. Soon we were on a comradely basis, and since they could not speak our language it seemed natural that we should learn theirs.

Our sergeant friend taught us from Baldwin's *Primer.* "I see the cat. Do you see the cat? Does the cat see me?" I can see him now, that blue-eyed, friendly man, relaxed under our nipa palms with his gun at his side, "on the ready" (in readiness for our fathers in hiding), using that simple book to teach a small circle of big-eyed little boys to read and write in English. I was very proud of the rapid way I learned, for none of the grownups I knew, not even my scholarly father, could read or write English!

I came to trust our enemies, to love them, and knew at last there was no difference between us, because we were friends.

In this I did not feel disloyal to my father and his cause. Friendship was a personal matter. It had nothing to do with war. It had no effect on my hatred for America.

What is the effect of hatred on a child? I had asked questions: How can men do such terrible things? How can God let them happen?

Not until I was a grown man would I know the answers and

then I had to find them for myself. I learned all men are good and all are evil and that serpents lurk in every Eden.

After Clemente was hanged and my grandfather tortured, I tried to stay away from the Plaza. But my friend the sergeant beckoned; and tempted, like Eve, by this possessor of apples and wisdom I forsook the pleasures of hatred and rejoined his classes in English.

Then, so swiftly and easily I do not recall when it happened, the sergeant and all the other soldiers were gone, the gallows was destroyed, and our Plaza was again a peaceful provincial park. My father was home, and all the other fathers were back with their families. Life was good and simple and safe again, and peace was something a small boy could understand.

Now we were under America, and where before our red, white, and blue Philippine flag had flown there now flew the American red, white, and blue.

Instead of shiploads of American soldiers there now came shiploads of American teachers and advisers to instruct us in the American way.

It seemed to make a great deal of difference that we were now under American rule instead of being a republic or in the throes of revolution, but the difference was not perceptible to a small boy.

The year 1902 saw final surrender, but the Filipino dream of freedom did not surrender. For the Filipinos had been promised eventual freedom by America, so all would be well.

My father was a leader of popular opinion in our town. He was fair-minded and temperate. He argued that since America had beaten us and then made its generous promise, the only honorable attitude for the Filipinos to take was to coöperate fully. He was among the last in our town to surrender and to take the oath of allegiance to the United States. But he was the first man in Camiling to learn English. In time he became a teacher of English. He made friends with the American school-teachers who came to our country and one of them, an American major, became such a close friend that he came to live with us in our home and was a sort of extra uncle to us children.

My father began the study of civic welfare that was ultimately to lead him into a political career. He studied the American form of government and became a leader in the fair government campaigns. He sought to see the good in all that the Americans were doing to help advance the Filipinos—new schools, better roads, medical and hygienic care. He praised these works and pointed out their advantages to his own people. He became the advocate in our province for the American way.

So enthusiastic was he for the new methods and so far-reaching was his publicizing of democracy that it was not long before Filipinos and Americans alike were urging him to run for office. He was elected municipal councilor, later municipal president (mayor), and eventually governor of our province of Tarlac.

When queried as to the reason for his change of heart the former revolutionary had his answer ready. It was based upon a promise he could recite by heart, as I would learn to recite it in my turn—America's promise as voiced by President William McKinley on April 7, 1900, when he instructed the Taft Commission:

. . . to bear in mind that the government which they are establishing is designed not for our [the American] satisfaction nor for the expression of our theoretical views, but for the happiness, peace and prosperity of the people of the Philippine Islands.

On these words my father raised his children in loyalty and respect for America.

My father was close and dear to me. But even he did not know the small rebel who surrendered at the same time that the adult turned his gun over to America and took the oath of allegiance. Until then I had been adamant in my hatred, not against the American soldiers who had become my friends but against the vague impersonal concept of contempt and power

over the helpless that they represented. But when my father
yielded, something in the child gave way.

I learned then to bow with dignity to the storm so that my
head might lift again.

For despite defeat my father's head was still high. By his
willingness to see the merits in and coöperate with the new form
of government he was developing into a leader who in the long
run would guide his fellow patriots back to freedom. My father
believed in the healing qualities of time. He explained to us
that even America had not always been free. But we would be
free, in time, and due to this American interlude the new Philippines would be further ahead in education and economic development than ever before in its history. Above all, we would
be permanently and irrevocably free.

My father did not live to see his faith come to fruition, but
in his serene heart he knew it was to be.

Now, when all over the world so many small countries are
struggling to hold their heads high under the yoke, let them
remember how it was with us and how long we waited. And
how, while we waited, our leaders died—Rizal, Bonifacio,
Luna, Mabini, Quezon—without ever knowing their country
is at last free.

Yet they led us to freedom. And they were not alone. We
had other Filipino heroes, unknown beyond our islands, but
we know them. The fathers of those among us who were
children in 1900 fought for liberty and some died for it; they
also are our heroes. My father fought on the losing side but
he is no less heroic in my eyes.

Our revolution is long since over, and Camiling is as peaceful a town as it was in my boyhood, but I have not forgotten
the crackle of gunfire in our hills and the body of our neighbor
hanging in our Plaza. Clemente's death is part of a remembered
nightmare and his name belongs in the ranks of the unknown
heroes who died for our freedom.

All through these infantile years of mine, which were also

the years of revolution, I had contrived to live outwardly the life of an innocent, active little boy. Anyone looking at the smiling, mischievous child I was then would have thought me without a care in the world. No adult could have guessed how deeply my emotions ran. Before I was five I had known the depths of human hatred and an equally passionate love for what I thought was right.

It had been simple in the beginning. My father's side was right. That made all the Filipinos good men and all the Americans bad. Morality was as simple to a small Filipino trapped in wartime as it is to the modern child watching a TV struggle between cowboys and Indians. The chubby-cheeked Carlos, who teased his grandmother by running away from lessons, was outwardly the child; inwardly an adult man seethed with longings for vengeance.

Now our enemies were our friends. Now the men I had dreamed of killing were guests at our dinner table; their children played with us. The helpless hatred of childhood had to die. But the passion born of the longing to be free did not die. Gradually I learned that freedom must be not only for Americans or for Filipinos. Freedom must be for all men in all countries before any man can be truly free.

So the righteous indignation I had known did not subside. It would remain part of me and hurl me into the fight for democracy wherever that need would arise. It grew as I grew, as I learned what the fighting in the hills around Camiling had been for and how the longing for freedom had grown in the Filipino heart until it would not be denied. . . . As it was to grow in my own heart and lead me in time to Bataan and Corregidor and eventually to the widest of all battlefields—the floor of the United Nations.

What does freedom mean to a child?

In my mind it was exemplified by our Philippine flag, perhaps because for so many years that flag was contraband. America, when it took over the Philippines, decreed our flag was not to be flown in any public place. My father was amenable to all American rulings since he had taken the oath of allegiance, and he kept it in every way except in the matter of the flag.

Despite the new law he displayed a large Filipino flag on the wall of his bedroom where he could see it first on waking and last at night. A similar flag was under the glass top of his desk in the library.

If the Americans wanted to snoop and confiscate his flags, he told us, let them try! The refusal to permit Filipinos to display their flag made him so angry that for a time he was tempted to withdraw his oath. But instead, he helped in an unremitting campaign for the righting of this injustice, which may seem minor to the conquerors but is not a small matter to the conquered.

My father explained to his family that in displaying the Filipino flag in his own home he was obeying the American ruling to the letter.

"The American law says we cannot display our flag 'in any public place,'" he told us. "Well, my bedroom is not a public place. It is personal and private. I am displaying my flag in complete privacy, and I shall keep it there until I can hang it in public where it belongs."

It makes me happy to remember he helped to win this fight that was of such importance to the Filipinos, although it was a long time in the winning. Not until 1916 were we allowed to display our own flag again in our own country. I am glad my father lived to hang our flag once more before the door. He who had taken part in so many battles for freedom was proud of this seemingly unimportant but so telling a victory.

American guests in our home in Camiling noted my father's flouting of the law, and had only kindly understanding for their defeated friend who chose to make this secret stand beside his beloved flag.

To him it symbolized our country's hope of freedom. To the Americans it must have symbolized all that was best in my father and his fellow Filipinos—their undying faith in that shared ideal.

Three

SO PEACE returned to Camiling, and in its restored pastoral innocence I grew into boyhood. The years of war passed through my childish memories like a witch story told to children. Our home and family circle had remained fixed as the stars. Camiling was the center of the world; our elders and God had the world in their keeping, so how could events turn out other than right?

The world might shake with nightmare, but I was safe.

I would remember this in later years when I prayed for the safety of my own children. They in their turn did not escape the Moloch of war. They were homeless behind enemy lines where I could not protect them. I do not think the experience did them lasting harm. Indeed, it gave them wisdom and understanding beyond their years. It robbed them of what should have been the light-hearted period of their lives, but they kept their courage.

I believe that was because their mother was with them and gave them the calm assurance that all would be well, as my mother had given to her children when we were trapped in a country ravaged by war.

Now I pray for the safety of my grandchildren and for all this world's children that war will not strike again.

In my own childhood, war, once over, left an elysian peace. Ours was a happy land. We were a happy people. No child of today can have that sense of the word being wide beyond all imagining and filled on every side with peace and good will toward men. In faraway countries dignified kings and queens

37

sat securely on their thrones, and with America aiding us and ourselves part of America we had no one to dread.

So I grew into boyhood, a smug, self-centered, generous-and-selfish-by-turns, complete little being, a thoroughly happy child. I will not say there were no storms or sulking rages; I was only too human. But the world was large and safe and very beautiful and I was still its exact center.

Any problems I might have at this time would be of my own making. And I made them, for I was healthy, inquisitive, active, and overly fond of conversation. I knew everyone and everything in Camiling, and discussed all with unrestrained freedom. I seemed to be everywhere at once. I talked with all I met. I told all I knew.

My parents were tolerant and wise. They never spanked me, but they let me know that social errors on my part let my entire family down, if not my country. Americans were with us, American eyes were upon us, and I had to live up to our standards as a Filipino. Filipinos as a race were always courteous, gentle of speech, and friendly, and I was expected to display these characteristics.

But I was insatiably curious. I asked questions of children and grownups. I had opinions and aired them. The gift of speech that was to be my support and my salvation was fully developed when I was still very young.

I have often wished my grandfather were living and that I might tell him that his little grandson Carlos resides in America and is paid one thousand dollars every time he steps upon a lecture platform! I wonder what he would say if he knew that the Americans he and my father fought against have come by the hundreds of thousands and paid in good American money to hear his chatterbox of a grandson.

I can hear him now, that gentle patriarch, at the head of the dinner table, groaning, "Please, Carlitos, can you not be quiet?"

My father also tried to curb me. He admonished me in Spanish proverbs. "Still waters run deepest," he would say, and, "Remember, a closed mouth catches no flies."

Nothing could cure my jabbering.

In those days children were not supposed to enter into adult conversations as they do now. But I was interested in every subject being discussed, and I could not let any opinion go by with which I did not agree.

My family groaned, but they heard me out, down to the littlest member. My mother listened in silence, turning her shining head from one to the other as we spoke. She seldom joined in our arguments, but her attention was flattering. My grandmother shook her head or nodded in agreement.

But my father listened with apparent respect, and he would argue against my impassioned replies. Since he was older and wiser he always outpointed me.

Then I would give up, saying darkly, "Well, you have won this argument, but there is always tomorrow."

The tomorrows went by very fast. They brought me to the America my father and grandfather had protested against, but where Americans now were willing to listen to a small man from a small country.

My having been permitted to express myself as a child has been of inestimable value. It gave me the courage to believe in my own opinions. Later I would hone my skill in argument on debating teams; it would serve me in politics and in the United Nations. I had ideas I thought were important, which must be expressed. I had learned to communicate my ideas when I was a child in the receptive circle of my family.

I am still trying to communicate the thoughts that seem important to me. Therefore I write and make speeches wherever and whenever I am asked. I never allow any opportunity to pass for publicizing my country and my people.

The ability to express our thoughts has raised us above the animals. To this date in human history it is the weapon, not too effective, which holds us to an unsteady peace.

So it was that when in 1946 I ran second to Eleanor Roosevelt
on the popularity roster of the W. Colston Leigh Lecture Bureau I would find myself smiling at the memory of Grandfather's pained remonstrances at my constant chattering.

It is one of my last memories of my grandfather. He died
soon after our revolt against America ended. I was still so young
that, while I have distinct memories of him living, I do not
remember his death.

In fact my memories are singularly free of unhappiness in
any form, once our revolution ended.

Poverty was all around us, but it was not visible to my young
eyes. Values are comparative; the modern Russian thinks of the
way his ancestors lived under the czars and believes he is fortunate. In Camiling there was none of the poverty I would see
when I was campaigning many years later in the Philippine
hinterlands and visited in the homes of families who could afford but one meal a day.

In my boyhood I was surrounded by cleanly, smiling neighbors, who enjoyed life in a tropical climate where fruit and
fish were abundant—and free.

In New York and other cities the tenement and the luxury
hotel are side by side. So it was in Camiling, where the nipa hut
stood by the landowner's casa. No matter what the size of the
house each had its own well, and the clotheslines out-of-doors
were always hung with newly washed clothing smelling
sweetly of sun and air.

There were many nipa huts in our *barrio* (precinct), Cabi-
ganan. The children who lived in them were our playfellows
then and are our friends today. They are always the first to
greet me when I return to Camiling. Some of their families
were quite poor, but we children knew nothing of poverty.
What is shoelessness to a small boy whose toes thirst for the
warm dust?

Some of our neighbors were our tenants. My family owned
the land on which their houses stood. Evidently this did not

interfere with our popularity, for when my father ran for governor our *barrio* voted for him one hundred per cent.

Many of my boyhood companions from the *barrio* have risen to positions of high authority. Several became political leaders. Among these was my neighbor and early grammar school companion, Paulino Santos. He was a poor boy with a brilliant mind, who won his cadetship in the Military Academy of the Philippines by competition and who later became head of the Philippine army. He was killed by the Japanese during the war. His granddaughter, Milagros, is now my code clerk in Washington.

These boys and I did what small boys were doing all over the world. We played marbles and baseball, stick ball and leap frog, climbed trees, stole fruit from the orchards and were chased by the farmers in what we considered hair's-breadth escapes, and crawled through the dark damp culvert that ran under our street with all the thrill of Tom Sawyer exploring his cave.

Rich or poor meant little in our lives. We dressed more or less alike in that tropical climate, as lightly as possible. We were clean because that is part of Filipino tradition, at least we were clean when we left our homes.

We were not entirely aware of the advantages of money, because we saw little of it. I imagine we were all fairly even as far as cash was concerned. My father, with a large family to provide for, was a thrifty man, and he saw no reason why a small boy should have money while he was well clothed and fed. My grandmother was more lenient, and she started me on a weekly allowance of five centavos.

With these large copper pennies clutched in my fist I was the first cash customer of the day at the *saba* (fried or boiled banana) stand. *Saba* is a popular dish in the Philippines both as a food staple and as a delicacy. Even though we always had plenty of freshly cooked bananas in our house my entire weekly income was spent on this delicacy, which tasted so much better away from home and out-of-doors.

There was no ice cream in Camiling when I was a child. Our favorite special treat was *gulaman,* a frozen concoction of shredded coconut, sugar, and gelatine.

Well do I remember my first sight of that remarkable modern invention, the ice cream freezer. One of my uncles had brought it from Manila to make ice cream for the church fair. It was a round, tublike affair with an inside container that turned with a crank. When I saw it first it was sitting on the steps of the church in the plaza, surrounded by everyone in Camiling who had gathered to marvel at the new contraption. There was never any difficulty getting boys to turn that freezer handle.

My father was so impressed with the invention that he bought one for our family, and after that we had ice cream twice a month, which was as often as the ice cart came to Camiling. There was no train then, so the great blocks of ice came lumbering over the dusty road in one of the great wooden wheeled carts drawn by carabaos. The ice chunks were packed in burlap and sawdust to protect them from the sun, but just the same they always arrived melted to half their original size.

We boys vied for the position of crank turner. That was a place of decided advantage, for the churning cream often swelled up and lifted the lid of the inner churn and small fingers could scoop up the delectable overflow. Sometimes the taste of rock salt went with the cream but we didn't mind.

I have never lost my love for ice cream, but the thrilling taste of that we made ourselves in the old wooden freezer has never been equaled, and I have indulged in my favorite dessert in all the leading restaurants and ice cream parlors in the world. It was the first thing I asked for after my escape from Bataan. But that ice cream of Camiling—boyhood was in the taste of it, a flavor never to be found again.

So much happiness to be remembered! Our "saint's days"— the equivalent of birthdays—the feast days and celebrations and holy days, family anniversaries and weddings, and, far apart, even the hushed sanctity of family funerals that held so much of beautiful ritual and love. Above all a child looked forward to Christmas, to the visit of the Three Kings and the gifts and feasting and parties, to the songs of early morning Mass, and to midnight Mass on Christmas Eve in the old church, made mystical by the glow of candles and fragrance of incense, the soft voices of the priests, and the sense of being safe with all one's family in the presence of God. And stumbling home later under the midnight stars, half-asleep and clinging to my father's hand, the ecstasy of the moment when, laughing at my weary plight, he would stoop down and scoop me up into his strong arms and carry me home. Then, drowsiness forgotten, came the joy of sitting at the table for the feast of Noel—the midnight Christmas meal and the *lechon* and *relleno*—a small member of a family group blessed by God.

I entered the primary grade in the brick schoolhouse on the Plaza with no obvious show of reluctance. I did not mind going to a real school as I had minded attending my grandmother's classes. This meant I was starting to grow up. Also, I was not alone; many of my young playmates from the *barrio* entered with me.

My mother recognized this move toward man's estate on my part and took over the responsibility of my allowance, increasing it to two centavos a day. These were spent promptly at recess for fried bananas, with no nonsense about waiting for lunchtime.

I had rebelled at my grandmother's tutoring because I had been the sole victim and because play had seemed more interesting in those budding years than learning my ABC's. Now I saw the advantage of that preschool training. I had a precocious knowledge of the rudiments of three languages—the Spanish reading and writing taught me by my grandmother, the English learned from my sergeant friend in the Plaza, and our own dialect, Pangasinan.

I went to the head of the class in all subjects dealing with language, and stayed there.

But I drew an absolute blank in anything pertaining to mathematics.

Many of my playmates from the *barrio*, now my classmates, were very bright in school. Several showed particular genius for mathematics, in which I showed a definite early talent for being abysmally poor. They could not understand why I, who did so well in every other course, was always low in math.

My first grammar school teacher was Mr. Leo J. Grove of Ovid, Michigan. He and his wife were two of the American teachers who had come among the "one thousand teachers" sent by the American government to bring modern education to the Philippines. He made a minor crusade of trying to teach me the multiplication table. He would poke my skinny chest with what seemed an enormous forefinger. "How much is two times two? Three times three? Four times four?"

And I simply could not remember. I was a scared little boy and he seemed awfully big to me.

My schoolmates were sympathetic. "Why don't you study?" they would ask.

And I became obstinate. "Why should I? Why do I have to learn math?"

"So you can keep your own accounts when you're a man and not be cheated," one boy explained.

"When I am a man," I countered, "I'll hire an accountant!"

And the truth is that I never was any good at mathematics, and I do have an accountant now who keeps track of my financial affairs.

My school friends gave up scolding and began coaching me. That helped, and in turn I helped them with their English. It was my first try at teaching.

In time I would regret my neglect of the science of numbers. I know now that the study of mathematics provides good mental discipline and I would have profited by it in many ways.

Curiously, by the time we came to study geometry I found I liked that subject and did well in it. But then geometry was logic, it required reasoning, and stimulated my mind.

From the beginning, school opened to their widest the yawning ducts of my insatiable curiosity. I wanted to know all there was to be known. That this ambition was to fall short of the mark was no fault of the wonderful American teachers, who had come to our Islands to help the Filipinos get started in the ways of democracy. They were more than teachers; they were missionaries and personal friends.

These builders of democracy in the Far East—the American men and women who gave modern education and the tenets of democracy to the Philippines—have gone unrecorded and for the most part forgotten, but their influence was as far-reaching as it has been abiding.

I have written of them many times, but never been able to say enough. The educator is always the secret leader of the future. How many, I wonder, know how important they are?

I knew. During the first years I spent in the Camiling grammar school I found out what I wanted to be. I, too, would be a teacher.

These emissaries from the far-off world of America were my family's friends, and the friends of my people and country. In every way they showed their respect for the Philippines, present and past. They taught us, in English, Philippine and American history together, so that we could see how close-knit were our ideals and dreams.

They helped develop a love of country in a generation of growing Filipinos. They taught us to regard the American way of life as our own.

Under their kindly guidance all my childish hatred of America was forgotten. These teachers were America to me and they became my heroes.

Now when America is being tested and the eyes of the world are upon her, she might do well to remember those pioneer teachers who came to us in the Philippines at the start of this century and drove into the minds and hearts of the children there the belief that all men are brothers under the canopy of heaven. They proved their belief in their teachings by showing respect for the Filipinos and for Philippine customs and traditions. There was no looking down, no superiority shown. They knew the inner story of the Filipino struggle for freedom and taught it to us just as it happened, comparing it in every way with America's own struggle, so that we felt allied to those heroes to America whose pictures looked down on us from our classroom walls—Washington, La Fayette, Jefferson.

These early leaders of democracy, and Abraham Lincoln, who was secretly my favorite, became very real to me.

How could they help but be real, when beside their pictures in our classrooms hung those of our own heroes—Rizal, Aguinaldo, Mabini, Bonifacio, Marcelo H. del Pilar, and Luna? These men from two worlds were allies of the free world. They were my supermen; my life would be built upon them.

A child has many fathers: his own and those men living or dead who capture his imagination. My first heroes were my father, grandfather, and uncles, because they had been fighters in a just cause. Now, from our American teachers, I learned more of the great Filipinos who had helped advance Philippine history. My grandmother had told me of them, and now I thrilled anew. To me the greatest of all was Rizal.

I would return home from school and go into the cool, dim living room where two painted portraits hung. I would stand beneath them, looking at the strong faces of two of the great men of the Philippines. My father had known them: his general, Antonio Luna of the Philippine Army of the Resistance, and Rizal. I shared my father's respect for them.

Rizal seemed closest to me, for he had almost become my cousin. Before he became the patriot-martyr, he had been in love with and engaged to marry a beautiful second cousin of my mother's, Leonor Rivera. For some reason, perhaps because her mother wanted for her a more stable life than could be provided by a revolutionary leader, she was not allowed to choose her heart's desire. Instead, she was persuaded to marry the Englishman Charles Kipping, who had fallen in love with her and courted her persistently. Their son, Carlos, later married my older sister, Lourdes.

Leonor Kipping was one of the famed beauties of her generation, and her portrait hung in the Museum of Manila near Rizal's until the Museum and all it contained were blasted to rubble by the Japanese.

I would stand a long time looking up at the portrait of Rizal. He had lived and died for the Philippines. Someday, I determined, I would find a way to be a credit to the Philippines—like Rizal!

What a strange upbringing was mine; as mixed as my country's origins. Certain leaders in modern education would hold it deficient in intellectual balance. I had my growing collection of heroes. From my grandmother and the town priest I had absorbed a firm belief in the saints and their miracles. Also from my grandmother, servants, and playmates I had collected an impressive list of fantastic illusions—I believed in ghosts, goblins, dragons, and other mythical monsters that are rife in Filipino folklore.

In time I would discard my belief in folklore, but in those days childhood could be a delightfully scary experience. Nor can I believe the bogey tales worked lasting harm. Surely it can be no worse for a child to delight in the slaying of a mythical monster than to gloat over the multiple slayings on a TV program.

I regret the modern offerings of gunplay and gangsterism to children in place of the hero worship we were permitted. A child longs for an ideal, the enlarged vision of self upon which he can build the adult image. The ambitions I have cherished and the good I may have done were in emulation of men who were my heroes—and are my heroes still.

One of the wonderful gifts from our American teachers was that they did not rob Filipino children of their Philippine heroes, and, in addition, they shared their own with us. In practical ways a child could understand they made the American dream seem worth-while.

In America, so we were told and believed, all men knew our Lord had created each of us in His image regardless of color, and that the divine spark that burns in me burns also in you.

Our teachers made us see the truth in that pattern when they sought the divine spark in the poorest of their pupils, nurtured it with their encouragement, and rejoiced when they saw that genius burst into flame.

In America, we were told, welcome was given to other countries' "your tired, your poor, your huddled masses yearning to breathe free," who had left persecution behind them in old, benighted places to live as free Americans.

We knew this was true when our American teachers visited our homes and invited us to theirs, when they showed their liking for our parents and their children played with us.

So we who were children as the century began came to believe in America as our religion told us to believe in heaven. It was the land of hope and freedom, where justice was the rule and not the exception, where all were polite to one another because all were equal, and all men walked as kings.

Yes, I thought, dreaming over my schoolbooks, lying deep in warm grass on the banks of the river, scuffling through the dust to and from school, someday I shall see this America where I will be equal to all!

And like so many others who have dreamed, I would in time see America and learn that all men do not stand there as brothers under the canopy of heaven, and that while all may be equal in God's eyes they are not so in the view of the prejudiced. This is America's greatest weakness, her Achilles' heel.

The racial problem is one she must attack within herself,

because it was America who first taught the world to believe that all men are created equal.

Our teachers, Mr. and Mrs. Grove, were frequent guests in our home. While Mr. Grove seemed relaxed and amiable there, I could not lose my dread of him, because he represented the mathematics I could not master in school.

But Mrs. Grove was my first English teacher in the Camiling grammar school, and to me she represented the magic world of books. It was due to her skill as a teacher that much of that magic rubbed off on me. I was a shining star in her class, and one of the dullest in her husband's.

She was quick to recognize my love of words and helped my interest along. She introduced fields of reading I might never have known but for her. Years after I had left school and much I had learned was forgotten I remembered the Groves, and I even remembered the American town from which they came—Ovid, Michigan.

I thought a great deal about them after I escaped from Bataan and came to America. I wrote a letter to them addressed to Ovid but it was returned, address unknown.

Then, in this same year 1942, the Pulitzer prize was given me at Columbia University, and in my speech of acceptance I said that the real winner of the prize was my first English teacher, Hattie Grove, who had taught a small Filipino pupil to value the beauty of the English language.

The speech was publicized rather widely and I hoped it would flush the Groves out of hiding wherever they were, but still no answer came.

Then, a few years ago, my speaking engagements included one at Miami. Just as I was about to leave for Florida a letter came from Delray Beach in that state. It was from Hattie Grove. She wrote that she and Mr. Grove had retired and he was in a wheelchair.

I telephoned ahead to the Miami committee, and as soon as I arrived a car was waiting to take me to Delray. I brought the

Groves back to Miami, where that night at the dinner at which I was to speak they were guests of honor.

We sat at the head of the table and there was a great deal to be said before the speeches began. We had not met since, I believe, 1912, in the Camiling grammar school.

"Why did you not get in touch with me?" I demanded, when I learned they had followed my career and saved every clipping concerning me.

They explained they had not wanted to bother me. "But we are so proud of you and of all you have done," they kept saying.

It was an emotional reunion. When I rose to speak I repeated what I had said the day I had accepted the Pulitzer prize, that Mrs. Grove, not I, was the true winner of the honor. The audience gave her a standing ovation and she was in tears. But she got up on her feet like a champion and made a wonderful little speech.

She wound up saying, "I am eighty-two years old and this is the happiest moment of my life!"

Her husband—how had I ever thought of him as formidable—leaned over to me with a twinkle in his eye. "She's a liar," he whispered gaily. "She's eighty-five!"

Mrs. Grove had brought a gift for me, her collection of all the clippings about me she had saved after my escape from Bataan. I took them, had them bound into a scrapbook, and sent it to her with my love.

My widening world of books did not end in Mrs. Grove's classroom. My father was a great reader and he liked to be read to. One end of our upper balcony was enclosed as my father's library and it was completely lined with books. Here he took his rest during siesta hour, lying on a sofa with his eyes closed while I read aloud to him. Many of the books were gifts from his American schoolteacher friends.

My own favorite was a set written for children, *Fifty Stories of Fifty Great Americans,* which had been given him because he was the first person in our town to learn English. These books fed my hero worship and my passionate interest in America.

Our readings were in Spanish and English, and my father corrected my pronunciation and my delivery in both languages.

He subscribed to the leading American magazines, so that we had in our home. *The Youth's Companion,* the *Ladies Home Journal, Harper's,* and another magazine which I believe was called *The Independent.* Their accounts of American cities made Camiling seem a tame place. I devoured accounts of tall cities and of highways crisscrossing a continent. Every person I read about was rich or famous, and although all were privileged all were equal.

We also enjoyed our Filipino publications. My father's favorite was the *El Renacimiento (Renaissance),* a newspaper printed in Spanish in Manila. My father loved poetry and read it beautifully, and corrected me gently as I read. So I was introduced to the poetry, written in Spanish, of our country's great lyricists—Fernando Maria Guerrero, Flavio Zaragoza, Manuel Bernabe, Cecilio Apostol, Jesus Balmori, and Claro M. Recto.

Guerrero, Bernabe, Recto, Balmori, and Apostol were my favorites. I memorized their poems and asked my father questions about them. I learned Recto was a political leader as well as poet. He was to play a great role in our development. As one of the country's distinguished jurists he presided over the convention that drafted the Philippine constitution. He was in turn a member of the Philippine Supreme Court and of the Philippine Senate. He is our greatest dialectician.

Age differences tighten as one grows older, and the young poet whose words in "Bajo Los Cocoteros" I memorized was later to become my friend, although we had many differences of opinion on national questions. He was to serve Japan in the puppet administration during the war, and be exonerated on the ground that he bent the knee to Nippon only to enable him to give continued aid and protection to our fellow Filipinos.

Young as I was, I was gaining a smattering of politics. The newspaper articles I read aloud to my father raised questions in my mind which he was delighted to answer. Then, when I was about eight, a personal interest showed me how fascinating politics could be.

My father was never what could be called a professional politician. He was an intellectual, and his studies of American democracy, new in his country, led him into a local campaign for good government. At this point the step from teaching to politics was inevitable.

He served first as Camiling's municipal councilor, then as its mayor.

The campaign when he ran for councilor changed family life for the Romulos. I learned then what happens to personal privacy when a member of a family enters politics. Our home was no longer a private dwelling. It was like a church, in that its doors might never be closed. Night and day people came and went. The rooms were always crowded. New arrivals were forever at our door. No matter what the hour all who came must be offered some form of refreshment.

We never sat down to dine as a family any more. There were no more intimate teasing family conversations, no family jokes. Everything we said was overheard. We children learned to be careful of expressing our opinions, and for a time my exuberance of speech was drastically curbed. There was also a temporary interruption of the siesta hours and the reading.

All our lives were changed by this upheaval. Perhaps my mother's serene existence was most disturbed, but one would never know that from her calm demeanor. She made the switch from domestic privacy to public turbulence as easily as she had maintained her calm the day our roof caught on fire. My wife would display the same serenity when in turn I answered the siren call of politics. Both women were home-oriented, happiest in the smaller circle of family and friends. I do not think either would have chosen this public mode of living.

My mother had led a busy life, commanding her own family domain. Now for my father's sake she widened the circle and accepted the new order. She threw open her doors and re-organized her household, until she was running a day-and-night catering service, ready to serve all who appeared.

My father came and went, always in a hurry, always off to make a speech somewhere or meet with his campaign managers. I longed to hear some of his speeches, but I was in school and could not. Yet I was certain they were like himself—blunt and honest and sound.

I was equally certain he was going to win.

That inner assurance, the certainty of victory, was something I was to experience many times. I was also to know the certainty of defeat, but never without feeling its injustice. I had in my make up the assurance of the victor, inculcated there by a father who would do his best to win, and who did win against a power-ful opponent. Later he ran for reëlection, and won again.

All this was heady fare for an eight-year-old boy.

A man in public life can have no secret life, no hiding place. Even now, when I am in bed in my room the telephone by my pillow can summon me from sleep and a secretary's voice relay to me a problem that cannot wait until morning.

After my father became mayor the telephone in our house rang at all hours.

For that remarkable innovation, the telephone, came also with his new position. I had never before seen one. Until my father's election there were only two in Camiling: one in the *presidencia* (City Hall) and the other in the post office. Anyone having business apart from Camiling would go to one of these public buildings. There were no secret conversations in our town.

Now that my father was mayor, he had the use of the phone

in the *presidencia*, and he was also given one in our home. Like
the others ours was a wall phone that summoned the operator
with a crank, and its installation was a seven-day wonder. We
children were not allowed to touch it, but we could bring our
friends in and point to it with understandable pride.

Its performance was not always one hundred per cent perfect.
Telephone poles in those days were tall shoots of bamboo and
far from strong. When the heavy rains came or when we boys
were flying our kites and got the tail strings entangled in the
wires conversation suffered a setback in Camiling.

My father tried to take his new office and its duties with
calm, but he liked being mayor. As I said earlier, he was seldom
able to hide his emotions. It was about this time I saw him furiously angry for the first time.

He had organized a wild boar hunt with his friend the American major and took me along on condition I keep behind the
men and out of the way of the guns. I obeyed, but somehow the
major got in the rear, and when a boar started up in a bamboo
thicket he fired. I heard the bullet whine close to my head. I
never again saw my father so angry.

As a rule he was sweet-tempered and tolerant of other people's errors. No matter how nonsensical my behavior he never
ridiculed me. He would correct me with an eyebrow whim-
sically lifted and a few sarcastic but not hurtful words. He
offered no criticism when about this time I confided to him I
had given up my ambition to be a teacher; I had instead decided
to become the greatest acrobat in the world. That was when I
was nine, and the first circus I had ever seen came to Camiling.

In those days a circus held a parade before giving a performance. The band was headed by a small boy holding a placard
advertising the attractions of the show. For this service he
would be passed free into the tent.

The opening day parade was held, and I was the small boy.
My reward was munificent. I received not only my own

promised pass for opening night, but an extra pass that I might "take a friend." I took my brother Henry.

Did anyone else in that vast tent enjoy the performance as much as I? I'm certain Henry did not. For on the following day I suggested that Henry also apply for a card to be carried in the parade that we might both get passes for the second night.

"Who, me?" snorted Henry. "I've seen the show!"

So had I, but a gargantuan appetite for circuses had merely been whetted. The circus played a week in our town, and each day I carried the placard in the parade, and each evening I was in a front seat staring upward, lost in dreams.

I had never known human beings could attain such mastery of flight as those glittering creatures on the high trapeze. I knew now what I had to be.

I rigged up a trapeze in our tallest tamarind and for days practiced swinging and twisting high in the air. I beguiled Lourdes into turning performer with me. She was to be a tightrope walker. But she was lukewarm to the idea, and after I took a couple of bad falls my father ordered the trapeze taken down.

There was a great deal else in Camiling to distract my attention. It was about this time that a friend from Manila, who would later be my brother-in-law, arrived from the capital in the first car ever seen in our village. It was a second-hand Hupmobile, and the commotion it caused was as exciting as my father's election. It was a nine-day wonder, parked before our house. The entire village collected in our street, and farmers came in from the countryside to see the wonderful "cart that travels without a carabao."

I took my first automobile ride in that car, never dreaming that it marked the beginning of the end of our Elysian age.

On the banks of the Camiling River I was circumcized, when I was ten, along with sundry small friends by the town herb doctor. We had looked forward to this event with longing and dread, the one because it marked the first step toward manhood and the other because we knew it would be painful. Somehow we were all very certain we would be brave, and true enough, when the day came, we were.

This rite stretched far back in the Philippine past. And as if we were required to see both sides of the coin at the same time, we were simultaneously preparing for first communion. These two events gave a true picture of Filipino life, with old customs and beliefs side by side with the new.

The preparations made in our household for my formal acceptance into the Christian faith made me realize it was a spiritual crisis in my life. There were not only the long hours spent memorizing the catechism, but I had to be outfitted from head to toe in shining white, symbolical of the purity within. In white suit, stockings, and shoes, aglow with faith, I moved forward with my fellow communicants in the old church on the Plaza, between pews filled with relatives, and down the aisle toward the altar.

The church was as familiar to me as my own home. I had been baptized there. Now it seemed more awe-inspiring than ever before. I was aware of the solemn presence of the priest, waiting between the altar boys before the altar. He was no longer a friend but a transfigured being.

Then above the altar I saw the reassuring painting of St. Michael. This was his church; he was the patron saint of Camiling. He was also my favorite saint. My grandmother had told me often of his bravery. She had told me of many saints, but I preferred St. Michael above all others because he had slain a dragon! An archangel who could challenge monsters and win was definitely the patron saint for me.

We were growing up. One of the symptoms was a tendency to separate into pairs of boys and girls and dance in one another's homes after school. We had no dancing class in Camiling. We taught one another the one-step and two-step and waltz.

Then we were outgrowing the brick school on the Plaza. It went only through the seventh grade, and when we graduated we would be ready for high school. There was no high school in Camiling, and I was wondering where my education would be continued, when a change in my father's career settled the problem.

While I was still in the seventh grade his friends decided that he had been so popular as Camiling's mayor he should run for governor of our province of Tarlac.

Once more our family entered upon the excitement of life in a home that was also campaign headquarters. Men came and went by night, by day. Posters were printed, speeches written. My mother moved calmly through the upheaval, welcoming all who came, moving her household affairs on an ordinary schedule despite my father's hectic plans. Our doors were never closed. Our kitchen stove never grew cold.

My father won! There was a massive fiesta in Camiling the night the returns came in. My father stayed in our house surrounded by his family, and we saw his happiness as victory grew clearer with each report.

What made him proudest of all that night was the fact that our own home precinct had voted for him to a man.

The celebration began all over the village, and concentrated around our house until there were only heads to be seen from our windows, shining in the flare of the torchlight parade. The torches were bamboo poles threaded with wicks and filled with petroleum.

There were bands, many and glorious, pounding away in triumph under our windows. To the sound of loud music my father was marched to the Plaza and I, standing under the platform in the effulgence of his glory, listened to the speeches made in his honor. My skinny chest was ready to burst with pride.

Then he spoke—my father. I had never heard him speak in public before. He made no effort toward oratory, but what he said was simple and honest and from the heart. The people of Camiling cheered loudest of all for him.

What circus could ever hold the thrill of this spectacle!

When I finally went to bed that night I was certain I would never be able to sleep. But I did fall asleep, for sometime later I was awakened by soft music and singing. Under our windows an orchestra and a group of singers were serenading my victorious father. They were singing the Kundiman, the Filipino love songs, hauntingly Spanish, sung in Tagalog in minor keys. I thought I would never hear anything more beautiful. Half asleep, I was thinking, "They are singing to honor my father. This is his reward for being a good man."

There have been unavoidable pitfalls along my way over the years, and although I never entirely lost sight of the ideal set before me that night it would be far in the future before I realized that I actually asked little more of myself than to be a good man like my father.

Four

NOW that my father was governor we moved to Tarlac, which is the capital of our province.

The move provided adventure in itself. Our household goods were sent on ahead in great lumbering *carretones* and *carromatas*, driven by the equally lumbering carabao and pony, and the family followed in these same unwieldy and uncomfortable carts. The dusty roads seemed endless, and we children were tired and quarrelsome by the time we reached the village of Bayambang. But before reaching Bayambang we were revived by the excitement of fording the Camiling River on a raft. At Bayambang we boarded a small slow train that brought us eventually to Tarlac. I started high school there and life took a sudden leap forward.

Tarlac is described as a small city, but it seemed large and cosmopolitan to a boy from a country town. At first we lived in a rented, furnished home. Although later my father bought a house in Tarlac, Camiling remained home to us all.

I expanded as a social being in the Tarlac years. We were a friendly family. It would have been difficult to be a recluse in a family as large and outgoing as ours. My parents had a gift for making friends, and our outlying family circles alone would have insured generations of social interplay. In our turn we children made friends and brought them home.

Life became fuller and more pressing. I discovered girls in high school, or perhaps they discovered me, for I cannot recall a time when I did not know that girls were in many ways more attractive than my boy playmates. I was still in my freshman year when I narrowed this discovery to one girl and began "dating" seriously, as it is called now. "Going steady" had no connotation of precocity in those days.

A high school romance could not be very serious in that well-guarded era. One walked home with a girl after school, carrying her books and umbrella, hung about her house evenings without courage to knock at the door, and danced with her as often as she would permit at the informal affairs given in our homes.

Urged on by romance I coaxed my sympathetic grandmother, who had remained in Camiling, into giving me enough money to hire a four-piece orchestra, which played in honor of my love at a small dance given in our home.

Ours was an idyl of the teens. The girl was a minister's daughter and very pretty, in my eyes beautiful beyond description. Nevertheless I did my best to describe my feelings, and in so doing found my first true ambition and ultimate goal.

As we walked home from school I would see an envelope tucked into one of her books which I was carrying. Without comment I would extract the note, slip it into my pocket, and replace it with another note filled with my effusive emotions of the day. Meantime we would chatter brightly, both pretending to be unaware of the exchange.

Once I had handed over her books and bade her a fairly formal good-bye at her door I would rush home to read her letter in exquisite privacy. The sentences were correct and spare, but I read into them all I longed for. Then I sat down to compose my reply, when I could let my heart soar freely and write all I longed to say and hear.

The ecstacy of first love was in those letters. I was certain this attachment was to last forever, and I poured into it my first love prose and my first poems of love.

She answered each letter, via the book, but she never mentioned my poems. This hurt, because ambition was taking shape in my mind. I wanted to write. I would be a poet, like Guerrero or Recto or Balmori.

I had now seriously determined to be a teacher. But why could not teaching and writing go hand in hand? So in the Tarlac high school I began my preparation for the career that would underlie and survive all others—that of writing.

An outsider might have wondered where I found time for this demanding occupation. School studies and homework, sports and social life apparently filled the days. But I had short cuts to leisure.

In the first place my romance was not entirely without its practical side. My girl was as smart in math as she was pretty, and I was as hopeless as ever at numbers. I had reached the conclusion that nothing dealing with numerals could ever be absorbed by my mind, and I gave up any effort in that direction. The object of my affections and several other classmates were generous in seeing that I managed passing grades in math, and in turn I wrote for them the compositions in which I excelled.

In doing this I was actually competing against myself, but I saw to it that I continued to get the highest English marks in the class.

In every subject except math I was what actors call a "quick study," so schoolwork never interfered with my interest in sports. I liked all our high school games but my specialty was sand-lot baseball. I would play till late afternoon, one of the shouting, running, swatting boys in our nine; then, at home and shut away from the world in the privacy of my room, I became another being, dedicated, solitary. No longer the teen-age student, the player of games, the callow lover, I struggled with the science of words and their meaning.

I was trying to write.

No one knew of this secret ambition. It had been born during the siesta hours on our balcony in Camiling, when I had read to my father in Spanish and English. Driven into me was an abiding delight in the sight and sound of words.

I had read then for his enjoyment and mine. The pleasure had proved of further value. In school I was often asked to read aloud, and my teachers would praise my ability. I liked to recite poetry. I had even achieved a minor success in my class-rooms as an elocutionist.

Now I had absorbed so much of good reading that I was aburst with the need to express my appreciation in writing. My growing emotions demanded expression. The daily love letters and the almost daily poems—never acknowledged by their fair inspirer—were part of this expression. But these were private, confessions seen only by myself and my love, and I craved wider recognition.

If I had any gift for writing I determined to find it out and not hide my light under a bushel.

My first short story required much rewriting. When almost every word had been changed many times I decided it was pretty good. Now what did a writer do, after his work was done? With much nervous pondering I mailed my maiden effort to a favorite magazine, written for boys, in English, and published in Manila.

Not until it was in the mail did I realize that the Philippine *Observer* was a Protestant publication, published by a Protestant minister!

I was ravaged by hope and trepidation in turns as I awaited each edition. The day came when I opened its pages and there was my story, under my name in clearest type. It was the first time I had seen my name in print. I was an author.

The sense of accomplishment I felt was overcast by dread, for what would my father say? What would this outstanding Catholic governor of a Catholic province do, when he found his son's name in a Protestant publication?

I need not have doubted my father. He had an innate respect for all faiths, for all people. Weak with worry I watched him turn the pages of the magazine I had not been able to hide from him; I saw his quick glance scan the fatal page. And his smile grew. He looked at me over the magazine. "Why," he exclaimed, "this is wonderful!" He read the story aloud to all who came.

The pride he showed was the starting bell that sent me on my way. Since that day I have won a few literary awards and honors, but none have meant more to me. I valued his praise because I knew his love and reverence for writing was as deep as mine.

Now that my secret was out I gave way to ambition and wrote freely. Poems and short stories poured from my agile pen, to be sent abroad with fervid hopes, and invariably returned. My second acceptance was actually a setback.

I had sent a poem to the Philippines *Free Press*, the leading weekly, published in Manila by R. McCullough Dick. He was owner and editor and a fine author in his own right, so I was intensely proud when he accepted my poem and published it. It won a prize, and I bought ten copies of the magazine. I was doubly affronted when my father read the poem and showed none of the enthusiasm he had had for the short story.

Instead, he commented tersely, "You know poets die of hunger."

I was deeply wounded. Into the verses I had poured all the admiration I felt for our wonderful American teachers. The poem was called "The Elect."

I felt better later, when I learned my father bought up all the copies of the magazine he could find and mailed them to our relatives for miles around.

Perhaps he was wise in trying to steer my writing into practical lines. His dry, humorous attack on my romanticism was badly needed. For I have no illusions about my early writings. While written in English, they were emotionally Spanish. Until recently Spanish literature was as rococo and ornate as Spanish architecture. Since it was my first language, the speech of my childhood, my first writings bore the Latin imprint. They were not only flowery, they were florid!

News writing was to cure me of overwriting. I had to learn to crowd words into the smallest possible amount of space, as

the "white paper shortage" is a bugaboo that rides every newspaperman's life. So it was just as well that my father shook my
faith in the muse as a means of livelihood.

I turned to playwriting. Camiling was planning a celebration
in honor of our greatest national hero, Rizal. In a blaze of patriotic fervor I poured into a play about Rizal all my lifelong
adoration of the revolutionary leader and his influence on the
Philippines. I formed a drama group among my Tarlac classmates and directed the production. Then in a troupe we went
to Camiling and produced my play on Rizal Day in gala pre-
mière. Shakespeare on a return visit to Stratford could not have
been more content than I.

Ambition had not struck with suddenness. I had made efforts
in one direction over the years, arrows pointing the way. Now
my sense of direction was firmly set. Writing and teaching were
enough for any man.

These adolescent years are important in the life of every boy.
I shall never cease being grateful to the father who helped steer
me through their eddies and currents. I was impulsive and
overly romantic; he was always ready with the right word, the
sensible, kindly hint of advice.

He led a busy life, for a governor's time can never be his
own. His office and his home were always swarming with people who had grievances to be adjusted or problems to be solved.
Still he found time for all his children, and gave to each his individual attention and concern. To me, he was always available,
always watchful of my best interests. He was less my guide during these impressionable teens than my sponsor, my adviser. He
let me seek my own way, and then, as in the matter of the poem,
gave his opinion only when I showed I wanted it.

All he did was done with deep love and knowledge of the
sensitive feelings of an adolescent boy. He had studied his children as individuals since each was born, to determine our in-
clinations and talents, and he had tried to guide us along ways
inherently our own.

For example, take my talkativeness. Did he know how valuable the gift of gab would be to me? He never curbed my chattering.

Once, when I was a very small boy still in short pants, he had taken me with him on a trip to Tarlac. The train from the small town of Paniqui was stuffy and slow and I, overly excited at the prospect of seeing Tarlac, chatted like a myna bird. Three young ladies of the Natividad family, friends of ours, sat with us during the trip. I began telling stories to help pass the time.

The young ladies and my father sat spellbound, or perhaps merely numbed, all the way to Tarlac, while I, a pint-sized male Scheherazade, spun tale after endless tale. The young ladies laughed until they were weak, whether at my stories or my earnest rendition of them I shall never know.

They were so amused my father made no attempt to check me but let me carry on. When we left the train at Tarlac I was still talking.

My father eyed me in a thoughtful way. "Where in the world," he asked, "do you manage to hear so many stories?"

I had no idea. I had that flypaper mind; nothing heard, read, or seen was ever lost.

After I grew to manhood I sometimes met those girls, now become women, and they would tease me about the way I had beguiled the hours on the trip to Tarlac.

My father often remarked that I was "quite a talker." But he said it without criticism.

And now in Tarlac, while I was in high school, my father spoke to me seriously one night after dinner. "Carlos," he said, "I think you are going to be an orator."

"Why, Papa?" I asked, for I intended to write and it had not yet occurred to me that the craft of words could be utilized in more ways than one.

He was in earnest. "I heard you, here in our home the other day, talking with a group of your friends. You were discussing some matter and the way you presented your arguments impressed me. I have heard many good speakers and I know that to speak well is a gift. Yes, I think you will be an orator."

So the idea was implanted in my mind, and in time I was to follow it through.

I had only one fault to find with my father, and that was one commonly felt by youth. While he was always very well-dressed and a pattern of neatness his style was far too conservative for my taste. I had been conscious of the way people dressed since I was a very small boy, and in high school I developed a decided leaning toward the flamboyant and unrestrained.

My father failed me as an ideal in this way. I had to look for examples away from home.

My first was a cousin of ours, Vicente Bengzon, who was attending a Jesuit school in Manila. He had visited us in Camiling when I was very small, wearing his school outfit—black coat, black bow tie, white pants, and black shoes. To add to his fascination at every step his shoes gave a raucous squeak.

I had no way of attaining his sartorial perfection, but it seemed to me I should be able to achieve squeaky shoes. I consulted various people and was given various kinds of advice. One told me if I stood my shoes in water overnight the soles would tighten and squeak. They tightened, but they did not squeak.

Someone else advised me to stand the soles in oil. Another had me wedge strips of rattan inside the shoe, against the sole.

I tried all these methods with varying results in punishment and pain, and then gave up.

Now a guest from America came to visit us in Tarlac, and I could not take my eyes from this Beau Brummell from the States! He was a judge, a Texan, and I was certain that what he wore was the last sartorial word. He had evidently come to the Philippines with no knowledge of our summer climate, for he had on a blue serge suit with a vest, tan socks, and tan shoes.

I determined someday to have an outfit exactly like this worn by the great man from America! A few years later I duplicated the Judge's costume with the first money I ever earned. I bought the blue suit, the tan socks and shoes, and wore them as a splendid surprise for my family for the first time on a Palm Sunday morning. When I came downstairs in my finery I found the day was hot and my blue coat already steaming.

My father, cool in tropicals, was sitting reading the newspaper, waiting for the rest of the family. He stared at me over the printed page. "Wherever did you find such an outfit?" he gasped. "And in this heat!" Then, glancing floorward, "And why the tan shoes?"

I had to search for another sartorial hero pattern; I found him after I went to the university.

University was already in my mind. My father was determined to give every child, girl or boy, the best education he could afford.

During my second term in the high school at Tarlac an event occurred that crystallized my aim at higher education. The first of the *pensionados* returned to Manila after their years of study in America.

I had been too young to remember the time of their going, but my father was keenly interested in this experiment as he was in all educational matters. The *pensionados* were one hundred and fifty of the brightest students in the provinces, who had been selected to complete their studies in the United States.

Under the kindly guardianship of William Howard Taft and at the expense of the United States government, they had finished their university education at various schools and colleges in America.

Now these bright young men were back, and immediately showed their capacity for organization. They moved into key positions in the government. They would in time assume leadership of the country. They founded the Philippine Columbian

Association. Its members were all educated in the United States, all boosters for democracy and lovers of America, and still the Columbian Association was to be the bulwark of Philippine nationalism. Quezon was to speak before it, and Roxas.

What an answer these *pensionados* were to the charge that Filipinos were a benighted race, incapable of self-improvement!

And now as I write these words I must record the fact that these erstwhile lovers of America are no longer her dedicated partisans. Some of them feel that America has let the Philippines down. They are not leftists. They have no leanings in the direction of Moscow. But they are disappointed that after the loyalty shown by the Filipinos toward America, the lives sacrificed and the losses taken, the Philippines have not been given as much consideration by the United States as have the people of India or Japan.

From the American point of view this may be an understandable oversight. America's main effort has been toward preventing the spread of communism in the Far East, and to propping up those countries that seemed about to fall under the hammer and sickle. In the Philippines we had shown we could be trusted; we carried out our own resistance against the Communists. As a result, since, as the saying goes, the halted streetcar is never run after our cries for assistance went unheeded. Promises we felt should have been kept were postponed or only partly fulfilled.

Chester Bowles expressed the American policy when he warned America, "keep a sharp watch on India, for if that country falls, it means the failure of democracy in Asia."

The failure of democracy in India might well be considered a calamity. But how much greater the calamity would be if democracy should falter in the Philippines, the only Asian country that since its founding has upheld the American ideal?

What loss of face then to America?

At the Bandung Conference American newspapermen

thought to honor me by reporting: "Romulo is pro-American. He is defending America against the Communist charges." They did me no service by those words. I was not defending America; I was defending democracy.

In Tarlac I read every word printed about the returned *pensionados* and the ways in which they were hoping their American training would help to advance the Philippines. My father and I discussed these young men endlessly. Then one of them, Jorge C. Bocobo, came to our high school to speak, and I was well in front in the audience. I was excited by everything he had to report about America and the *pensionado's* experiences as students in that wonderful country.

All the time he talked I was thinking, "Someday I'll go there!"

I would meet Bocobo again. Later he became successively President of the University of the Philippines, Justice of the Supreme Court, and Secretary of Public Instruction. He is one of our great intellectual leaders and a true nationalist. Many years later a Filipino dance group called "Bayanihan," organized by the Philippine Women's University, would triumphantly tour the world and give the Philippines excellent publicity. It displayed the Filipino folk dances, which Dr. Bocobo, as President of the University of the Philippines, was the first to develop and cultivate as part of his cultural program for our state university.

Another of the *pensionados*, who later became my friend, also visited Tarlac about this time. He was Dr. Victor Buencamino, who had chosen to study at Cornell and who became our country's first veterinarian. He arrived in Tarlac astride a motorcycle, wearing goggles and leather leggings—in our eyes a creature from outer space.

The machine age was on its way to Luzon.

I had even seen my first airplane while on a visit to Manila to attend the carnival. Open-mouthed, I stared skyward while an American stunt flyer, a woman whose name I never knew, climbed into a tiny single-seated plane on the water-front park, the Luneta, and took off into the air. I couldn't imagine any human being having the daring to do such a thing; for a woman to do it was beyond my comprehension. Not for several years would I see another plane.

Yet how many times since have I whipped across the oceans by passenger plane, army bomber, and jet!

The *pensionados'* visit to Tarlac and their accounts of the democratic living and glorious advantages to be found in America left me with an unquenchable desire to see that country. I had felt this since my earliest years, when my friend the sergeant had introduced me to Baldwin's *Primer* and told me of his country over the sea—a land where apples grew and men did not hunt one another by night.

"Someday I am going," I would tell my father, and he would nod in serious agreement and say, yes, someday I must go. With all his many responsibilities and his many children I know he was seeking a way, while I was in high school, to send me for a few years of additional education in the United States.

At this time, however, we were completing plans for the continuation of my education in our country's capital. I had finished my first two high-school years in Tarlac and we were moving to Manila, where I would enter the Manila High School in my third year.

My father's tenure as governor of Tarlac was over. He had served for six years. To further the education of his children he brought his family to Manila and rented a house on Calle Cabildo in the old Walled City.

My ambitions were swelling. I was ready for the big city and was confident it was waiting for me.

Nevertheless a large share of a boy's heart would be left in Tarlac. There were good friends and happy memories, and saddest of all was the parting with the minister's daughter. When I said good-bye to her I was positive the love I felt would never die, but when in the following fall I entered the Manila High School as a Junior the first love in Tarlac became a dream, misted over in the roseate effulgence of a love that was new.

Five

FROM the very first, Manila was my city. Since my introduction to the former Philippine capital as a student I have visited every great city in the world and there is none more beautiful. I fell in love with Manila at first sight, and in turn it opened its heart to me.

My plans called for four years of study—my last two high-school years and a two-year English course at the university in the hope of obtaining my Bachelor's degree in Liberal Arts.

I plunged into work and the life of a great cosmopolitan city. Camiling became a child's remembered paradise, Tarlac an adolescent's dream. Life in Manila was real and earnest and filled with action. I took part in activities both in and out of the classrooms that would rob me of much of my sleep for the next dozen years, but I have always been too interested in what is going on about me to need a great deal of sleep.

My enrollment in the Manila High School was an experiment on my father's part. He had radical ideas about education, and as a former educator he was interested in studying the difference in advantages between public and private schools. He decided to divide the educational systems between his two eldest sons. As a result I was selected to attend the public high school, with the intention of ultimately going on to the state university, while Henry, my older brother, who had announced his intention of becoming a physician, was registered in the Ateneo de Manila, privately run by the Jesuit Fathers. Later he attended the University of Santo Tomas. This historic university, founded in 1620, would be made into the infamous concentration camp by the Japanese during World War II.

My father lived to see both of us graduate from the schools he had chosen, but what conclusions he drew from their advantages or disadvantages we never knew. He was equally proud of us both.

The public school system as set up in the Philippines with the help of American teachers got me out into the world quicker and I believe better equipped to make a living than most of the young men I knew who went through longer years in private schools. I am not referring to my brother, who in choosing medicine had chosen the long, arduous, and always exemplary way.

Fortunately for me study was easy as always, and I had time and energy to spend on more interesting matters.

There were two debating clubs in the Manila High School, the Cryptia and the Rizal. I had found my voice and was eager to use it. Perhaps I recalled my father's prophecy that I would someday be an orator. At any rate I applied for membership in the Cryptia, which was considered the superior club.

One had to pass a preliminary test in the form of a debate before being put up for membership. Three titles were written on paper slips and placed in a hat. I drew the subject, "Should capital punishment be abolished?"

Now it happened that at this time I was heartily in favor of capital punishment, but since I was to argue in the affirmative I reversed my guns and made a speech in full-voiced advocation of its abolishment. I was unanimously invited into the club.

My adviser entered me at once into the preliminaries for the annual debate. I won in the semifinals and was one of three chosen to compete in the finals, where once more I found myself declaiming passionately for the abolition of capital punishment. I gave my all to the contest, but one of the boys on our side developed stage fright and forgot what he had planned to say and we abolitionists lost.

But I had tasted blood. My father had been right and I was going to be an orator. I entered every contest. Then came the oratorical contest, which I have described in an earlier book, where I won first prize with my heartfelt declaration on the subject, "My faith in America."

My father was deeply touched by the speech. "That settles it," he told me. "Someday and somehow I'm going to send you to America."

I got my first job while in high school. It was temporary work as a parttime Civil Service clerk in the provincial treasurer's office at twenty pesos a month.

Recently I checked over my Civil Service record. There I was, down as a clerk with my service rated as "satisfactory."

This twenty pesos was the first money I had earned. When I collected my first month's pay I bought a peso rosary for my mother. The rest I blew in on the aforementioned blue serge suit and tan shoes that so startled my father. I got little wear out of that outfit, but I continued to pay for it for many lean months, at ten pesos per month.

Between school and the new job life was full, but I found time for romance. My new love was a mestiza, a classmate at Manila High; and again I carried books and poured out letters and poems. Again my romance was not impractical, because I admired not only her appearance but her intellect, for she was a brilliant student both in physics and biology, subjects I had added to my own curriculum and in which I found myself completely hopeless.

In turn I helped her in her literary subjects. The pattern was growing familiar.

Literature was still my chosen field. In my spare time I continued trying to write. Through my father's political activities I had become aware of the great power newspapermen could wield. I saw some of the leading gentlemen of the Manila press from afar, came to know them by face and name, and envied these alert, aloof beings who daily swung the opinions of a city their way.

The idea came to me with startling suddenness. I wanted to write. Why not write for a newspaper?

I told my father this ambition. If I could get work on one of the Manila papers, I said, I could give up my job as a clerk and learn to write while working. It would not detract from my schooling, I added hastily.

My father thought the matter over but said nothing, until a few days later he introduced me to his friend Victoriano (Vic) Yamzon. "This is my son," my father said. "He wants to be a newspaperman."

Yamzon looked me over with friendly curiosity and waited for me to say something. For once I was speechless. Yamzon was the number-one reporter of Manila, the star of the American newspaper, the Manila *Times*. I was awed by his good looks and his perfect English.

They both seemed waiting for me to voice my ambitions, but I continued mute. Nothing more was said. My father did not mention the subject again.

As the days went by I could not forget the meeting with Yamzon. I grew angry; I had muffed my chance. A few weeks later, without a word to anyone, I walked boldly into the Manila *Times* building and asked admittance to Yamzon's office. Once more in that dazzling presence I lost the power of speech.

Yamzon waited, more curious than before.

At last with an effort I broke through the vocal barrier. "Mr. Yamzon," I babbled wildly, "I want to be just like you."

He grinned. He knew what I meant. Then he looked serious. "Come in tomorrow morning and I'll recommend you to Mr. Thibault for a job as cub reporter."

I knew my *Who's Who* of Manila journalism. L. H. Thibault was from America, and the city editor and business manager of the Manila *Times*. The paper also had the added luster of nobility, for Wilmot Lewis of England, its editor, was later to become Sir Wilmot, Washington chief correspondent of the London *Times*.

I found my voice. "What's a cub reporter?"

"That means you'll just be starting out so you won't get a salary. After you've served your apprenticeship as a cub and become a full-fledged reporter then you get paid."

"How long will I have to be a cub?" I asked.

"That's up to you," Yamzon answered. Then he started. "Say, why wait for tomorrow? Come with me and we'll talk to Mr. Thibault right now."

I followed him in a daze into my first editorial room. What followed happened easily and was quickly settled. Yamzon introduced me to Thibault with a casual, "Here's a young man who wants to be a reporter."

The manager gave a quick glance at his star reporter from over a mound of newly printed sheets and typewritten "takes." Then he turned his gimlet look on me. "Be in tomorrow at eight," he snapped.

That was all there was to that. I was a newspaperman. I was a cub reporter and determined not to be a cub for long.

At eight the next morning I was again before his desk.

Thibault looked up from his never-ending task of editing to brief me on the science of newswriting. In two sentences he laid the premise that was to support me through many years of reporting news. I've cited these laws many times, for I've found no better advice for fledgling reporters.

Cram everything you know into the first paragraph—that's called your lead; go on from there.

Memorize the four W's—who, where, when, and what—those are a reporter's ABC's.

Although I would receive no salary, he added, I would be allotted two streetcar tickets a day.

He then mentioned offhandedly that my first assignment would be the Senate.

I was astonished. Green though I was, I knew no cub was ever sent to cover that august body. Yamzon was the Senate reporter for the *Times*.

He saw my concern, and went on to explain that while the Senate was well-covered by seasoned reporters who knew its politics and were up on political facts, still he felt there was room for a wide-eyed youngster with a fresh point of view and an inquiring mind. I was to browse around the outside of Senate affairs and pick up such extra tidbits as could be found. These I would incorporate into a column to be called "Senate Doings."

I was to start this task on the following day after school. He then jerked his thumb toward a typewriter, told me it was mine, and apparently forgot me. . . .

I sat at the typewriter desk in that noisy, littered "local" room and was blissfully happy. Reporters came and went, copy boys rushed to and fro waving short "takes" and long galleys. Wet inky proof pages fluttered under Thibault's hand. Bent over the mountain of copy he did not look up.

There was a quickness, an excitement, and a knowingness to all this that attracted me with passionate interest. I knew this was my life. I listened to the arguments, reportings, discussions going at Thibault's desk—the pounding untidy heart of this activity—and heard from the adjoining room the jerky roar of the presses. What was going on out there?

I knew I would find it. I was going to learn the newspaper business from one end to the other. A great deal was going on in this *Times* office I did not understand, but I was going to understand it all.

Not once did it occur to me that it was unusual for a cub to become a columnist on his first day. I did not know that most reporters work years before being awarded that plum of newspaper assignments, a column of one's own.

Thibault had told me mine would carry no by-line. That did not bother me. Names of news writers were seldom printed in Manila or anywhere else at this time. Anonymity would help

me to conceal my job on the *Times* from my father, for until
I had graduated from the cub division and had a salary I did not
want him to know about it. The family could think me in study
hall afternoons or playing baseball. Being a newspaperman was
my secret, I hugged it to my heart.

"Romulo!" It was my first desk call and it sounded like
thunder.

A fire alarm had sounded over my head and Thibault was
beckoning. The other reporters were busy at their typewriters.

"You," said my city editor, jerking an iron thumb my way,
"cover that fire!"

He gave me the location and I dashed out as if the city of
Manila were threatened with combustion. The fire was in a
shed and quickly extinguished. Panting, I returned to my office,
to my own desk and typewriter. Just as my fellow reporters
were doing, I inserted the short paper sheets under the roller.
Then I realized I did not know how to type.

A furtive survey of the room reassured me. Some of the best
newsmen in Manila were in that local room and none of them
seemed to be other than two-finger virtuosos on the lettered
keys. Just the same, some of those men were rapid typists.

What man can do, I can do has always been my motto.

I hunched over the desk and began to write. By hunt and
peck on the typewriter, in true reportorial style I pounded out
my first news story on a machine as noisy as a harvester.

This was to be my masterpiece. Three pages of throbbing
prose were pecked into being. I had every intention of writing
much more, but Thibault had looked at the clock, then at me,
and sent a copy boy over to snatch the last page from my typewriter. So it was that midway in inspiration I learned the nature
of a deadline. Thibault took the time to remark that stories not
ready by deadline never saw print, and I wistfully watched my
first news story vanish into the maw of the composing room.

Now I learned that I was free for the day, and that the first
edition would "hit the streets" that afternoon at two-thirty. At

that hour I was posted in a strategic position in the ice cream parlor La Favorita. Seated at a table by the window I nervously consumed dishes of ice cream and watched the pressroom door like a hawk waiting to pounce. When the first horse-drawn delivery trucks rolled up to that door I was out with my five centavos on the ready for the first paper off the press. The hot, damp, inky smell of those limp sheets was wonderful and would always be. Even now, years from the reportorial life, I love the stinking fragrance of a paper right off the press.

My story was not on the front page where I had confidently expected to find it. I tore through the pages, column by column, line by line. At last, in a collection of local odds and ends labeled "Police News," I found my masterpiece shaved down to a brief item known as a "take."

Well, there would be other assignments. But it took courage to report before Thibault's desk after school the following day.

He was too busy to say much. "Read your story yesterday?"

I spoke more coldly than a cub should to a city editor. "Yes. I found it. Finally!"

He looked up at that. "Then you've had your first practical lesson in news reporting. Brevity and a sense of proportion. If you needed three pages to describe a fire in a shed how much space would you want if Malacañang Palace burned to the ground?"

A subdued cub set off for the Senate.

In its pressroom I found the Valhalla of that newspaper world of which I had dreamed. These godly men, who covered the high offices of my country, were of heroic stature to me.

They were absorbed in their own impressive affairs and paid little attention to a green cub doing parttime reporting when he was out of the classroom. I was fifteen and to my annoyance looked younger. They were men of years of experience, thirty-five to forty years of age. They were leaders in the newspaper world, and later they were all to become civic and political leaders in the Philippines.

I looked upon them with awe as men who were established
in their careers. I did not know they were on their way to
greater power and feeling their way as I was feeling mine.

Yamzon was top man in this group of experts. He was my
sponsor and found time to introduce me to his colleagues. Their
newspaper writings were unsigned but they were famed in the
city, and I recognized each man by name. They were fine writers and distinguished men.

Among them was Manuel Briones, a member of the Spanish
Academy; Claro M. Recto, whose poetry I knew by heart,
having read it to my father in Camiling; Arsenio N. Luz;
Luis Improgo Salcedo; Francisco Varona; Ramon Torres; and
Vicente Almoalla, star writer for the powerful Manila *Daily
Bulletin* and Yamzon's chief rival.

These men took a slightly superior attitude toward me at
first, but Yamzon's introduction brought me into the fold. They
took turns walking me through the Senate chambers, explaining
the workings and introducing me to all we met who might be
of help to a new reporter.

They invariably introduced me as the son of Governor Romulo, which I discovered did not handicap me in the least.
Everyone we met seemed to know and think highly of the
gentle, studious Governor from the provinces.

These older reporters might easily have ganged up on an
eager-beaver boy reporter muscling in on their terrain. Perhaps
they were kind because I had no idea I was doing that. I was
fascinated by all they told me and all I saw, and without their
concerted help I could never have produced my opening column on "Senate Doings."

As a result of this help, it was singularly good for a first column and I took pride in it.

My only regret was that I could not show it to my father and
tell him how highly he was regarded by the men I had met in
the Senate building. But I would not let him know until I had

a salary to show. So I wrote my column for three months before my father learned I was working on the *Times*.

Considering the trend my life would take later on I cannot think of better training than was given me during the three months I worked without salary on the *Times*. I worked hard. I would follow a lead through to its end if it took all night. I learned to assemble facts, to write as well as possible the thing I wished to say, and above all, to save space. I read every word written by the older reporters I so admired and studied the way they handled reports and interviews. This was training of the best kind for a newspaper career.

Although I did not know it then I was also receiving free training in the school of diplomacy.

During my three months as a cub I learned the importance of connections and of preserving them whether one liked the connectee or not. I learned not to show disapproval or anger and to delay ill will under the cover of expediency. I learned to distrust certain politicians and to trust others and to treat both sides fairly. I might dislike a man and all he represented, but if he was a source of news I accepted him as a good source if not as a good man. It was not my business to judge and condemn. I was a reporter, a shell in which the voices of other men resounded.

With this tolerance I won the trust of men in key positions, and from time to time they would give me exclusive items. My little column was creating a small but growing circle of readers.

Among its followers was my father, and I drew out his comments with breathless anxiety but dared not tell him the authorship was mine.

Evidently the *Times* thought it was all right, for at the end of three months Thibault told me the paper had decided to keep me on. I would now be a full-fledged, salaried reporter.

My first thought was, "Now I can tell my father!"

My financial affairs during these vital three months had been decidedly rocky. All I had to sustain my high-school days and my afternoon working hours were the two daily streetcar tickets and the small allowance given me by my father. This left little leeway for the ice cream that was my indulgence. Now in a pleasurable daze I heard Mr. Thibault say my salary would be seventy-five pesos a month, and as added largess I would receive each month a full booklet of streetcar tickets.

My mathematical sense was as weak as ever, but I was able to calculate the princely income of seventy-five pesos a month! The peso was then worth fifty cents in gold.

I doubt if I actually believed in this windfall until I collected my first month's salary and carried it home intact to show my father as proof that for three months I had been a columnist on the *Times*. He made no attempt to conceal his delight, and his praise went to my head.

"From now on," I told him importantly, "I want no more allowance money from you. I'm independent. And what's more, I expect to pay for my board."

The indulgent parent became an outraged patriarch. "As long as I am alive," my father stormed, "no son of mine is going to pay board in my home!"

Sub rosa, I offered my earnings to my mother. To my surprise she accepted the money without comment and from then on I turned nearly all I earned over to her.

One month later I was sent for by Frank Holland, city editor of the *Cable-News*, the American rival sheet of the Manila *Times*. Holland was an editor out of *The Front Page*, and his dramatic personality hit me like a blow. He was bald, he was smoking a cigar, and he wore an eyeshade that cast a fascinating green tint over his bulldog features. He was tough, keen, all dynamo. I took one look at Holland and knew someday I would own an eyeshade like that. Another hero had entered my life.

Holland wasted no words. "Rommy," he started in, as if he had always known me, "I hear you're doing an up-and-coming job of reporting on the *Times*. We have a vacancy. How about coming to work for us at double your salary?"

Double? That was one hundred-and-fifty pesos. Just like that! While I was still counting, I remembered. Yamzon and Thibault had been wonderful to me. There was that little matter of loyalty.

"I'll have to consult my friends on the *Times*," I said.

Holland squinted under his green shade. "Don't take too long. If you aren't back by ten tomorrow I'll have to look for someone else."

I rushed back to the *Times* and found Yamzon there. Breathless, I poured out my story: the offer, my sense of loyalty, my gratitude to him for getting me my job on the *Times*. Under these circumstances, I asked, was it right for me to go over to the *Cable-News?* "At double the salary," I added, modestly.

Yamzon blinked. "Grab it!" he told me.

"But I like the *Times!*" I wailed.

"Son," he said, with more warmth than he had ever shown, "the newspaper game is a tough game. It won't look out for you. You have to look after yourself. When you see a better spot than the one you're in don't ever hesitate. Grab it!"

I was wretched with indecision. I went to Thibault and told him all. He looked at me just as Yamzon had, then in almost the same words he gave his advice.

"Don't wait. Grab it!"

I still was ridden with doubt. I confided my problem to every member of the staff I knew.

Their enthusiasm for my leaving was so unanimous I began to suspect I was not very well-liked on the *Times!* I would realize later how generous they were in their attitude. This was long before the Newspaper Guild was formed and many a good newspaperman would die in a harness grown burdensome because out of loyalty he had stuck to a job without a future.

I still favor loyalty. It is the key quality for which I have chosen my young candidates for diplomatic training. But it must be tempered with reason and an eye to one's personal future, and not given blindly.

That night was spent in mental wrestling. Morning came and I was still uncertain as to the justice of deserting the *Times*. Ambition won, and I am glad it did. I was in the *Cable-News* pressroom at ten o'clock.

Holland didn't seem surprised to see me. "Now get this through your head," he said grouchily. "One-hundred-and-fifty pesos is a lot of money. We're only giving it to you because of what we've heard about the way you've worked on the *Times*. We're paying you twice as much as they did, so we expect you to do twice as much good work for us."

He explained what was expected of me, and it was indeed double if not triple the work I had been doing.

I would not only continue to cover the Senate, but I would also cover City Hall. Added to these duties would be a new innovation borrowed from newspapers in America. I was to collect the vital statistics and print a daily list of all who had married, died, or been born.

"Where will I get these lists?" I asked.

"Board of Health for the births and weddings. Cemetery for the deaths."

"But those places are at opposite ends of town!" I burst out, for nothing had been said about car tickets and I could see my fine new salary melting before the demands of travel.

Holland threw in one last splendid touch. "You'll have streetcar tickets unlimited. As soon as one book is used up just go to the cashier and sign for another."

I had arrived.

As further proof Holland pointed to the desk next to his own and said it was to be mine. It was the spot of honor in the local room. I remembered my desk at the *Times* in the littered corner far below the salt and wondered blissfully why I had ever hesitated.

When I told my mother I was receiving one-hundred-and-fifty pesos for after-school work she told me to stop talking nonsense. When I assured her it was true she was overwhelmed by a mixture of pride, anxiety, and dismay. Was it right for a sixteen-year-old boy to be earning an income of that size?

"Think of it," she kept repeating. "For a boy still in high school to earn so much, and your older brother who is in private school has not made even a centavo!"

This was not entirely fair, since Henry had chosen medicine, which takes years more study than a general course, while I had chosen a way which for me was an easy and facile one.

When I told her to choose a gift from my largess she found it impossible to make up her mind. One might think she had never been offered a gift before. But I insisted the first money from my new salary must be spent on her, and eventually, after much soul-searching, she settled upon a kimono. Nearly all the rest, as before, I turned over to her without comment from either of us.

My schedule would have wilted the stamina of anyone older and less determined. I spent a full day in school and was ready to start my news rounds about four-thirty. Time could not be wasted, so I worked out a travel pattern that started at City Hall, which was near the high school. There I cultivated sources until a list of marriages and births would be typed out and waiting for me, and at times I could even arrange for them to be phoned into the newspaper office. From City Hall I went across town by streetcar to the Cementerio del Norte, where my friend the caretaker was waiting in his office by the gates with the names of the newly interred. From there I rushed to the Senate, arriving around five when the sessions opened. As a rule they ended about seven, but often I did not wait for the closing. I listened until my interest waned, then took a farewell tour around the building to pick up whatever leftover crumbs were to be found in those august halls. Most of the time I left the Senate around six, hurried back to the *Cable-News*, and turned out my pockets. With my various lists and notes spread beside the typewriter I began pecking out my reports.

Sometime around seven, with other reporters, I would wander off to a small Chinese restaurant on the corner for a light snack, then I would be at my typewriter again, working often until midnight.

No matter how late I worked, I was up early the next morning and in my first class at nine.

Sleep did not matter. School was losing first place in my new scheme of life. Life was concentrated for me in the local room of the *Cable-News*, where the presiding genius was Holland.

From my desk beside his I watched him every minute I was free. Under the green shade the x-ray gaze was steady, as he read, edited and discarded, clipped and chose from the never-diminishing mound of copy, wrote headlines and subheads, and made up the front page.

I asked no questions. I watched and listened and puzzled out for myself why things were done. I eavesdropped at conferences between Holland and top members of the staff as to the choice of lead stories and scareheads and the "balancing" of the front page that it might have items of interest to catch every eye. I studied every column as the editions came to my desk, trying to figure out why certain stories were given top play and others were underplayed. What was a sure-fire head? Which story had human interest? Which contained popular appeal?

I was in the newspaper business for good, and I planned to master every angle. Whatever I tried, I wanted to be my best. I had been that way in sports, in my studies, and in the debates. Now I was out to win again. Holland was my master. I was forming myself as a newspaperman in his image.

I was no longer satisfied with the dream of being a star reporter. I wanted to be an editor like Frank Holland.

Another hero entered my life, who in the long run would prove to be the most important of all. I have often told how as a

high-school senior I perched with other students atop the old
Spanish wall and watched Manuel L. Quezon step through the
gate broken in that wall to honor his triumphal return from
America with the confirmed Jones Act. This was one of the
finest moments in his life, and it was my first glimpse of the man
who was to mean so much to me.

Our nation was not yet a commonwealth. Quezon was President of the Senate but all knew he was destined to be the future
president of the Philippines. "Mr. President," men called him
even then.

On this day he was the hero returned. The Jones Act was the
first definite pledge of future independence given us by the
American Congress. It permitted the Philippines to establish its
own legislative body. It was our first great triumph since we
had lost the struggle against America, and we owed it to the
persistence of our people, to America, and to Quezon.

He was the idol of Philippine youth. We who were young
on that day—would we ever forget that gallant, debonair figure,
the radiant smile, the smooth, black hair shining in the sun?

We devoured every mannerism, every detail. Apart from his
heroic qualities, Quezon was the epitome of elegance. He was
wearing the first two-tone sport shoes we had ever seen, black
and white, and his tie and kerchief matched!

I had found another sartorial model on which to pattern my
appearance. Clothes had always been important to me, and
Quezon's appearance impressed this importance upon me for
life. A man who is well-dressed is at ease and sure of himself.
He is acceptable to others and to himself.

Within the week all the students I knew had two-tone shoes
and matching ties and kerchiefs.

Imitation did not stop there. We copied Quezon's walk, his
manner, his way of dancing. He had learned the tango in the
United States and we learned to dance it Quezon's way.

Now I had a living, three-dimensional hero to study, and I

wanted to know all about him and to know him personally. My
interest in politics increased with the return of Quezon.

Politics had taken hold of my imagination when my father
ran for mayor of Camiling. Afternoons in the Senate chambers
had increased this interest. I knew politics was the greatest
working power any country could develop. It would be of
utmost importance to the Philippines. Quezon was the focal
point of that growing power.

From my seat in the press balcony of the Senate I watched
Quezon in the presidential chair. I heard him speak. I might
have approached him perhaps in my reportorial guise but I did
not. I felt privileged to watch a true patriot who had greatness,
as well as good looks and charm. I was content to worship my
idol from afar.

It was due to this enraptured distant observation that I
stumbled onto the first great landmark in any newspaperman's
life—my first front-page story.

Time meant nothing to me if I was interested. There was no
Newspaper Guild to check my hours, so if a story excited me I
stuck with it until its possibilities were exhausted.

I was in the press gallery at the Senate, almost dropping off
to sleep and wondering whether or not I should rush through
my assignment that night and attend the carnival. The time of
carnival, which marks the start of Lent and the end of gaiety
in Manila, is always one of laxity where work is concerned, and
one by one the other reporters had left the gallery to hurry to
the auditorium where the first of the great balls was being held.
Before leaving they told me the day's session had been dry as
dust. Evidently the Senators had the same opinion, for most of
them seemed drowsing in their chairs.

I longed to be off to the celebration, but duty clamped me to
my seat. Quezon started to speak. I sat up hoping some chance
observation might translate into the next day's news.

Then I was galvanized. Quezon was in one of the angry

moods I had heard other reporters describe with awe. He was all fighter and leader—the unquenchable soul of the Philippines. He held a newspaper in his hand—it was *La Vanguardia*, owned by the Roces family, which had been attacking him—and he shook it over his head as he raged against its policy. What an artist of drama he was in his anger!

His wrath shot through that lethargic meeting like an arrow. I was hanging over the balcony rail, open-mouthed, too excited to take notes. It was a scene more dynamic than any I had seen played on a stage. It had been a long time since the Senate chamber had vibrated to such a storm. I turned around in search of other reporters to share this intensity, but I was alone in the gallery.

In fiery words Quezon denounced Alejandro Roces, his paper, and his policy; then, with a gesture of supreme contempt, he hurled the paper to the Senate floor.

I waited until the session ended, then galloped back to the *Cable-News* as fast as I could go. Nearly all the staff had left, but Holland was still at his desk. I started to babble my report, but before I could finish Holland gestured toward my desk.

"Get to it," he said.

Hunt and peck on the keys, I slashed through the Senate excitement. Every word Quezon had spoken came back as clearly to me as if it were a recording. My retentive memory had never before faced such a demand. I recalled his every intonation, each gesture, his mounting fury, the dismay of his Senatorial listeners, and that final crashing moment when he had hurled the Roces paper to his feet.

All the admiration I felt for Quezon was in that story. It was not impersonal; it burned with his anger, which I felt as if it were my own.

Holland read over my shoulder as I typed. His green shade was pushed back on his bald head and his eyes were snapping with excitement. He was all newsman then, nose down on the hunt. As I came to the end of each page he snatched it from the machine, scanned it with x-ray agility, and bellowed for a boy to rush it into the pressroom, at intervals exclaiming, "Wonderful! Wonderful!"

They say the test of a true newspaperman is his ability to turn handsprings with excitement over each new story. Holland had that ability. I learned, as I typed madly under his burning attention, that I had too!

My story filled three columns on the front page of the *Cable-News* the next day. Ours was the only paper in Manila that had the story.

There is just one first front-page scoop in any reporter's lifetime. I don't know how I survived the dullness of classes that day. My story was unsigned, but every newspaperman in Manila would know!

I set out after classes for the Senate, prepared to accept with becoming modesty the laurels that were certain to be offered me by the Senators and my fellow scribes.

My hopes fell as I entered. Felipe Buencamino, Jr., Secretary of the Senate, was waiting at the door, and obviously he had been stationed there to intercept me. I had never seen anyone look sterner.

"The President has called all the reporters into his office," he announced. "He wants you there right away."

"What have I done?" I demanded, words to be spoken by me often in an all too impetuous life.

No answer came from the guardian of the temple and with quaking knees I followed him into the office of the President of the Senate.

I had never entered it before. I was as nervous as in my boyhood days when a farmer had caught me stealing mangoes. Quezon was famed for singling out reporters who had roused his anger. I had heard his diatribe against the publisher Roces and I could picture myself reduced to quivering jelly on his elegant rug.

The office was a splendid place. I knew that even as I advanced timidly toward his desk. Those blazing, beautiful eyes, intent as a leopard's on its prey, were fixed upon me, and so was the attention of all my fellow scribes.

Standing before Quezon, close to my hero for the first time, I felt the emanation of power. It was like a psychic wave, impossible to describe. Why some men have it and others do not I have never been able to learn, but Quezon had it to an extraordinary degree. It was a positive magnetic charm that could control and compel—and terrify, as it did me in that moment before his desk.

As frightened as I was, my reporter's eye did not miss an object in that room. I noted the fine rug and the handsome office furniture, the silent, watching ring of reporters, and, flanked by two secretaries, the elegant graceful figure standing behind his desk—Quezon.

The desk was beautiful, of shining narra wood that was mellow as old ivory. It was bare except for the morning edition of the *Cable-News*. His beautifully groomed hand pointed at my scoop, three columns of irrefutable accusation in cold print.

"You are Romulo?"

I felt very small and young—David surrounded by Goliaths. My muttered "Yes" was an adolescent squeak.

"And you wrote this?"

The eyes and voice of the inquisitor, the circle of the tribunal. I was on the rack. I wondered if I would ever know a worse moment or if I would ever be able to live through this one.

He snapped, "Do you take shorthand?"

My answer was lower and squeakier than before. I had been too nervous to think of adding "sir" to my answers. Then I quavered, "Is anything wrong with it?"

"Wrong?" Suddenly the sun burst through clouds, the wonderful warming Quezon smile poured over me, his hand went out and clasped mine. "My God, boy, it's wonderful! You've not only reproduced my speech you've improved on it. Let me shake hands with you."

Then the others were around me pounding my back and shaking my hand with the generosity of newspapermen, who will fight tooth and nail to prevent being scooped and laud to the skies the opponent who has scooped them.

I basked in their praise. At last I was upper echelon—accepted and approved by my heroes of the press. But my eyes were on the smiling, friendly man behind the shining desk—Quezon, hero of heroes from that moment on. In that first meeting he might have ordered me as he willed. I was his creature. Quezon could win any person he chose with the warm, personal charm that was his greatest asset as politician and man.

Perhaps he wanted to insure his victory when he called me back to his desk as I was filing out of his office with the others. He spoke in low, personal tones. "They tell me you're Governor Romulo's son. I've always admired him. Tell me, where are you studying?"

I explained I was just about to graduate from the Manila High School and planned to enter the university in the fall.

"And your major?"

I told him, liberal arts.

His last words were, "Keep in touch with me."

I left his office knowing I was a marked man.

Six

THE meeting with Quezon changed me. I was obsessed with the memory of the moment when that frightening figure of power had relaxed and become all friendly charm, a man I wanted to please and follow. I worked harder than ever in school and at my reporting, hoping to continue to hold his interest and respect.

He had shown definite interest in a cub reporter who had worshiped him from afar, and he continued this interest. Each time he entered the Senate chambers and passed under the press gallery he singled me out for a wave and friendly grin. "Hello there, Romulo."

This set me apart from my fellow reporters and caused me to set my sights on a higher goal.

I began an unremitting study of the two men in the Senate closest to Quezon. The meeting with the Senate President had been my first close-range glimpse of power. These men were power's next of kin.

They were Buencamino and Elpidio Quirino, the latter would be our postwar president in the Philippines. These men had been pleasant to me since I started as the Senate's youngest reporter. As I made my late afternoon rounds in the halls I often tapped meekly at their office doors. Sometimes they would ask me in and even favor me with choice bits of news. Since these tidbits were always items the other reporters were not given I had proof of their liking. Now that I had passed Quezon's burning-eyed survey their kindness was even more pronounced.

Sometimes their doors remained closed. Sometimes all doors

seemed closed to me. Things were going on inside those rooms
in which a boy outsider had no share. How I envied the two
who were never barred from any office, not even Quezon's!
They were close to him, in his confidence, all-knowing.

How did men attain such places of power?

I was only a high-school student. I felt puerile, timid, unsure
of myself. I had none of the confidence of these leaders I so
admired and no idea how that confidence could be developed.

How did they get that way?

I was haunted by the memory of that inner chamber that
held the heart of Philippine affairs. I remembered the terrifying
presence that had become kindly and human to a small, scared
reporter. And I made a promise to myself that if ever I attained
a position of authority I would try to remember to be kind.

It was a promise I have tried to keep.

Why was I so obsessed with respect for power? What inner
demand kept my nose to the grindstone when I should have
been enjoying light-hearted youth, and why, after half a century, does it drive me still?

At home my skyrocketing career was followed with pride
and dismay. Why this probing into political interests beyond
my years? Why was I determined to make every waking hour
count? Why wasn't I content with high-school friends and
games and studies and girls and dances as were the other boys
of my age?

And the answer, too easy to speak, so difficult for others to
understand, was the charge laid upon me in babyhood. I was a
Filipino. The need to uphold the dignity and honor and pride
of my race had been impressed upon me at my grandmother's
knee. I had absorbed it from my parents. The study of my
country's history in my growing years had translated this pride
into facts. Mine was a good race. Ours was a good country. I
loved every foot of it that I knew—Manila, Tarlac, Camiling.
I had been reared in a wonderful country among wonderful

people and I wanted all the rest of the world to know and respect the Philippines.

I grew in importance as I grew in years because I was a Filipino. To do my best, to increase and never lessen my country's pride was the underlying motivation of all I might attempt. To that end I had flung myself into sports and studies, into the debating clubs and journalism. I had to be outstanding, to make the greatest effort to win, to prove I was capable not in spite of having been born a Filipino but because I *was* a Filipino.

This has been the driving force of my life. It has also been a restraining force. There were many times I might have given way to loss of temper or dignity, and would not because I am a Filipino.

As one of the new generation of Filipinos under American authority I had the advantage of the new educational and governmental methods America introduced. It was up to me and the others to show the Americans that we had profited. America had promised us our independence. It was up to my generation to prove worthy, to prove that all they had done for us and all we were doing to aid our own self-development was worthwhile.

Someday the Philippines would be free, like America. It rested upon my generation to be ready when that time came and show the world what we could achieve.

All the students I knew were talking, working, planning toward that end. If I had talents for voicing their longings, for assuming leadership I was determined to develop them fully. We knew what the rest of the world thought of the Filipino, if it thought of him at all. He had been taken over by the Americans. The sovereign powers ruling in other Asian countries were spreading adept propaganda to prophesy that we never would be able to develop as a nation and that America would be foolish indeed ever to give us our freedom.

So all that my generation had to look forward to rested upon that single word—freedom. It is the most important word in any language. It was the basis of a new life that had been promised us and for which we determined to prove ourselves worthy.

We had faith in ourselves and in America. I retained my faith in America—my prize-winning high-school oration proved that. I had brought it with me from Camiling to Tarlac to Manila, and there I must admit my burning idealism received several dousings of very cold water.

The Americans I had known in the province of Tarlac were sincere, dedicated people who had come to the Philippines to help the Filipinos and were prepared to share our lives. They liked us and showed it. They appreciated our history, our values, and our sense of pride. They were living examples of the democracy they had come to teach, and we could not have had finer. I was certain all Americans were friendly, wise, and fair, like our friends in Camiling and Tarlac.

Then we moved to Manila where disillusionment was slow but irrefutable. We still had many American friends. But gradually I became aware of a cancer of ill will growing in the city. It was turning against us, the Filipinos.

There was an American element in the city that associated with Americans only and was openly contemptuous of what they called "the natives."

I heard such reports and refused to believe them. In the first place, I argued, Americanism was a form of faith, and no true American sneered at another race. America itself was made up of many races, and all were equal. And again, so I protested, the Americans were people of breeding and would never behave unpleasantly in a country where they were guests.

So I argued, so I believed, and I had to find out for myself.

The America I had imagined, having heard of it, read of it, and dreamed of it all my life, was a looking-glass world into which I would step someday to prove to my own satisfaction that all the glowing reports were true. Meantime I was content to know it existed as an example of Christian charity for all the earth.

My eyes were opened on the afternoon I dropped into the Manila Army and Navy Club at the invitation of an American friend.

Since this is a deeply personal account of myself I am sure I have made it painfully clear that I had at that time a high sense of my own value, as a person and as a citizen. A large and affectionate family circle, a larger group of Filipino and American friends had not served to lower my self-esteem. As a governor's son doors opened before me and I never questioned my right to go wherever I was asked and chose to go. Two years in the Manila High School, where my journalistic and debating successes had made me a very large toad in a very small puddle, and my brief but telling career as a gentleman of the press had added to my self-assurance.

I was accustomed to entering the offices of our government leaders. I was accustomed to associating with Filipinos and Americans, to dining, visiting, meeting with both on intimate terms of friendship. I had grown up believing that all Americans believed as they had taught us to believe—that all men are equal.

As I walked into the Army and Navy Club that afternoon the question of racial distinction never occurred to me.

A club servant met me at the door. He was a Filipino and did not mince words. "What do you want to come in here for?" he asked bitterly. "This is an American club for Americans and they don't want Filipinos in it."

I knew he was telling the truth and that the worst I had heard was true. It was the first humiliating experience of my life. I have survived it, but I have never forgotten its ugliness, and I never shall.

Many writers have described the ease with which I meet all types and situations and explain the fact that I accept and am accepted because I take my welcome for granted, I carry no chip on my shoulder. I carried no chip until that day when I found myself barred from a club in my own country, and I dropped it on that same day.

For I returned to high school sick at heart. I was an embittered, unhappy young Filipino, and I might never have lost that bitterness if I had not chanced to run into Michael J. O'Malley. He was my school principal and my favorite member of the staff. To him I poured out the story of my humiliation. How could I believe in America if Americans behaved that way?

His friendship and understanding may have saved America an enemy that day. There is no emotion so devastating as humiliation.

"Carlos, the members of that club are military men," he told me. "Army and navy people are alike all over the world. They don't care too much about associating with anyone not in uniform. Even in America they stick together. They're Americans and I'm an American, but I'm not army and they don't want me in their club any more than they want you, and for my part I haven't any interest in going there."

In those simple words he knocked the chip off my shoulder for life.

I have told this story of O'Malley many times before, along with an account of our joyous reunion in San Francisco where he was the first old friend to greet me in the United States after my rescue from Bataan, but I repeat it here because it is the most important incident in my early life.

I had been mortally wounded and would never forget. I made up my mind to fight the injustice of unequal treatment on racial terms wherever it appeared, and I have done that all my life, in my first editorials, in speeches, in books and articles and interviews, on TV and over the air, and on the floors of the American Congress and the United Nations. It was the bus boy at the Army and Navy Club who started me on this lifetime crusade, and I am on it still, and am grateful to him.

This was one episode of my high-school years I did not report at home. There was another, too, which was kept secret from my family circle for some time—my first plane ride.

Any sort of trip by air is a humdrum occurrence today, but

my first trip marked the end of an age for me and a glimpse of
the future world. It was not an adventure that would have been
shared with sympathy by my parents.

My flight was a newspaper assignment. I was to go up in one
of the first planes ever to soar over Manila. I accepted with
mixed feelings and almost turned back at the field. The pioneer
two-seater crate resting on the Luneta looked no larger than a
baby carriage. It was almost on that exact spot that I had seen
my first plane go up, years before, with an American woman
at the stick. It had taken some time for aviation to come to
Manila, but it was here and I was to be one of its pioneers.

I considered flatly rejecting the honor, but one does not turn
down an editor's assignment.

When I clambered into the first of the narrow seats I made
sure I was well strapped in. There was nothing between my
head and the sky.

By the time the flight was over I had run out of prayers. As I
staggered onto the ground I looked around in a dazed way. It
seemed to me I had survived with heroic fortitude and that
crowds should be there cheering. I was the only person I knew
who had ever been up in a plane.

A quarter of a century after this I would stand on the balcony
of the Herald Building overlooking this very spot and see the
great sky monsters of Nippon lifting in sinister formation over
our doomed city. MacArthur had telephoned; Quezon had
warned me from Baguio; the Japanese were over the Philippines! How many changes since that day on the Luneta when I
went up in my first plane.

My second meeting with Quezon came at about this time. An
open feud had broken out between the President of the Senate
and General Emilio Aguinaldo. The General had been a thorn
in the side of America during the revolution but he was one of
our greatest Filipino heroes, so this disagreement made many
people unhappy, including my idealistic self.

Aguinaldo was supposed to have entered into a business deal or at least loaned his name to a project with an American. Quezon claimed a national hero should never have permitted his name to be used in such a way. I was in the gallery with the other reporters when Quezon in a furious tirade condemned Aguinaldo's act. He raged. He smote the table with his fist. One of the Senators rushed forward to see if the President had hurt his hand, and Quezon, blind with anger, struck the man away.

I duly reported Quezon's actions and words.

On the following afternoon I was again in the gallery in time to hear Senator Emiliano Tria Tirona defend Aguinaldo's actions. He spoke with bitterness, and Quezon with equal bitterness renewed his attack on the General.

A battle between giants was being waged on the Senate floor.

As I was hurrying out of the hall with my notes Buencamino stopped me. "Come into my office," he requested.

Now what! I wondered, apprehensive as always. But the Secretary appeared friendly, and after we reached his sanctuary he gave me a smile that seemed to hold a glimmer of conspiracy.

"The President was talking about you last night, Rommy."

"Yes?" I was still worried.

Buencamino winked at me. "He has plans for you. You'll be asked to his Pasay residence one of these days."

Anxiety perished, to be supplanted by a strange icy calm. So this was it? This was the way things happened? I was starting the long ascent upward. I looked at Buencamino and wondered at what point and in what fashion he had set out toward his position of assured command.

I gathered it would be a matter of days before I heard from Quezon. I waited, watching for the mail, leaping at every ring of the phone. When the summons came it was through Guillermo Cabrera, another of the Senate secretaries, now one of our most competent judges.

How casual were the words! "The President wishes you to have breakfast with him in the morning."

Awed, I hung up, thinking that is power! One man summons another to breakfast and the guest goes knowing his future is in the hand of his host. I had a conviction that my destiny was rushing to meet me and would be upon me in the morning.

It was my first visit to Quezon's home. I was far from calm. I felt I was about to change from youth to man, and I did not have the appearance to match my good fortune. I was miserably aware of my boyish countenance and the clear skin that had never been touched by a razor.

Quezon was the picture of a man of distinction, as he sat in a handsome brocaded robe, waiting for me in the breakfast room at a table set for two.

I remember little of that breakfast visit. I recall only that I choked down some orange juice and Quezon made some light conversation. He asked me teasingly if I had reported his debate with Tirona as accurately as I had his attack on Roces, and I assured him that I had.

Only at the end did he strike a serious note. "How soon do you enter college?" he asked.

I told him, "Next June. High-school graduation is in a couple of weeks."

The dark expressive look burned through me, then he asked with paralyzing suddenness, "How old are you now?"

I had to tell him, mumbling, "Sixteen."

I caught a full view of myself in a hall mirror as I was leaving —dewy-skinned, round-cheeked, bursting with healthy adolescence. All I needed to complete the picture, I thought bitterly, was a Boy Scout uniform.

Why hadn't I grown as rapidly as that man-size patriot within? I was betrayed by my own downy youth.

Just the same I left Quezon knowing Buencamino was right, the President had his eye on me. Time would reveal Quezon's plans. My immediate need was to grow up.

Adding to the pressure of final exams and my job, I served as editor in chief of our class annual. This gave me the opportunity to write my opinion of myself and my future. The report gave my motto as "Excelsior" and my ultimate ambition as that of becoming a farmer.

Both these statements were true. I was ambitious, but no matter what I might do in the active world I hoped some day to own a farm as my people had for generations at Camiling. Don't think I had any intention of personally cultivating my property! Not I. My intentions were to be a gentleman farmer who rode out each morning on a handsome horse to inspect his burgeoning fields.

It is an ambition still to be achieved.

Graduation is always a sweet sorrow. The two last high-school years in Manila had been happy and active, although shared on a co-existent basis with my newspaper career. Now there were promises to be made, friendships pledged to last for life (many of which would be kept), and a few tears shed by the girls, most of them by the girl with whom I had shared my rare leisure hours. There was the sadness of parting with the teachers—why did I always like mine, especially Mr. O'Malley—and the emotional congratulations of relatives gathered together to see the boy launched toward manhood and an unknown destiny.

I was confident of that destiny. Two more years of schooling at the university and I would be ready for fulltime living. Life branched before me with many paths and I had but to chose one. I was certain that I would make the right choice.

So far I had been able to do all I had set my heart on. I was convinced that luck was a matter of knowing what one wanted and then being willing to work to make the wish come true.

But then I was only sixteen.

Seven

WHEN I enrolled for the two-year course in the College of Liberal Arts in the University of the Philippines I did not give up my afternoon job on the *Cable-News*. The two years would give me my Bachelor's degree and I could decide then whether I wanted to devote myself to teaching or to journalism or somehow to divide my time between the two.

Meantime I prepared to savor campus life fully and I plunged with enthusiasm into a variety of activities. I do not wish to give the impression that I skimmed over studies. It was simply no effort for me to memorize anything that did not include figures. I could remember dates for they were history, and I could read history with unceasing pleasure. Literature, my favorite of all studies, could be memorized with a reading and never be forgotten.

So there was time for the activities of the debating team, the dramatic club, and extracurricular newspaper work, for I was immediately elected editor of the *Varsity News*.

There was also time for girls, which as usual narrowed before long to one particular girl. At that stage I was given to complete fidelity, to one love at a time.

As editor of the college paper I was a man of distinction on the campus. My newspaper training made the *Varsity* sheet easy. I cast about for topics to enliven its pages. I fancied myself in the role of a liberal editor ready to sponsor any noble cause the campus should uncover. Youth is always in favor of the radical and the new, if it is normal youth, and our student body of the University of the Philippines was a normal group. We read

The Forum and *The Nation* and the *New Republic* and discussed lost causes passionately. And because I was an editor on the campus and a Senate reporter off campus, my opinions were sought and accepted with flattering attention by my fellow students.

I became the fighting editor who had never fought a battle, but I was ready. That is the main argument against armament—prepare for war and one will develop.

It amuses me now to remember that my first campus crusade was a highly unchivalrous attack on the Dean of Women. At the time it seemed neither droll nor lacking in courtesy. She was urging the college powers to deprive me of my campus city editor.

Cornelio Balmaceda, my assistant on the *Varsity News*, was a brilliant student in the Law College of the University. He would later be Secretary of Commerce of the Philippines, one of the best we ever had. He wrote and we published an article criticizing a reprimand given another student who had somehow managed to offend the Dean of Women.

She retaliated by going to the Law College Dean and asking for Balmaceda's suspension. The sentence was about to be carried out when I sprang into the breach with an editorial flaming with indignation.

My father's example of unremitting courtesy toward the fair sex must have been in the back of my mind for I did not attack the Dean personally, I simply said nothing to indicate my faith in her judgment. I suggested that since Balmaceda was not chief editor of the *Varsity News* and I was that I was the guilty party, responsible for publication of the article. For that reason, I declared, if Balmaceda was suspended I would walk off the campus with him.

I asked that the Dean of the Law College deny the request for suspension.

This was my first clarion call before the gates of the Bastille, and it was unheeded by the campus royalists. Balmaceda was suspended, and in a two-man walkout we left the campus together.

And we stayed out, too, until the suspension was rescinded and we returned to the college, still together!

It was an uncertain victory and made me suspect the printed word was not always enough. Opinions on paper were strongest when backed by opinions in speech. Quezon won his victories by way of the spoken word. I became more determined to excel in oratorical contests.

The debating club became my outlet in expressing all I was feeling and thinking. The world was filled with injustices I burned to see righted. I argued all the leading issues of the day that in any way concerned my country and its people.

My protests were limited to the pages of the *Varsity News* and the debating society, but my reputation as a firebrand was growing. I had found my voice and it was not long before I found a cause in which it could be raised.

L. H. Thibault, my former editor and the business manager for whom I had worked on the Manila *Times*, roused my creeping suspicion of anti-Filipino prejudice among the Americans in our city. He wrote and published an editorial attacking our University President, Ignacio Villamor. His son, Colonel Jesus Villamor, was later to become our outstanding ace and a hero of World War II.

In my opinion the editorial was motivated by prejudice. It seemed to me Thibault was attacking Villamor not as an educator but as a Filipino, as if a member of a nonwhite race was incapable of serving as the head of a great university. Mixed in with my emotional resentment, I can see now, was the memory of my experience at the Army and Navy Club. This was not the sort of attitude the American teachers who had come to our country would approve! It seemed to me cruel, unjustified, non-American, and not to be tolerated in any country that was flying the American flag.

Nor by any peoples under or apart from that flag.

So the editorial I wrote for the university paper burned with all the resentment that had been growing in me since the day I had been warned from the door of the American club. Now I readied double ammunition for my slingshot—I was prepared to back up print with the power of speech! The editorial concluded with a summons to all members of the student body to a mass meeting to be held on the campus in protest against the Manila *Times*.

At the hour set students began gathering and an estimated half-thousand were present when I got up to speak. It was the first real unrehearsed speech of my life and it came from the heart. I was remembering all our patriots, dead and living, from Rizal to Quezon. The interrupting cries of approval and cheers of my fellows went to my head like strong drink, and at the end, in my most resonant tones, I summoned them to follow me in a march of protest to the Manila *Times* building.

I started off over the campus and my audience fell in step to a man. Cheering, we marched through the city to the *Times* Building—our Balintawak, our Bastille.

In his local room Thibault was warned of our coming. He telephoned the police for protection. Before the authorities could reach him the students were upon Thibault. We swarmed into the *Times* building, into the pressroom. Those who could not find places inside swarmed at the door like angry bees. I was shoved forward to Thibault's desk to act as spokesman. Our opinion of his editorial attitude toward our president was voiced to the accompaniment of angry booings and shouts from outside.

Thibault was nervous and showed it, but he eyed me as I talked with a cynicism that left no doubt of his realization that he himself, by giving me my first newspaper job, had set my feet on the rocky road of protest that brought me now to his door.

I told him we were there to demand a retraction and an apology for the insult to our revered President, in print.

Before I finished, strong hands grabbed Thibault from the

rear and tossed him protesting into the air. But it was only a couple of our sturdiest varsity players hoisting him onto his desk so that all could hear.

From that elevation Thibault wiped his brow and announced that his editorial had been written in good faith. In fact, he said, it was written by a Filipino member of his staff.

I stood by our guns. "That may be, but we believe your paper has attacked our President's capacity to run the University because he is a Filipino."

Thibault protested that had not been the editorial's meaning. Then, before our stony silence, he yielded. "I will be fair," he said. "I'll print your *Varsity News* reply and my explanation in tomorrow's edition. Meantime, I want you all to know that I personally have the highest respect for President Villamor."

It was vindication! We marched back to the University, cheering every step of the way.

That march to and from the *Times* building put me into the millrace for life. In a small way I had helped spark and carry out a campaign of protest. I had found two voices with which to fight—one in print and one spoken. I had used both with success. It was my first taste of power.

Now in newspapers, newsreels, and on TV I watch hordes of young people marching in all countries. All over the world youth is on the march. They brave the guns of police and soldiers, fire hoses and jail, the wrath of their elders and the hatred of those in power. They face disaster and death.

Why are they angry? What is it they are trying to say? And why do we not listen and try to understand?

I remember those days of my own angry youth and our march on the *Times*, and I can smile, remembering how dedicated we were and how we felt that marching with us were the revolutionaries of all time. All we wanted was a few words of understanding, an explanation. We won that and we were happy and proud.

I suppose casual observers in the streets of Manila that day regarded us as a parade of noisy school kids. Outwardly we were. Inwardly we marched to the rhythm of long-ago pipings on Boston Commons and to drums that beat on the slopes of Valley Forge. And—to the cry of Balintawak!

We were striking our first modest blow for the acceptance of the Filipino into the family of man.

Would Quezon have approved our action? Did he like the collegiate editorials I wrote and the arguments I was making for freedom? I had no way of knowing. He was as far away as ever. But in two brief meetings he had flashed a bright light that had cleared the way ahead for me. I knew where I was going. Quezon was leading my country and I was following Quezon.

My hero worship was as profound, and as distant, as before. I had nothing as yet to offer him, to draw his attention my way. He knew my age, my school status, and my hopes. If the time came when he might find need of me, he knew he had but to call.

Meantime I crammed every day with activity.

The University dramatic club took a great deal of my time. Perhaps every public speaker is at heart an actor. The stage had great charm for me. I liked seeing plays and acting in them. I hoped in time to write them. The writing and producing of the Rizal play at the Camiling celebration had whetted my appetite for drama. The interest carried over into University life and I found the plays we put on in the dramatic club a delightful means of self-expression. The debating club dealt with facts; the drama club yielded to enchanting nonessentials. I was a hard-working, thoughtful young man who enjoyed losing his serious identity for a few hours in an imaginary world.

The club produced several plays a year, and in one, something of Molière's I believe, I was cast in the role of a beggar who incites a mob to action in a long incendiary speech. Just before curtaintime an excited report reached us backstage. Our idol Quezon was in the audience!

Rushing with the rest of the cast to the curtain peephole I saw my hero, flawlessly attired, suave, smiling, in the presidential box. And I had to appear before this impeccable model in beggarly rags!

I had my long speech to fall back on. I gave that all the emotional drive I possessed.

Afterward, while we were still in our costumes, Quezon came backstage with his friends. I greeted him, in my grotesque makeup and rags. There was amusement in the dark eyes probing the mime's façade.

"So?" he inquired. "You act as well as write?"

There was no answer to that. I was silent.

Then the Quezon charm turned on me full blast. "Rommy, why don't you come to see me?" he asked gently. "In my home, Saturday, before lunch?"

He was gone, leaving me to remove my makeup and costume with trembling hands. How could I carry on normally until Saturday? And "before lunch"—what did that mean? Was I to have lunch with him? I knew I would be too nervous to eat.

Then I remembered he had called me "Rommy." It was the nickname used by my friends. How had Manuel L. Quezon known that?

A country's head is at once the best informed and worst informed of all its citizens. I am still not certain why Quezon came to the University theater that night.

He knew he was my hero. He was the hero of all Filipino youth. Quezon was an idealist, but he was a pragmatist as well, and the needs of the Philippines were his all-in-all. If any talent of mine could serve those needs in the smallest way then I would be grist for his mill.

I doubt if Quezon saw me at that time as anything but a bright youngster who might be of use to him. Years would pass before I knew he had come to value me as a friend.

That glowing, speaking look had burned through the stage's frippery to the essential being. I had his summons; I would go.

This time Cabrera, his private secretary, waited for me at the door of the Pasay residence and took me directly to the President. Quezon was not alone. A group of men were standing around him; I recognized them all. They were the country's leaders.

Then they stood facing me, my judges, serious, watchful. There was a sense of portent in the room.

Almost a year had gone by since I had answered Quezon's first summons. A great deal had happened since to strengthen my assurance. I was no longer a high-school senior; I was in my first year of college. I felt older, surer, more certain of myself and my opinions.

There is a great change in a boy's life between sixteen and seventeen.

So without qualms I faced the leader of my people and his closest advisers. I knew, respected, and admired them all. There were Quezon and Buencamino, José Abad Santos, later our Chief Justice who would be killed by the Japanese; Conrado Benitez, one of my professors from the University; and Dr. José P. Laurel, Supreme Court Justice, who was later to become president during the Japanese occupation.

Quezon spoke, addressing me man to man. "Rommy, we are going to bring out a new newspaper in Manila. We're calling it the *Citizen*, and it will be the first Filipino paper to be printed in English in this country. It's being organized to compete against the Philippines *Free Press*. (The *Free Press* had been unfriendly toward Governor General Francis Burton Harrison, a close friend of Quezon's.) Benitez is going to be the *Citizen*'s editor and we want you for his assistant."

Then they stood waiting, waiting for my answer. Opening before me were the dazzling vistas of privilege. What might I not accomplish among men like these? With a leader like Quezon?

And why, longing to cry out my grateful acceptance, was I smitten dumb? All I had to voice was a single word.

I could not speak. Was I always to face decisions that tore me apart? Less than a month before I would have leaped at this offer. Now a strange quirk of fate barred me from the Elysian fields.

Only three weeks before! Once more it had been a night of carnival and again I had turned my back on festival to toil in the night office of the *Cable-News*. It was late, but I would not leave before completing my columns for the following day.

I missed Holland's presence in the office. My editor-hero had accepted another job in the United States and had left Manila. I missed him, and the paper was poorer for his leaving.

It is never easy to replace an editor of high caliber, and his place on the city desk was being temporarily filled by one of the men from rewrite.

This man was out when I arrived in the office, and when I went out to dinner he was still absent. Holland's old desk was piling up with copy requiring immediate attention. The rest of the staff had gone home or to the carnival.

When I returned from dinner the city desk was no longer unmanned. Evidently the desk man had found the job of acting editor too much for him to handle, for he was sprawled over the heaps of unedited copy, drunk. The pressroom reeked of whiskey.

I opened the windows and rushed into the composing room. The linotype machines were idle. The foreman was in panic.

"What are we going to do?" he wailed.

I rushed back to my own desk and phoned Irving Posner, the publisher of *Cable-News*.

"There is some trouble here," I told him. Then, not wanting to tattle on a fellow reporter, I explained tactfully, "We're having some difficulty in getting out the paper."

Posner snapped back, "Whatever is to be done, do it."

The pressmen and I removed the sleeping one from Holland's old desk and I took his place.

The months I had watched Holland at work had prepared me for this night. I remembered him, the green eyeshade, the cigar, the decisiveness with which he worked, as I picked up his scissors and the thick editor's pencil. I worked as if I had been making up an edition all my life. Stories were slashed and pasted and fitted into dummy sheets. I wrote headlines and subheads and single-handedly made up every page.

Only after the last "take" had vanished into the pressroom did I go home.

The next afternoon Posner was waiting in the office. He did not mention the night's work. "From now on you're city editor," was all he said.

I was the youngest and newest member of the staff and I was taking the place of my vanished hero Holland. I thought of the steady look under the green eyeshade, the quick way he made up his mind when he hired me.

As city editor I would have to give orders to seasoned reporters twice my age. The prospect made me uneasy, and I told Posner so.

"Any man doesn't take your orders," he said grimly, "just let me know."

Actually I was never to have any trouble of that sort. I never asked a reporter to attempt anything I would not have been willing to do. I appreciated their efforts and let them know. I do not believe in withholding praise; I know how much it has meant to me.

I felt badly about the acting editor I had replaced. I told Posner I wanted him kept on. It was my first request as an editor, and it was refused.

According to Posner the man had committed the unforgivable crime of letting his paper down. The guilty one shared his opinion. When finally he showed up in the office Posner told him he was through, that he had his ticket to go back home, and added that he was making me city editor.

"You're making no mistake," the dismissed man answered. "That boy Romulo is the best man you have on the staff. We'll be hearing from him."

Before leaving he came to me and offered his hand. "I want to thank you, Rommy. You saved the paper."

Only a true newspaperman could say that and not blame me for being unable to save him his job.

Now that I was an editor I was given three-hundred-seventy-five pesos a month, more than twice my former salary, and an office of my own. I moved the desk that had become part of me into it.

That triumph was only three weeks before this offer from Quezon!

I was hesitating because of my new position and fine salary on the *Cable-News*. I was its editor. On the new paper I would be only a subordinate under Benitez.

I hated yielding that advantage. Above all I didn't want to give up my beautiful new desk.

But Quezon was my hero and the leader of the new Philippines. I went with him.

Eight

POSNER understood my affection for my new *Cable-News* desk. When I went over to the *Citizen* I took it with me. It was with me through subsequent offices and jobs, and was lost with the Herald when that building was bombed by the Japanese.

My first act as assistant editor of the new sheet was to acquire a green eyeshade, exactly like Holland's.

The cigar was outside of my circle of emulation. I have never learned to like tobacco. As an editor I often shared a cigarette at the invitation of a reporter but I never liked it.

The green eyeshade served several purposes. It made me feel like an editor, it helped disguise my youth, and it served as a shield against observation—for I cat-napped. During the next two years I would never get enough sleep. I worked nights only, but the nights seemed never to end, and I would be up, sometimes after an hour's rest, to start for school. I was never actually tired, for I have always been able to fall asleep at any moment and under any circumstances and the merest touch of complete oblivion refreshes me.

It is a knack I share with the indefatigable Eleanor Roosevelt. I have fallen asleep in foxholes and in theaters. I can fall asleep in the midst of a sentence and waken perhaps five minutes later to carry the sentence through to its logical end.

So during these years when I was attending university classes by day and acting as assistant editor on the *Citizen* at night I napped at the breakfast table, in classrooms, and in the Senate chamber. My most refreshing naps were taken at my desk in the *Citizen* office, where propped over the copy I was presumably editing, the green shield over my closed eyes kept the secret of my slumbers from Benitez and the others on the staff. If anyone spoke to me I answered. At the ring of the telephone I was the warhorse at trumpet call. I seemed to be able to keep track of everything during these brief, saving periods of blackout.

By this time I had achieved some importance on the campus. Because I was assistant editor of a paper founded by Quezon, rumored to have in some way captured the attention of the President, perhaps marked for advancement, the Philippine Columbian Association elected me to membership. I had hoped someday to be permitted to join this group of Filipinos who had studied in the United States, all of whom were close to Quezon. One by one he was absorbing them into the government.

Although only students who had studied in America were eligible, an exception was made and I was asked to join as an honorary member. I was deeply impressed by the honor because the Association was growing in influence and I knew belonging to it would be an advantage. It was winning a reputation for wielding its power in righteous causes, and shortly after my admission it found a cause worthy of its mettle.

I do not like remembering this episode, but I dislike even more the fact that it ever happened, so I think it should be told in full.

My experience in the Army and Navy Club had not been forgotten. Other reports came from privately run country clubs in and near Manila. Certain Americans in the Philippines were developing a definite campaign of social ostracism against Filipinos.

If this was permitted to continue we might find ourselves in the position of the Chinese, who in a Chinese city were confronted at park entrances by signs forbidding the entrance to the park of "dogs and Chinese."

As a newspaperman I was able to collect sufficient proof that certain American representatives of democracy and freedom, members of the Army and Navy Club and the Manila Polo Club and the Baguio Country Club had entered into a gentlemen's agreement to bar Filipinos from these places.

What sort of Americans were these who set themselves up as superiors in a country they had usurped? I have made it my business to find out. I have been studying this type of American for close to half a century, and let me say now that the insults proffered high-ranking Americans in alien lands can be laid directly to his door.

The American who moves to another country and takes up life there is at first strange and even a little uncertain. Then he finds he is being regarded by the poorer natives with awe because he comes from that rich, powerful country, America. He has servants, perhaps for the first time in his life. If he is with one of the services, he can buy through commissary channels so that all necessities and many luxuries are his at little cost.

He is showered with gifts from the native-born who hope to win his good will, his protection, or his friendship. He accepts this largess as his due and is likely to refer to it as "loot."

An average businessman in his own country, who at home belongs to Rotary, contributes to the Community Chest, goes to church if his wife insists, and treats all around him with fairness and respect, finds himself in another country an overlord among underlings.

In an impoverished land, where the power of his American dollar rides over the poverty of the inhabitants, he becomes condescending and even arrogant. He clings to his American friends, his fellow countrymen in an alien land. They are like exiles. He and his wife are inevitably inculcated with the propaganda of race snobbery.

When I was a very little boy and tried to puzzle my way through this injustice I decided it was possible because the native was not free. I still think that may be the right answer. Because we Filipinos were not free, Americans who would have small social standing in their own country could look down upon us as "natives." A Filipino girl might come from a good family and a cultured home, perhaps receive her education abroad and be accustomed from birth to servants and luxuries and gentle living, but no matter, she was *native*.

This is the triumph of the arrogant mediocre.

There have been of late reports of growing resentment against America in the Philippines. Why in the Philippines! It is everywhere in Asia. But in the Philippines the feeling is against individual Americans rather than against the American ideal. *The Ugly American* was not a myth.

I regret to say the worst offenders in the Philippines have been members of the armed forces and their wives. Michael O'Malley was right when he pointed out that the man in uniform draws lines against the rest of the world. Since the day I carried my first racial hurt to that kind teacher I have worn the American uniform and I know how insulated life can be for the army family. But it has done lasting harm in the Philippines and other countries.

Humiliation is the one hurt that is never forgiven. We have seen everywhere in the world counterwaves against past humiliations surging against white people. The tide is rising and the waves will ride high unless leveled off by equality.

I felt these hurts and knew that a showdown was inevitable between certain American factions in Manila and social leaders among Filipinos. It came when I was in my freshman year at the University. The chosen arena was the Country Club at the beautiful mountain resort town of Baguio.

As I have said, the members of the Philippine Columbian Association were our social and intellectual elite. They had studied in America, where they had been royally treated by Americans, and it was a shock to them to return to their own country and find that some of the Americans living there were not willing to meet them on equal terms. To these American-trained young men this seemed an insult to the very spirit of democracy and their first impulse was to withdraw in proud hurt, as so many others in similar circumstances have withdrawn.

Then they decided to bring the matter into the open. First there had to be definite proof of the injustice. A test group of carefully chosen, presentable young men was appointed to drive to Baguio and seek admission to the clubhouse. This group of refined, cultured men, headed by Conrado Benitez, college dean and editor of the *Citizen*, presented themselves at the door of the Baguio Country Club and were turned away.

We formed a committee of Philippine Columbian Association members and carried the complaint to Quezon. The Senate President heard us with flashing eyes and gave brief orders. We were to locate the owner of the land on which the clubhouse stood and order him to cancel the club's lease immediately unless the ban against Filipinos was withdrawn.

It was our first victory in a race war in the Philippines, a war of which few members of either race would know until it was over. Quezon had led the siege.

The number-one gathering place for the elite in Manila was the Manila Polo Club. Its membership was composed in the main of American army officers, prominent American civilians, and members of the white race who were Philippine born. This last group included the Elizalde brothers, society men and polo champions, and the Roxas and Zobel brothers—all of Spanish blood. Among the more enlightened members of this white man's social citadel a movement was started to admit their Filipino friends to membership. Some of these I am glad to say were high-ranking American officers. The move was stubbornly opposed by the racial supremacists.

Again a test case was prepared. The subject chosen was Manuel Nieto, and a better choice could not be found. Nieto was of pure Spanish blood and every inch the aristocrat. He was cultured, socially at ease everywhere, and would later serve as our distinguished Ambassador to Spain. The most exclusive doors in Europe and America have opened to him. But Nieto at this time was aide-de-camp to Quezon, and because of this close association with a Filipino leader he ranked in prejudiced eyes as a Filipino.

His name was put up by the liberal group in the club. He was blackballed to such an extent that someone remarked the count was like caviar.

His sponsors, including such prominent members as Roxas and the Elizaldes, immediately formed a committee of protest. Other fair-minded members flocked to the cause, and within a few days the largest and most important faction of the club withdrew its membership. The Manila Polo Club was almost deserted.

The withdrawn group reorganized and built another club-house on beautifully landscaped grounds in the outskirts of Manila. It was named Los Tamaraos (the wild water buffalo). The new club was finer and costlier and more desirable in every way than the old, and the best polo players in the world brought their teams there in dramatic competition. It was a club built by and for the people of the Philippines, but Americans were welcome there. It became the leading club and the social center of Manila.

The deserted Manila Polo Club perished. And so, due to war, has Los Tamaraos. It was destroyed by the Japanese. But a new polo club has been built in Manila at a cost of two million dollars and it is the finest clubhouse in the Far East. Its members are selected for their human values and not by the shade of their complexions.

We cannot escape snobbery. We like associating with those whose interests and intellectual attainments are on a level with our own. But to decry by race is a crime against the democratic and religious faith in which America and the Philippines have developed. Race prejudice cannot exist in these or any countries without lasting harm.

Now, on warm evenings in Manila, I watch groups of white-clad, laughing young Filipinos, among them sometimes my own sons, going in and out of the Army and Navy Club with never a thought of being denied entry. The same freedom exists at the Baguio Country Club. Then I know how greatly my world has changed since we who were young as they are now fought the battle of the country clubs in Manila, and I wonder how many of these gay youngsters know they owe much of their social freedom to a man named Manuel L. Quezon.

The progress of justice is slow and often painful. I know that advances such as these will be brought about in the long run by evolution. But young hearts can break in the waiting and young pride suffer. I believe the advances are coming faster than ever before. In spite of all I have seen of atrocities and war, of the rape of Manila and the charnel place at Belsen, I still have faith in the innate goodness of man. I believe that eventually man rights every injustice he has wrongly committed.

I believe this, because I saw it happen in the Philippines. No serious problem has ever arisen between the Philippines and the United States that has not in the long run been settled to the satisfaction of both countries. And there have been many problems, as is inevitable when one country is established and the other feeling its way.

The denial of the Filipino's right to display his own flag might have created a serious problem. That has happened in other countries, for example in Panama, where a revolution almost started recently over America's refusal to permit the Panamanians to display their own flag.

The majority of Filipinos felt badly about this rule, but they waited patiently, hoping for the right to be restored; it took time but the law was changed and Filipinos were allowed to fly their flag again.

Then there was Quezon's long-drawn-out fight with General Leonard Wood, the American Governor General who was firmly set against Philippine independence. Quezon carried his complaints against Wood to Washington. They were undergoing careful consideration when Wood's death ended the con-

Mrs. Carlos P. Romulo photographed in front of General Romulo's portrait, painted by the famous Filipino artist Fernando Amorsolo.

(*Top left*) General Romulo's mother, Mrs. Maria Peña de Romulo.

(*Top right*) General Romulo's father, Gregorio Romulo, at his desk in the governor's office, City of Tarlac in Tarlac province.

(*Left*) General Romulo's family (*front row, left to right*) Gilberto, Lourdes (Mrs. Carlos Kipping), Soledad (Mrs. Cesar Bengzon), and Josefina (Mrs. Alfredo Eugenio). Standing behind are Henry and Carlos.

President Manuel L. Quezon's autographed portrait, inscribed to General Romulo.

To my dear friend
Carlos P. Romulo - a patriot.
Manl. Quezon.

Members of President Quezon's War Cabinet, 1942–1944 (*left to right*), Secretary of Information and Public Relations Carlos P. Romulo, Auditor General Jaime Hernandez, Secretary of Finance Andres Soriano, Vice-President Sergio Osmeña, Colonel Manuel Nieto, President Quezon, not shown, Resident Commissioner J.M. Elizade, Major General Basilio J. Valdes, Arturo B. Rotor, Secretary to the President and the Cabinet.

Photo by Harris & Ewing, Washington, D. C.

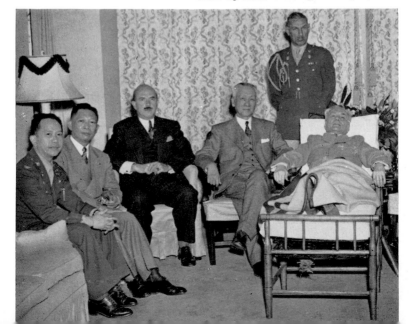

Romulo as colonel in the United States Army, 1943, aide-de-camp to General MacArthur.

General Romulo with Vice-President Sergio Osmeña, August 1, 1944, when the latter took his oath of office as president of the Philippine Commonwealth in the office of the Department of the Interior, after the death of President Manuel L. Quezon.

Photo by Harris & Ewing, Washington, D. C.

Philippine Department of Information and Public Relations

President Sergio Osmeña, General Douglas MacArthur, and Brigadier General Romulo on barge just before landing in Leyte, October 20, 1944.

Brigadier General Romulo makes an on-the-spot broadcast from the front lines in Leyte over the *Voice of Freedom*, November 1, 1944. Arthur Feldman of the Blue Network is at his left. General Romulo reported to the people daily over this station on the activities of the Philippine government and the progress of the liberating forces.

Philippine Department of Information and Public Relations

On the bridge just before the landing in Leyte (*left to right*), Rear Admiral Daniel Barbey, Major General Walter Kreuger, President Sergio Osmeña, Admiral Thomas C. Kinkaid, Brigadier General Romulo.

The day the reunited Romulo family arrived in Washington, D.C., from the Philippines in April, 1945, after more than three years of separation from the General. (*Left to right*) Mrs. Romulo, Roberto, the General. (*Rear*) Gregorio, Carlos Ll., Jr., and Ricardo.

General Romulo taking his oath of office as Philippine Ambassador to the United Nations before President Manuel Roxas, August, 1946. (*Left to right*) Vice-President and Secretary of Foreign Affairs Elpidio Quirino, President Roxas, General Romulo, and Speaker Eugenio Pérez.

General Romulo, Chief Philippine Delegate, signing the United Nations Charter, San Francisco, 1945.

President Ramon Magsaysay congratulating General Romulo after he conferred on him the Golden Heart Presidential Award, highest Philippine decoration, September 13, 1954.

General Romulo, as President of the United Nations General Assembly in
1949, during the ticker tape parade with President Harry S. Truman, on their
way to attend the ceremony of the laying of the United Nations headquarters
building cornerstone.

General Romulo, as president, presiding over a United Nations Security
Council session, January, 1957.

General Romulo, retiring as president of the United Nations General Assembly, bids farewell to Secretary-General Dag Hammarskjöld.

General Romulo with the Prime Minister of Indonesia, His Excellency Ali Sastroamidjojo, on the way to the Asian-African Conference at Bandung, Indonesia, April 18, 1955.

The present residence of the Romulos, called "Kasiyahan" (Tagalog for "contentment") in Forbes Park, Makati, Rizal, Philippines.

General Romulo, Philippine ambassador, with Mrs. Romulo celebrates his birthday, January 14, 1953, at the embassy in Washington. With them are their sons (*left to right*) Carlos Ll., Jr., Roberto, and Ricardo.

Associated Press Photo

The Romulos in their Washington residence on Garfield Street in 1956, the year before Carlos Ll., Jr., died. (*Front, left to right*) Mrs. Chloe Cruz Romulo (wife of Gregorio), Mrs. Virginia Romulo holding Miguel Antonio (second son of Carlos Ll., Jr.), General Romulo with Carlos III in front of him, and Mrs. Mariles Cacho Romulo (wife of Carlos Ll., Jr.). (*Second row, left to right*) sons Gregorio, Ricardo, Carlos Ll., Jr., and Roberto.

troversy. The long battle has been held responsible for Wood's death and it certainly contributed to the ill health of Quezon.

Wood was followed in the Philippines by Henry L. Stimson, who saw the justice of the Filipino stand and took an attitude entirely different from Wood's.

We protested when Nicholas Roosevelt was appointed as vice-governor because he had written articles inimical to our hopes for independence. Washington did not ignore our protests and Roosevelt's appointment was withdrawn. Roosevelt was sent to Hungary instead.

It has taken time to right some of the errors that have arisen during the half-century of Philippine-American relationship, but sooner or later justice has always won.

Errors are still in the making. Even now, in this enlightened and dangerous time and despite all the tragic and disastrous lessons taught the white race as the result of color prejudice around the world, an attempt is being made in some American officers' clubs in the Philippines to renew the exclusion of Filipinos. American friends of mine, newly arrived in the capital, have brought me reports of warnings given them within the club by certain members.

"Don't start bringing any of your Filipino friends in here," they are told. "We don't want them."

That is the sort of talk heard in other countries where a roused population has brought the question of blood lines to pillage and murder. It was the sort of talk that made Japanese anti-white propaganda palatable to Far Eastern people before Pearl Harbor. It gave birth to the atrocities of the Chinese Reds and the Mau-Mau of Kenya. It has lost great nations their place in world leadership and sunk them to second- and third-rate powers.

In the Philippines pride of race was forgotten by men who fought side by side for the same ideals. Why—at this time— a renaissance of hatred? What is behind it all?

Because there is this new difference—we Filipinos are now

a free people. We are no longer under the jurisdiction of any
government save our own. We are a proud people, and we have
been taught by Americans to believe in that pride and in our
equality with all men. We were brought up under democracy.
We are a democracy.

To permit any members of any other race to debase our faith
in equality can only result in tragedy that will shock the world.

Cannot these renegades from democracy, no matter what
their wealth or social position or official rank, see that by paying
lip service to democracy, while entrenched behind the color
line, they are playing with lightning? Can they not be made
to understand that in their self-willed arrogance they are
strengthening the flood of propaganda pouring out over the
earth from Moscow?

While studying at the university and working as subeditor
of the *Citizen* I took on several extra jobs to fill my "spare" time.
I worked in the Bureau of Commerce and Industry, as its assistant chief of Intelligence Division.

At home my family no longer viewed my late hours and
overwork with foreboding. I throve on tension. Their attitude
changed to the pleasing one of mass admiration, tempered in
the cases of my brothers and sisters with well-intentioned teasing. What was I trying to do, lift my race and country to higher
estate single-handedly? Well, that was about it, although I
wouldn't admit it.

My father beamed as he read aloud every word of mine that
saw print. Sometimes he criticized or advised, and all he said
was sound. My grandmother in Camiling took unflagging interest in all I did. Her little Carlos had always had her faith and
her prayers; she was content. And my mother smiled her gentle
smile and said little, but I knew that her feelings ran deep.

My career so far had been extraordinary for one so young. I
remember thinking I was doing all right to be assistant editor of
a political sheet like the *Citizen* at a salary of more than three

hundred a month, and to handle a government job in my spare time, while still a seventeen-year-old student.

Three hundred pesos was a great deal of money in those days, and also, as the saying goes, think of the prestige!

So, basking in the approval of my family and fellows, I was ill-prepared to face disgrace when it fell.

One of my jobs as Benitez' assistant was supplying "filler" for the *Citizen*. Seated nights before my cherished desk with the green shade keeping my eyes from the overhead glare, I scissored brief items from other papers and magazines to fit into small leftover spaces in our columns.

One evening a small item in *Life* magazine caught my eye. In a humorous, good-natured way it made fun of the draft. I did not notice its meaning as much as its wit. I clipped out the amusing item, tossed it into the "filler" basket, and forgot it.

As I said, the *Citizen* had been founded by Quezon and his confreres in opposition to the Philippines *Free Press*. At this time our rival was printing a series of attacks against Governor General Francis Burton Harrison. Then, shifting its tactics, it had widened its assault to take in Quezon.

The Philippine National Guard was friendly to Quezon and resented the *Press* attacks. They set the wheels of justice rolling against our rival. Its American editor had been brought into court and was being threatened with deportation.

It was a touchy state of affairs. At this point my ridiculous little item concerning the draft chanced to fit an empty space in a *Citizen* column. Small as it was it fell with a deafening crash into the chasm deepening between the two rival newspapers.

This was exactly what the American papers in Manila had been waiting for.

They demanded retaliation, only it was not openly called that, and being influential papers they were able to alert Quintin Paredes, Attorney General and one of our best legal minds, in their behalf.

Benitez and I knew nothing of this action and were pursuing

our editorial duties in our separate offices when I heard a howl
of anguish from his room. He had been visited by a dour individual who bore two papers, one for each of us. I opened
mine and echoed Benitez' howl.

"Rommy, what have you done now?" Benitez was frantic.

I? My conscience was clear as a babe's. I was certain it was
Benitez who had committed some abysmal crime. For it was be-
fore our eyes in cold print: "Conrado Benitez and Carlos P.
Romulo, editors of the *Citizen*, are hereby summoned . . ."

And the ugly words leaped: "CHARGED WITH SEDITION."

Sedition? In our panic we couldn't even remember the mean-
ing of the word. We had to look it up in the office dictionary.
"A charge of insurrection," it said, "of creating a commotion."
Well, that last part was true, but all the commotion was in the
Citizen office.

Hideous thoughts raced through my mind. I was certain that
my family and I and all our descendants were disgraced forever. Was I to go down in Philippine history as my country's
first subversive?

A frantic check at the Attorney General's office did nothing
to calm this fear. We learned they were rallying all their official
power in their determination to "throw the book" at us.

My worst moment was explaining to my father how it happened that I, a governor's son, was to appear in court on a
charge of sedition.

After we learned the reason for our summons Benitez and I
looked up the wretched paragraph and studied it from all angles.
It still seemed like a harmless joke to me. Certainly I had no intention of poking fun at anything so serious as the draft act.
But the Attorney General and his legions rejected this point of
view and saw nothing amusing in the item. The dignified Benitez and I were going to be tried on one of the most serious
charges a government can bring.

Our futures were looking steadily blacker when help came
from an unexpected source. The Philippine Columbian Asso-

ciation came to our rescue. While I was still only an honorary member I had made myself active in its interests. Benitez was of course a member. The group stood by us and employed attorneys for our defense. In their zeal they hired a redundancy, which became apparent when we made our appearance in court on that solemn morning. Present as our defenders were the three foremost lawyers in Manila: Jorge Bocobo, Mariano H. de Joya, and Francisco Delgado.

All were distinguished attorneys, in fact each was a stellar legal light in his own right. So many lights were blinding before the bar. There was a flare-up of competition as three brilliant minds met head on.

Bocobo rose and made some sort of proposal to the judge. Instantly De Joya was on his feet—"I object." Delgado disagreed with both of them.

The prosecutors from the Attorney General's office sat back and grinned. I leaned over to Benitez and groaned, "Here's where we both go to jail!"

Fortunately for us at this point the judge took over. He refused further argument and summed up the case against us in short order. He wound up by stating that in his opinion there was no reason to question the loyalty and patriotism of either of the two defendants.

Benitez and I were not only acquitted—we were acquitted with honors! But it was my first brush with the law and it left a painful memory.

The Philippine Columbian Association having taken me under its wing in this crisis was able to help me through another. I was about to graduate from the College of Liberal Arts and I longed for a scholarship to America. One of the Association's members, Tomas Confessor, was Chief of the Intelligence Division of the Bureau of Commerce and Industry. He sponsored me. Confessor became a national hero during the Japanese occupation. When asked to surrender to the Japanese he wrote a letter that was a classic in loyalty and patriotism. His courageous challenge and his aid to the resistance movement in the hills won the admiration of General MacArthur and President Quezon. When we returned to the Philippines he was made Secretary of the Interior and was subsequently elected Senator.

I was terribly excited at the hope of a scholarship. Since grammar school I had wanted to see America, and my interest had grown more intense with the years. My father had often told me that he would manage somehow to send me there. "Someday you are going to America," he had said many times.

I had prayed for a way to manage on my own. Now Confessor provided the answer. The Bureau of Commerce and Industry, where I was working part time, was planning to send a man to New York for special business training along American lines. It was announced that someone working in the Bureau would be chosen. Confessor recommended me to the Bureau Director, Fidel A. Reyes, who in turn proposed my name to Secretary of Commerce Dionisio Jakosalem.

Director Reyes was another national figure revered by the Filipino people. It was he who as city editor of *El Renacimiento*, my father's favorite paper, wrote a scathing editorial entitled "Aves de Rapiña" (Vultures). The editorial attacked Dean C. Worcester, an American official. Worcester filed a libel suit against the newspaper and won. Reyes and his chief, Teodoro M. Kalaw, were convicted and both became national celebrities.

I was chosen to go to New York. I would be sent by the government to Columbia University to study foreign trade service. I had no idea what sort of future that might be. It was enough that my dream of many years was to come true.

If this opportunity had not been given me, my father would have found means to send me to study in the United States. Filipino boys have been going abroad to study since 1860.

I had hoped to graduate from the University of the Philippines cum laude, but for that honor all "ones" were needed and after examinations I found myself with a "two" in math and a "three" in geology.

The low mark in math was no surprise, for I had long since lost hope of receiving more than a passing grade in that hated study. But I did have an alibi for the "three" in geology, which was the final mark that robbed me of graduation laurels.

That class, with Randall Rowley as teacher, was held at the somnolent hour of the afternoon between one and two o'clock. Now I was able to do without sleep any or all hours of the remainder of the twenty-four, but that hour is siesta hour in the Philippines and since babyhood I had devoted it to restful napping.

While it had been many years since I had been able to devote that period to sleep still the tendency remained, and no matter where I might be at one o'clock I would find myself nodding. Geology had no charms to keep me awake, so I jerked and dozed through that class only half-aware of what was going on.

I had worked sometimes all of the preceding night on the *Citizen's* desk and I needed sleep. It was doubly unfortunate that the class in a subject which I hated was held at that particular hour. Rowley made no allowances for my need to sleep.

I had found that a drink of cold water would revive me temporarily. I decided on this measure one warm afternoon and asked to be excused from class. Downstairs by the water fountain in the school corridor I met several girls I knew and joined in their idle banter. As we were chatting a presence went past and I recognized Professor Rowley.

I shot up the backstairs and into the classroom ahead of him. When he came in he did not glance at me. Instead, looking over the heads of the students, he began a stern pronouncement.

"There may be some among you," he said with meaningful scorn, "who hold to the opinion that because one edits a newspaper one is qualified to leave the classroom whenever one chooses and gossip with the girls downstairs, and still hope to pass this course. Well, let me tell you here and now it can't be done!"

"Any member of this class hoping to graduate will have to
prove his quality if he expects to get a passing grade."
It was a thrust direct and I took it to heart. I went to the
drinking fountain no more. I propped my lids open with my
fingers and stared at the pages and tried to remember what
geology was all about. It was meaningless. Try as I might I
simply could not catch up with the others, and so it was I
received that final and fatal "three."

Nevertheless I did graduate and was given my Bachelor of
Arts in March, 1918; and in July of that year I gave up my job
on the *Citizen* and left for the United States.

Once more I was leaving a love I had been confident would
last forever. The lovely girl I had squired through two years
of high school and two years of college was not to be forgotten.
On my last birthday I was sixty years old and among the hundreds of congratulatory messages one was from her.

I remember with deep tenderness my early romances. I believe they recall me with equal affection, for they have all remained my friends.

There was something mysterious about my departure for
America. The night before I was to sail grief filled our home like
a fog. I could not understand why my family should be so
wretched when I was so exultant. They came to the pier to see
me off, and all were in tears except my mother, but even she
seemed terribly sad. It was upsetting to have my family behave
as though I were departing for the eternal shades.

"See here," I burst out finally, "this isn't a funeral, you know!
I'm not going away forever. I'm just going to the States to
study."

But they wept afresh and would not be comforted. Not for
another two months would I know the reason for their tears.

After I was settled in New York I received a letter from my
father. He wrote that on the day before I was to leave, word
had reached Manila of my grandmother's death in Camiling.

The family had entered into a conspiracy to keep the truth from me, not wishing to spoil the happiness of my trip across the Pacific—my first journey away from home. Their tears had not been for me, but for her.

In my furnished room near the Columbia campus I gave way to belated grief. Camiling seemed pitifully far away. I remembered my grandmother as the dearly loved tyrant of my babyhood, the teacher of my childhood, and always my adviser and guide. I remembered her—tiny, indomitable in her love, fierce in her pride.

She had built that pride into me.

How her faded eyes had flashed when I told her I had been chosen to go to America! She knew I would do my best to absorb all of that wonderful country we had discussed so often.

I was in America to learn, for country and for race, and for her.

When I had last visited her in Camiling my grandmother had been frail and old, but I knew on that day of dark sorrow in New York that a strong supporting pillar had fallen from my life.

Nine

IN JULY, 1946, I flew back to Manila from the United States. World War II was over. Japan had been defeated and the Philippines set free. At last we Filipinos were to be awarded our long-dreamed-of independence, promised half a century before.

As Philippine Resident Commissioner living in Washington, I was returning home for the ceremonies that would change our country's status from that of a commonwealth to a republic.

Our plane dropped down on Wake Island to refuel. During the brief stopover I walked along the beach to get the kinks out of my legs. Rising out of the Pacific, close to shore, was the battered hulk of a wreck—a relic of war.

Somehow it looked familiar. I went to the water's edge and was able to make out the name, faded by sea water and the years. Lettered along the bow was *Suwa Maru*.

Time leaped back twenty-eight years. It was another July day, 1918. I was young, slender, blazing with ambition and hope, leaving Manila on that ship for my first visit to America. Yes, I had been young on that day, and the *Suwa Maru* had been young, bright with paint, and well-manned with neat Japanese sailors. Now we had both suffered the rigors of war. The *Suwa Maru* had served her time as a Japanese troop ship and gone to her watery grave during the shelling of Wake Island.

In 1918 I was thirty-five days crossing the Pacific. The journey did not seem long then, although we left Manila in July and I arrived in New York, via Canadian railroad, barely in time for the September enrollment at Columbia.

How many times have I crossed the Pacific since that maiden voyage? My last flight between Manila and San Francisco was made in eighteen hours.

Recently my wife and I took our two small grandsons on a flight to Manila. I doubt if the Pacific looked any wider to their young vision than it did to mine when I was twice their combined ages and setting out to learn a new way of life in another world.

What dreams were mine on that journey! And what were theirs, for who reads the dreams of even the most beloved child?

I doubt if a more fervent young idealist ever set sail for a different land. My American teachers in the Philippines pictured a utopian country I had further tinted with my own rosy imaginings. Everything I had studied about America and all that I had heard from returned Filipino students served to enlarge this image of the perfect country where all men were friends since all men were free; all were well-fed, well-clothed, well-housed, well-educated; all were equal.

I was firm in this belief, for had I not seen in my own short lifetime the changes Americans had made in my own country? In the past two decades under American authority the Philippines had made greater advances than under hundreds of years of Spanish rule. One had only to remember the schools, the good teachers, the opportunities given the young, the highways, agricultural and economic advice, hygiene and medical care— a new generation was growing whose faces would never be pitted by smallpox.

I believed in America as the golden land of the free because the teachers who had come from that country had in every way lived up to the standards they taught.

My father had been bitterly anti-American but he and his Filipino friends had changed their point of view when America lived up to its promise of justice for the people it had conquered. As a small boy I had seen hatred turn to friendship and resentments shift to new faith. As I grew, the dream of justice had grown.

The intent of good will to all men was the basic concept in the American mind. This we had been taught. This we believed.

When I won first prize at the university with the oration, "My Faith in America," I had spoken every word from the heart. I had kept that faith, and the prayer of someday seeing America had been answered. Now, still in my teens, I was on my way.

The *Suwa Maru* made a stop at Hong Kong. I left the ship to send a telegram to my father, letting him know that so far all was well. The clerk in the telegraph office was British. He addressed me in Chinese which I could not understand.

"I'm not Chinese," I explained in English.

"Then you are Japanese." Not a query, a statement.

"I am a Filipino," I explained with as much dignity as I could.

He might never have heard the word, and Hong Kong is just across the China Sea from the Philippines! His superior attitude classified anything I might be or say as unworthy of his interest.

Just before the attack on Pearl Harbor I found myself again in this telegraph office, filing the series of articles on the Far East that were to win the Pulitzer prize. The British message clerk might have been the same clerk who had looked down his nose at me a quarter-century before.

"Where is the American who wrote this for you?" he asked, glancing with contempt over the pages he had seen me write.

These men were small segments in the white pattern of Asia, a pattern seeped through with violence and bloodshed. And still those who believe in racial superiority will not learn!

But I was learning on this first flight from the nest that I as a Filipino was not as important as I had been led to believe. In my own beautiful country a Filipino had his human worth. Was he a total blank outside the Philippines? The British message clerk in Hong Kong gave me the first inkling that the Filipino was an unknown entity.

We sailed on to Yokohama and again I went ashore. The Japanese thought I was Chinese.

In Shanghai the Chinese spoke to me in Korean.

As we continued our slow junket across the Pacific an uneasy suspicion grew in my mind that the Philippines was not the center of the world. It had never before occurred to me that the country I loved so much was a small and unimportant nation. Had its long fight for freedom and its heroes gone unnoticed in the world that we in the Philippines believed was moving forward toward democracy?

The emotional jolts I had taken only made me the more determined to take full advantage of the opportunities in America. On my way across the Pacific I made up my mind to absorb all America had to teach—and more. I would show Americans what a Filipino could accomplish when given a chance!

At last ambition was full grown and I knew what I wanted of myself. A boy set out from Manila in July, and a man arrived late in August on the west coast of America. I left the *Suwa Maru* at Seattle to meet with her wreckage twenty-eight years later off the shore of Wake Island.

The trip across Canada by train was disconcerting, for was it possible that this vast stretch of Canadian country was equally matched by the breadth of America? I had never dreamed of such vastness, such empyrean space. No wonder North Americans were so expansive in their manners! And so generous! Everything was vast beyond anything I had anticipated—the mountains, the land that stretched from horizon to horizon without a roof to break its emptiness, the cities we flashed through culminating in New York.

New York swallowed me up. I had seen it in pictures, read of it, and heard of it all my life, but I was unprepared for its reality. What other city on earth had a skyscraper to compare with the Woolworth Building? I rode atop a Fifth Avenue bus —where have those buses gone—from the Columbia campus to

Washington Square, as overwhelmed by wonder as I had been at my first circus.

I braved the subway at Times Square and was hopelessly lost underground. When I finally learned to "follow the green light" and boarded the shuttle to Grand Central Station I felt like a true New Yorker. I was enchanted to learn that the green light indicator system was based on the labyrinth at Crete.

In the subway trains and elevators my lack of inches made me a prisoner pressed between giants; I could see nothing but backs.

On my first ascent in an elevator one of the passengers was a lady. With great difficulty I removed my hat. It was promptly crushed flat. After that, when I removed my hat in crowded elevators, I held it at arm's length above my head.

Columbia University was as confusing in the beginning as the city. The campus seemed endless and the buildings far apart. Matriculation was difficult, and I spent days of always dashing somewhere and always being late. At last my schedule was in order and I knew where my classrooms were and life became orderly. The names and faces of my professors became familiar and I picked up a speaking acquaintance with some of my classmates.

My lodgings were a furnished room on 106th Street, not far from the campus. The furnishings were comfortable and the landlady took particular pains to make me feel at home. In fact I was shortly basking in the attentions paid me, without realizing none of the other Columbia student roomers were being treated as well. But they noticed, and one student living in the house mentioned it to me.

"You've certainly made a big impression on our landlady."

"Why is that?" I asked.

"She says your folks are big stuff back home—that your family is rich and titled."

I was puzzled. "What can have given her such an idea!"

He pointed out various objects in my modest room. "See

those? Silver. Damask. Everything with your initials and your
crest."
My face towels. My napkins. My personal supply of table
silver. All were embroidered or engraved with the initials
C.P.R., Carlos Peña Romulo.
They were also the initials of the Canadian Pacific Railroad.
I had acquired these possessions on my train trip across Canada. In the dining car I had been impressed by the fact that the
initials on the silver and linen were my own. I asked the waiter
if I might keep one spoon as a souvenir of my journey.
He was a colored man and expansive.
"You just help yourself," he told me kindly. "Take all you
want of them. That's what they're here for."
I thought this very kind of the railroad, but tried not to be
greedy. Still it seemed foolish not to provide against possible
light housekeeping in New York. I chose a table service for
two—knives, forks, several sizes of spoons—and several nap-
kins. The waiter hovered over me, helping me choose.
"There's lots of towels in the washrooms, too," he said.
"They got the same letters on them and you'd better stock up.
Whatever is lost here is included in the company's 'profit and
loss.' " He was so kind and helpful.
Everything I chose was splendidly marked with my initials
and if I remember rightly a "small but costly" British crown!
No wonder my landlady was impressed.
I hope the Canadian statute of limitations has run out!
During my first weeks at Columbia I made few friends. There
was no time to be wasted. My sins of omission had found me
out and I was paying for all the years I had turned my back on
mathematics. To prepare for foreign trade service one has to
know accounting, and in order to learn accounting one has to
know mathematics. I had to start from the beginning, studying
the math I should have learned years before, and work in
double harness while trying to keep up with current subjects.
I struggled with the mysteries of accounting while taking

those courses in math. It was a harrowing experience, and it
served me right.

In my first week at school something happened that puzzled
me. I met several Negro boys. They were pleasant, nicely man-
nered young men from the South and I liked them. Sometimes
we walked from one building to another, talking together.

Then on a day when I was alone I was joined by two white
students I knew, who were also from the South.

One started right at it. "Romulo, about those black boys.
You know, don't you, you have to make up your mind? We
mean," he persisted, "are you going to be with us? Or with
them?"

Because this was America I was bewildered. It couldn't be
happening to me or they couldn't mean what they seemed to
say. So I made no answer at all and they walked away.

I had to find out. I hunted up another white student and
reported the conversation to him. I finished by asking, "Now,
what was that all about?"

His answer came quietly. "Don't you know we have a race
problem here?"

No, I had not known. Nothing I had heard from the lips of
the *pensionados* returned from America, nothing I had studied
or imagined had prepared me for this.

In my few weeks in America I had been well-treated. People
had gone out of their way to be friendly. Why was this hand of
friendship offered to me and withheld from that pair of well-
intentioned, nice-mannered, dark-skinned lads from the South?
It did not take me long to understand.

As the Filipino I was an unknown entity and a rarity. There
were few of my kind in the States, and perhaps not more than
a half dozen of us enrolled at that time at Columbia. The Negro
was known and and he was legion. The two colored students
were not suspect as individuals, but because they represented
a swelling pressure that was causing concern in white America.

Painfully, my eyes were opened to the America I had

dreamed about so many years. Now, watching, I saw the feathers of disillusion floating wherever I looked. Negroes peered wistfully through the windows of even the poorest restaurants and dared not enter. At our enlightened university the Negro students sat together and apart in the rear of the classrooms.

If this went on at one of the most progressive universities in America what could conditions be in the South?

In my first bitterness I wondered if we of the Philippines had not been reared on fairy tales. But no, I knew one thing: the American teachers had been sincere. They had wanted to believe as they taught us to believe, and basically what they said was true.

I remembered their teachings and I suddenly thought of my father reading to me when I was a little boy a newspaper account of Booker T. Washington's visit to the White House. President Theodore Roosevelt had invited the great Negro educator there as his personal guest. My father had explained that this was the first time a Negro had been a guest in the presidential mansion, and he—my father—thought the invitation had been a splendid gesture on the part of the American president.

"This will help the fight for equality," my father had said.

And I, a child, was thinking that since equality was already the way the people lived in America, why should it be fought for?

Now as a Columbia student I knew the fight was still going on and I felt let down and unhappy. But giving way would not help. And the ideal was still before us.

So I hunted up the two white students who had spoken to me.

"You have asked me which side I am on," I told them seriously. "You say you want me to be with you. And I want to be with you. I like you. But I like those other fellows too. Why can't I be on both sides?"

I have no idea why it worked, but it did. From that time on I was friendly with all the racial groups on the campus.

The incident taught me that if I kept my head and my temper that I could remain friendly with all.

It was a valuable lesson. It has helped me along my way. One need not bellow to be believed. Ears seal automatically against anger, and unreason takes over when argument becomes tirade.

In the same category is the use of swearing by way of emphasis. I seldom swear, because I have great respect for the power of words and it seems to me that profanity lacks the power to express intelligently. Anything I wish to say can be expressed in my limited vocabulary, and to me foul words are the refuge of the drunk, the hysterical, and the inarticulate.

The pinprick of doubt had assailed me, but I was still in love with America and still happy at Columbia University. I had admired and envied the *pensionados* who had been the first from my country to study at this great American school, and now I was one of them. The half-dozen or so Filipino students at Columbia were all there as the guests of the American government. Curiously enough, while we were all friends we did not herd together. We were in America to understand it and we liked knowing Americans.

There were so many facets to this country. I had been told only one side—the theory, the gleam. I refused to believe I had been deceived. My innate sense of well-being kept me the incurable optimist. I was going to discover the best in America, and the best was everything I had hoped it would be—for me.

In my passionate determination to see the finer side I found all I had expected in material achievement. There were good railroads, fine hotels, an efficient postal system, a plenitude of cars, schools in the smallest hamlet, and prosperity everywhere. On my free days I walked through midtown Manhattan, the core of sophisticated New York, and I was exultant.

"This is life," I told myself, "in a nation that has reached its

full development. Someday we will live like this in the Philippines."

Then I found my way by chance into the slums of the great
city. Here was a side of New York and America never described
in the schoolbooks. I had pictured everyone in this magical
country as being well-housed and well-fed. Was everything we
Filipinos had been taught to accept as our ideal only an illusion,
and could equality never be achieved?

My doubts grew through the years when I visited Washington, the brain center of the United States, as the guest of my
father's friend and my guardian in America, William Howard
Taft. He had been Governor General of the Philippines and
was now Chief Justice. His son Bob was my particular friend.
Governor General Taft was highly esteemed in the Philippines.
It was he who proclaimed American policy in the Philippines as
"the Philippines for the Filipinos." His name is enshrined in the
Filipino heart.

In Washington I was even more shocked by the dreadful
slum areas. We had depressed areas in Manila but I, as a student,
had never seen them. And somehow poverty is never flagrant
in a tropical zone. Our poor wore rags, but the rags were
clean. The poorest mother could forage food for her children—
a basket of fruit, a bit of fish from the sea.

I could not understand why a country as rich as America
would permit such conditions to exist.

As I adjusted to classroom routine tension eased and I began
to feel at home. Even the hated math became easier and the laws
laid down for keeping accounts less confusing. I kept my aching head over these studies the sooner to be rid of them, for
after they were behind me I promised myself at least one year
of the subject I loved most: comparative literature. No matter
what career I might enter, the writer in me would never be lost.

I knew now words would be the base of all I might attempt.
The books I had read, my father's guidance in my reading, yes,

all the way back to my grandmother's stories, these contained the words that had fed my imagination and my ambition. With words I could move men and mountains, I could carve into any design I wished my future and my world. With words I could develop my personality to its fullest and help to bring recognition to the Philippines.

It was a pretty large order for a small student in a large, strange country, but I was confident. Make of it what you will.

Before the first month ended I had joined the debating society. I took part in the debates for the next four years. It was a jolt to receive as my first subject: "Should capital punishment be abolished?" I had drawn that question word for word out of a hat when applying for admission to my first debating society in Manila. The question had followed me halfway across the world. I did my best with it.

Gradually I was beginning to convince myself with the many arguments I was obliged to collect advocating the abolishment of the Mosaic demand of a life for a life.

It was on the debating platform that I first saw into the kindly inner heart of America. I noticed that when I pled my side of the argument I was soundly applauded, and realized finally that this approval was not for my subject, but for a young man from Asia who was tackling a large question and in English. Wherever we debated I heard this applause, even when my side failed to win. It was a gesture of kindness, the democracy I had expected to find. But why, if given me, why not to all?

Perhaps they did not know that the English in which I tried to express my thoughts was the speech of my childhood. I had learned its rudiments from the Baldwin *Primer* of my American sergeant in Camiling. I had been reared on American publications and English classics, and I had a great respect for the art of human speech. English was but one of the flowering branches, one of the best.

Because of this respect I regretted then, as I do now, the slipshod vernacular into which so many Americans were lapsing. It is part of the relaxed pattern of the times and one notices it all over the world. In Manila one hears our students, "Gotcha! Waddayaknow!" Even when they are speaking in Tagalog the carelessness is there.

I regret this breakdown after the centuries spent in the development of exquisitely precise human expression. It seems a pity that a trend toward jargon should be permitted to destroy the treasure handed down by generations of great authors and poets.

Now that I have studied and spoken English for more than fifty years I realize I have but scratched its surface. Language has always seemed to me man's most marvelous gift. It enables him to communicate. It ties his life to others. It has lifted him from his place somewhere close to the apes to a position near the angels.

In my case speech has been my treasure chest, and everything I have achieved in life has been won by words. (Even when I persuaded my wife to become my wife, how I dipped into my supply of eloquence then!)

I began making friends on the campus and girl students were among them. I liked girls and I missed girls, my sisters and their friends and my own girl friends, particularly the one I had left at the university in Manila, certain I would never forget. They had accustomed me to feminine companionship and I missed it. But I was shy about asking my male friends the all-important question: How does one go about making a date with an American girl?

After three months as a dateless bachelor student I decided I had to figure this out for myself. A man had to be brave.

I chose my victim with great care. She was pretty, but not formidably so, and had an easy manner that seemed encouraging. Also, and for some reason this seemed helpful, Anna was from Brooklyn.

I ambushed her between classrooms and struck a conversation, which to her may have seemed casual but which was my opening gambit in a carefully plotted campaign.

Did she like the theater, I threw in carelessly.

She did indeed.

So did I! (Hopefully.)

Had she seen Frank Bacon starring in *Lightnin'* on Broadway?

No, regretfully, but it was one of the plays she wanted to see.

Then I threw my all into the ring. If I could get tickets to this sold-out attraction would she go with me?

She would. It was as easy as that. I had my first date in America.

The next problem was to get tickets. My allowance was not exactly lavish. After recovering from the shock of the cost of two tickets to a Broadway hit I found myself left with exactly eleven dollars to splurge on the rest of the evening. This would have been a lavish sum in Manila, but I had an idea New York was going to expect more of me and made discreet inquiries among the more sophisticated men on the campus.

It was the consensus of opinion that a popular night club was a nice place to wind up an evening. I stowed that fact in my mind and went forth to my first appointment with romance.

My date had suggested that since she lived in Brooklyn I was to wait for her at the top of the subway entrance at Fourteenth Street. I was prompt and so was she. Since it was some distance to the theater where *Lightnin'* was playing I insisted on our taking a taxi.

The fare I remember was eighty-five cents. At the theater entrance I handed the driver one of the two bills in my pocket and told him to keep the change. His effusive thanks would have roused the suspicions of anyone more accustomed to the habits of New York cab drivers.

We enjoyed the show and after the curtain fell I impressed Anna with my casual suggestion that we drop in at a night club. In the men's room at the club I dove into my pocket to tip the

attendant and found one lone dollar bill. I had grandly presented the cab driver with my ten dollars. No wonder he had
been so grateful.

Anna was waiting at the table studying a large menu. "Cover
charge" was printed boldly on its front. Until I saw her there I
hadn't made up my mind what to do. Then I thought of the old
adage: when in trouble tell all. So I showed her my dollar bill
and told her.

She laughed, while my face grew redder and redder. Then
she opened her purse. "It just happens that I have ten dollars
with me, Carlos, and I'll lend it to you."

And that is what she did, slipping the bill to me under the edge
of the tablecloth. We had a fine time and I borrowed the money
to repay her the next day. So I learned why American girls were
considered good sports.

I made more and more friends, on and off the campus, and
there were no more empty evenings and weekends. But still
there was a loneliness. Comradely casual dates with girls were
not enough. I missed my family. I missed my girl. I had "gone
steady" for four years in Manila and I craved a permanent love.

I fought this longing for months. I told myself I was in America on a mission and had no time for girls. I was here to help
make the Filipino known.

Lack of that recognition was my greatest personal disappointment since leaving the Philippines. I had traveled and
found no one who knew of or was interested in my country.
Wherever I went, in New York or Washington, I was still being
taken for a Chinese.

But in the Philippines, we were of importance as Filipinos.
We were not to be classified with other Asians. We were citizens living under the American flag.

For all I experienced and heard in the United States we Filipinos might never have fought and lost—or even existed. Americans knew of Admiral Dewey, not of Aguinaldo. If they ever
thought of the Philippines it was as a collection of small islands

in the Orient that had been claimed by Admiral Dewey in a contest nobody could understand.

I had left a country I knew was as beautiful and vital as any in the world, and I had traveled in China, Japan, and Canada to the United States, to be greeted like an arrival from Mars.

Somehow I was going to make the Philippines known to the world. Relations had to be improved on an international scale, and while I was nobody, an alien freshman lost in a great American student body, I determined to do my bit.

To begin any sort of crusade one must find a flag to wave and to follow. I found an emblem in Rizal Day. That day was nearing. In the Philippines it would be commemorated everywhere in honor of the country's greatest hero. There it corresponds to Washington's birthday in America.

But who in America had heard of Rizal? This was the "gimmick" I needed. I could begin by showing the Columbia students that my country also had its heroes.

The campaign began with organizing the scattering of Filipino students on the campus and promoting a Rizal Day at Columbia University. Earl Hall on the campus was chosen for the celebration.

There were groups of Filipinos living in New York and Brooklyn. Each group had planned separate celebrations on Rizal Day. We brought them together into one common group, for a major ceremony.

Once organized, we were a cross section of Philippine life. We were students, professional men, laborers, waiters, and entertainers. In Manila we would have had little in common. In New York we had Rizal.

Rizal Day was a big success. American and Filipino notables were on the platform and Filipino singers and dancers on the program. Among the singers I remember best the popular star Nemesio Ratia and his dramatic rendition of Henley's "Invictus."

"I am the captain of my soul."

I was at the right age to be transported by those words.

Arsenio N. Luz presided as chairman of the day. He was a newspaper editor from Manila who was taking a postgraduate course at Columbia.

I believe Dr. Nicholas Murray Butler, President of Columbia University, made a speech, and I know I made one, because after the ceremony a young American girl in the audience came up to the platform to congratulate me. She was a fair-skinned Saxon type with a serious, gentle charm that sent all my resolutions about having no time for dalliance flying out of the window. I knew then how lonely I had been in America. We spoke briefly, and I knew I would not be lonely again.

I might have won higher honors at Columbia if it had not been for that girl. On the other hand I would have missed a lot of happiness. Every minute I could steal from my studies we were together. She would come to my room and wait while I studied—with the door left open for the benefit of my landlady, who kept a sharp eye on the extracurricular activities of her roomers—and it was enough for both of us that she was there. The finest way to discover a country or learn a language is through love.

Her presence made even the detested bookkeeping bearable. Slowly I was developing a concept of the nature of mathematics, but I would never learn to like numbers. To this day I detest them.

She was not a student. Latin-American friends had chanced to bring her to the Rizal celebration. She had a deep interest in the Orient. I helped her to understand my world as she in turn widened my understanding of America.

My happiness in finding an American sweetheart did not blind me to the discrepancies I continued to meet between American belief and American practice. I met with conditions that left me in a state of despair, for if such injustices were permitted in a country that exemplified democracy what hope for the future anywhere?

So many things were calculated to cut down the esteem or hopes of someone considered inferior by reason of color, and the most shocking part was that these acts were often carried out by people who regarded themselves as the cream of Christian America.

For example, during my second year at Columbia a friend of my father's came on a visit from the Philippines, and I wished to entertain her in some distinctive New York way. By this time I considered myself quite a boulevardier in the big city and without too much trouble was able to secure good seats down front for *The Ziegfield Follies*. As we settled down to enjoy the show I was proud of my companion. She was older than I and a woman of great distinction in the Philippines, where she was one of our first women doctors. Dignified, beautifully gowned, with dark hair and clear skin, she was outstanding among the women seated around us. I noticed several looking at her and thought their stares were admiring and well-justified.

During intermission some of our neighbors left their seats. My companion and I sat on, lost in gossip about Manila.

A hand fell on my shoulder. An usher was leaning over me. "The manager wishes to speak to you in his office."

I excused myself and followed the boy to the front of the theater. The manager was waiting. He seemed nervous. "You are a student?" he asked.

"Yes, at Columbia."

"Chinese?"

"I am a Filipino," I answered, as so many times before. "Now, what is this all about?"

He was deeply embarrassed. "I am sorry to say this," he stammered, "but there have been complaints. Some people sitting in the same row with you—they say you are with a Negress."

I was sick I was so angry. That black, curly hair of my friend's—that was all they had to complain about! Her skin was as light as any other woman's in the row.

As calmly as I could I explained my guest's honorable position in our country and the fact, which was true, that she was in America at the invitation of a high-ranking government official. When I mentioned his name the manager paled. Seeing the impression made, I ordered the manager to telephone this official at once, and gave him the private telephone number in Washington. Washington would know how to deal with this insult, I added. This was all true and my indignation was very real.

The manager begged me to return to my seat and forget that anything had been said. I did not want to go back, but I could not desert my guest. To spare her feelings I had to return. She wanted to know why I had been called away and I muttered something; she did not press me.

That night the long-stemmed *Follies* beauties pranced for me in vain. I did not enjoy the rest of the show. I spent my time scowling at the laughing faces around me. They all looked fair and kind. Which among them, I wondered, had wanted to humiliate the fine, selfless woman at my side, who was their country's guest at the invitation of one of their leading officials? How dared they!

How I longed to rise up in the aisle and demand to know which among them was guilty! But I could not make an issue of the incident for my friend's sake and for America. I hope she has never learned of such happenings in America, because she admired its ideals as much as I.

What has struck me hardest during my life in the United States is the difference between the American in his own country and the American abroad. He becomes another person in another country.

Many non-American friends of mine have commented upon this. They visited America and are welcomed with open arms. They return to their own countries and the Americans there are unfriendly. Expatriate Americans stick together. Mutual fear of criticism makes them afraid to entertain the foreigner as freely as they would in their own homes in America.

I was to puzzle over this schizoid attitude for many years before I began to understand. My opinions on the subject were not personal. I realize I have nearly always been the exception to the rule. There are many reasons for the fact that no barriers have been raised against me. One was my arrival in New York when there were so few Filipinos in the United States that they had not raised the uneasy suspicions of the white supremacists.

Another factor made me the exception. If barriers have melted before me it is because I have refused to admit they were there. I like everyone, I know my own value and that of others. I like all kinds of people and respect all opinions. And if my trust fails I do not brood over the failure.

My thanks for all time go to my teacher Michael O'Malley, who knocked the chip off my shoulder before prejudice had the chance to sink in.

I do not hold with bitterness. I learned early never to permit myself the luxury of wanting to get even. If I am hurt, and I am easily hurt, I may weep at the injustice done me but I make myself forgive and forget. I envy nobody. I hate no one. I am happy when my friends succeed and I delight in my own successes. I have always worked hard, and I have been too busy to cherish ill will.

One day a friend of mine asked me if someone he heard speaking ill of me was my enemy. I told him that possibly he was my detractor but certainly not my enemy. Enemy to me implies mutual hatred and I could not find it in my heart to hate anyone.

This has been my philosophy, and it keeps me content and industrious and fond of my fellow men. It kept within reason a feeling that developed during my four years at Columbia—a growing discontent or disappointment in America.

Even as a student I recognized the need for change. Something was terribly wrong. The Negroes I saw in New York and Washington were submissive, shoved together in slums, a depressed people huddled together in freedom's land—the country held up to us in Asia as the land of the free. Men of dark skin were afraid to speak the truth, afraid to protest against outrage.

They hung their heads when reproved. Untaught, underpaid, and underprivileged, they walked softly and in fear. Only in their own ghettos did they dare lift their voices.

I saw these black hordes in their slum areas and wondered what crimes they had committed save that of being born to the Negro race.

But I walked freely. I was asked everywhere. America the beautiful was being beautiful indeed to me. It was for the deprived I suffered and felt shame, not for what they were, but for the way they were treated.

My interest in politics grew. Only politics could make America, and in time the Philippines, right as countries should be. A new hope rose in the world. It was the League of Nations. I looked on that as the rising flame of freedom. I had a new hero— Woodrow Wilson.

My hero-worship made a personal dilemma in my life, for it was difficult to have a close association with the Tafts and be their frequent house guest in Washington while openly worshiping at the Wilson shrine. But I passionately admired Wilson, most of all for his dream of writing a never-ending peace. On my Washington visits I went to hear him speak again and again. His enemies were mine, and I despised them, I am certain, far more than Wilson ever could with his cool, temperate mind.

Wilson's picture was on our classroom walls in the Philippines, close to Washington's and Rizal's, for it was Wilson who had signed our Jones Act, our first giant step on the road to freedom.

In his fight for the League of Nations Wilson was the voice of a world that would be free. I prayed for its success, and for him.

Henry Cabot Lodge was fighting Wilson. I shunned Lodge as intensely as if he had done me a personal wrong. Couldn't Lodge see that in fighting the League he might be responsible for the deaths of millions?

The League was defeated. But the hopes it had raised remained to haunt the conscience of the world. Someday, I was certain, there would be a new League of Nations. There would have to be. The tides of evil rose as man became more lethal. From the time of Wilson's defeat I had my own burning personal dream of a league, a world organization, wherein all peoples would band together in a common cause against man's greatest enemy—war. I even drew vague sketches of the building that would house those delegates of the nations. It would be a tall cathedral reaching to the sky.

How fortunate am I among men, for that once penciled dream, now a reality, is the first thing I see when I come by plane over New York City.

I was not the sole dreamer, I knew later. Men all over the earth were sketching that dream building.

If only Woodrow Wilson had lived to see it there. If he had won the League for the nations, how many lives, how much torture, how much unleashing of world hatred might we have been spared! If the United Nations had existed in Wilson's day and seventeen nations had said to Kaiser Wilhelm, "Stand back!" his soldiers would never have goose-stepped into Belgium. If Mussolini had been warned to stay out of Africa, if Hitler had been reprimanded by all the free nations those human horrors could never have wreaked their manic vengeance on the world.

Let those who scoff at the United Nations think that over! It has its faults, but what better court has man devised?

Wilson came back to America, ruined, defeated, ill. Rumors of his physical and mental breakdown were sent flying out of Washington. Hatred does not last with me, but its impact is sickening when I am in its throes. I have never despised any group of men as I did that committee of Senators who visited Wilson's home to check the rumor, insisted upon entering his bedroom, and even lifted the blankets of the bed where he was lying to see if the report that the President was paralyzed was true!

One of the profoundly touching experiences of my life took place in the Military Institute at Staunton, Virginia, at the Woodrow Wilson Centennial ceremonies. I was guest speaker, and I stood in a circle drawn on the platform. Within that circle Woodrow Wilson had stood, when, before his oath-taking as President of the United States, he made the pronouncement that he would favor the independence of the Philippines.

He was the first American president to make that promise. Because of that pledge, his signing of the Jones Act, and his services on behalf of freedom, he is a hero in the Philippines.

At last I had struggled through the mathematical torments and was free to return to comparative literature. I reveled in those classes. I did my best work in them. I was fortunate in my literary adviser, for he was Carl Van Doren.

Years later, his brother Mark, the poet, and I would receive honorary degrees together from Adelphi University in New York City.

My years in America ended in the spring of 1922. I would leave Columbia with my M.A. My American sweetheart and I had our plans all made.

We would be married in New York directly after the graduation exercises. After a brief honeymoon visit to the Philippines we would return to New York. I would find work on a newspaper.

What a different course my life would have taken if we had carried out those plans.

We were blissfully certain of our future. Whatever differences might have arisen between us I am certain none would have been based upon race. There was never any sense of difference between us and there could have been none. I felt fully prepared for life and marriage. I had grown up during the university years.

Our idyl was interrupted by the burly but un-Cupidlike figure of William Howard Taft. I do not know how the Chief Justice of the United States learned of our modest little romance. Perhaps as my guardian in America he kept a closer watch on my personal affairs than I suspected. For no sooner were Commencement Day ceremonies over than my landlady ushered into my room a dignified emissary from Washington. It was one of Governor Taft's secretaries, and he let me know at once his sole purpose in coming to New York was to pay me this visit.

"The Chief wants to see you in Washington," he said.

"What for?" I asked. I was startled and uneasy.

"He wants to see your college reports."

"But I have graduated!" I waved before his eyes the magic diploma for which I had toiled four long years. "See? Master of Arts!"

He was not impressed. "How soon are you leaving for home?"

I began to understand. I said coldly, "As soon as I am married I shall return to the Philippines with my wife."

He showed no surprise, although nothing had been said before about any girl in my life. Of course he had no need to ask. I found out later he had combed my list of friends for information. I had been undergoing a thorough investigation while believing myself alone with my love.

The aide left without comment, and the next morning I received a telephone call from Washington. "Carlos, I hear you have graduated," Governor Taft said. "Congratulations! Why don't you come to see us in Washington and return to the Philippines from here?"

"I have planned . . ." I began, but he cut in with a sharply incisive, "Come anyway! I want to talk to you."

It was an order. I was on the next train for Washington.

Taft was to me what modern writers would describe as a "father image." His family was my family in America. Benign, paternal, and kindly, he kept an eye on my reports and was always interested in knowing how I was getting along.

The Chief Justice was a formidable person to face. His steely eyes probed like fine wires.

"So you're planning to be married."

"Yes sir." I had never been meeker.

"Have you talked this over with your parents?"

I admitted I had planned to do that after the marriage. It was to be a surprise. . . .

My guardian waved my explanations away. "I think it is your duty to go back to Manila. Consult with your parents, stay with them for a while, talk things over, and think it over. Now, how soon are you leaving?"

I was caught off guard. "Well, I must see about getting my tickets, and . . ."

His voice had the ring of steel. "Your tickets are already bought. You have a reservation on the train leaving New York tomorrow morning for San Francisco. The train connects at San Francisco with the boat leaving for Manila. Your cabin on that boat is reserved. Have a good trip."

William Howard Taft looked soft, at a distance. The hand he shook in farewell ached for hours.

He was my guardian and I had to obey him. I returned to New York glazed with suffering. My love and I had only one evening left for the most sorrowful parting since Romeo's from Juliet.

We walked Riverside Drive for hours, my girl and I. Through our tears we saw the moon washing the striated Palisades across the water and vowed all the old vows, "by yon constant moon." Despite our grief we were certain love like ours could never die.

Still in a daze of sadness I boarded the ship at San Francisco. I had looked forward to this triumphal return home. Now I remember nothing of that trip across the Pacific except the nights when I walked the decks alone, melancholy as Hamlet, and lifted my suffering face at intervals to that same "constant moon."

When a year later I returned to Washington and by chance met my lost love again we were as aloof as if newly introduced. During that year our minds and hearts had changed. She had found other interests and I had met the girl I would eventually marry.

"Go home and think it over," Taft had ordered during that harrowing interview one year before.

I had gone back to Manila and met Miss Virginia Llamas.

Several years later I introduced my wife to Senator Robert Taft and he beamed on our happy young faces, and then gave me one of his shrewd, keen glances. "Well," he said, smiling, "don't you think Dad was right?"

How right he had been! And how wise. I will always be grateful to him. I had thought him a monster, void of sympathy and romance. He had seen me as I was, immature and infatuated and in the throes of a puppy love that had seemed deeper because of my loneliness in a strange land. He had realized that the companionship my girl and I had shared on the Columbia campus was not the material of lasting love.

Now after almost thirty-seven years of marriage I know I could never have been happy with any woman other than the one I married. William H. Taft was indeed my benefactor.

As each of my boys has approached manhood I have told him, "Don't marry right away! Look around you, meet girls, and then, when you finally choose the one you know is right, be faithful!"

A successful marriage is like a successful business and must be based upon lasting understanding and complete honesty. Race, I am confident, will be of increasingly less importance in this changing world, but the advantages of a shared background and ideals will never be lost.

Ten

THERE is no better medicine for a broken heart than new interests. Back in Manila I found that four years in America had added luster to my reputation as a young man who was going places.

I took up life at home and found it good to be with the family again.

My father was now assistant director of the Census Bureau. He had worked long and well in his country's service and this was actually an honorary job.

I found him little changed and my mother not at all. If his motions were slower than before that made him more like other men. He had always been ultrarapid in gesture and speech. These were good days for my father. His two oldest sons were through school and he took pride in work well-done. My older brother, Henry, had just graduated from Santo Tomas medical college. Two weeks after my return from Columbia my father hung my brother's brass sign before his door, stepped back, and looked at it with an expression of pure happiness.

Dr. Enrique P. Romulo

I know how happy my father was on that day! He had given my brother and me the best he had to give and we had done what we could to show our appreciation.

The next day I found him crawling up the stairs, his face contorted with anguish. He was operated on at four that afternoon. The pancreas had ruptured. By three o'clock the next morning he was gone.

We had been a united, loving family. Now the center of our life was missing. My mother remained dry-eyed but I knew her heart was forever empty. My sisters wept and would not be consoled. I remembered how our father had tried to curb our tears and his own, and I fought for control and tried to silence my sisters.

"Restrain yourselves," I begged them. "He always wanted us to control our emotions."

But they could not, nor could I. We were like our father and this was the first true heartbreak of our lives.

My mother accepted widowhood with dignity. She carried on in the home and kept her children about her. I stayed on with her and set about the business of active living. Jobs were to be had for the taking. In my first enthusiasm I took all that were offered.

If only my father had lived a few more weeks! Soon after he left us I was appointed Assistant Professor of English at the University of the Philippines. How happy that would have made my father, who had always been the teacher and guide at heart. He would have been happier still at another appointment I received at the same time, for I was made one of Quezon's secretaries.

Now I was one of those I had so envied as a cub reporter, the secretaries who were the confidantes of Quezon. I had wondered how they reached their positions close to power, and now I knew.

I had seen what a man in Quezon's position could achieve. I had admired him without reservation. From my new position, close to the heroic statue I so admired, I would learn in time to see the defects in the stone.

As Assistant Professor at the university and private secretary to Quezon, I would be in my classroom from nine to twelve and from two to four, then in Quezon's office until eight or nine in the evening, depending on the lateness of the Senate session.

There were partial evenings free, and they were soon filled.

Six months after my return from America I became assistant editor of the *Herald*, which was the first Philippine daily printed in English. Benitez was editor, so our positions were the same as they had been on the *Citizen*. Now again on the *Herald* we supported Quezon. That was all right with me. I believed in Quezon and his policies with all my heart.

Now I was holding down three jobs and had three salaries. I collected my first lot and brought them home to my mother. I was remembering the storm I had caused when I had offered my father part of my salary. Again, Mother took all I gave her and said nothing.

My routine settled down to an unremitting headlong pace, but I never found time to be bored.

Each morning I was up early. I reached the university at nine and taught until noon. At twelve I dashed home for lunch. There was time for a very brief siesta and at two I was back in the classroom; by four I was at work in Quezon's office in the Senate building. After that I went home for dinner, and then on to the *Herald* office.

The *Herald* was a morning paper. I would work until the edition was ready for the press, sometimes at midnight, sometimes two or three in the morning. No matter how little sleep I had, I was up at eight the next morning.

My talent for catnapping was perfected during this period. Between classes, under Quezon's very nose, or at my desk in the *Herald* office—the same desk that had been my companion since my first subeditorial job—I indulged in the brief moments of total blackout that were all I needed. I could fall asleep anywhere and under any conditions and I always felt energetic and well. My mother kept a comfortable home, I was content with my various jobs, and for a time was busy holding them. I was too busy to give any thought to marriage. That was too permanent a situation for a young man on his way.

But girls—that was different. I could always find time for pretty girls and we have beautiful girls in Manila. The Romeo

and Juliet idyl of the Columbia campus faded in the light of a
new interest, but charming as she was, she could not claim much
of my time. I was too taken up with all those jobs.

At this time I was a serious and reflective young man, although I doubt if anyone meeting me casually would have
thought so. The years in America had deepened my innate
capacity for questioning. Now more than ever I was certain that
America's first intention for the Philippines had been right—
Christian, democratic, free. America had taken charge of my
country on the promise that it would be trained for freedom.
Why then the promise and not the act? Why not the definite
pledge that on a certain day we would be free?

I had seen freedom in America, imperfect but indicative of
what freedom could be. The four Columbia years had fixed
that ideal more firmly than ever in my heart. Someday we too
could vote for the man of our choice; someday we would be
citizens of an independent nation.

Someday—McKinley had promised, and Taft, and Woodrow Wilson.

And now living in Malacañang Palace, in our midst, was
Leonard Wood, Governor General of the Philippines, who was
openly antagonistic to our national leader Quezon and against
Philippine independence. He was working through Washington channels to withdraw from the Filipinos all the rights for
self-government we had won since the century started and our
subjection began.

Now I knew how those two gentle family men, my father
and grandfather, had felt when they took up their guns and left
their homes to fight first the Spanish usurper then the American.

The time had passed for guns. On my desk was the typewriter upon which I would wage my wars. My ammunition was
words, and with these I followed Quezon into the fight.

Despite the differences that were to come between Quezon
and myself from time to time, I see him still as the ideal leader
every country needs—the man whose strongest motivation was

love of country. He had minor flaws, but his patriotism was never in shadow. He knew exactly what the Philippine ideal should be and he was willing to give his life to it, and in the end he did.

Throughout his entire career Quezon fought a steady fight for more self-government for the Philippines and eventual emancipation from American rule. It was a crusade he had been led into by Sergio Osmeña, who as first speaker of the Assembly, our first legislative body under American rule, had outlined the ultimate plan for our self-government.

Osmeña mapped out the dream. Quezon set it to action. He had won the Jones Act for us. He was constantly urging Washington to place more and more power in Filipino hands. He discovered bright young men and helped them attain key positions to strengthen Filipino faith in our own power to govern.

And all he was doing, or trying to do, was being steadily undermined by his arch enemy, General Wood. Wood was not only stopping Quezon on every advance but he was trying to persuade America to rescind rights already won by Quezon.

It was an insult to Filipino leaders of conscience and intelligence to find themselves outranked in their own country by Americans. But this was done, and by American protocol. Americans outranked the Filipinos on all governmental levels.

Americans might think this is a trifling issue. But would American people in government be pleased to have Filipinos take social precedence in Washington and find themselves in their own capital seated below the salt?

It may not have been important, but it was a constant source of hurt to Filipino leaders.

Quezon was struggling to place more Filipinos in places of authority and to have more concessions made to their dignity. Since the Philippines would eventually become self-governing, he argued, their training should start as soon as possible. He was always planning ways to wrest more concessions from the

United States that would increase Filipino participation in the
government and enhance their dignity.

Quezon wanted more Filipino members in the cabinet. Governor General Wood was fighting to reduce the power of that
cabinet. It was move and countermove in open enmity. On
rattling typewriter keys I kept pace with the contest and did my
best to win support for Quezon.

Open war broke out between the two when Wood made a
deliberate attempt to interfere with Secretary of the Interior
José P. Laurel's powers as head of his department.

A night meeting was held in Quezon's home. The entire Filipino cabinet was present. It was resolved that they should resign in protest against Wood.

This dramatic and shocking move gave force to Quezon's
fight to elect Ramon Fernandez, of the well-known shipping
family, to a seat in the Senate. His candidacy was skillfully opposed by Juan Sumulong, head of the Democratic party and the
brains of the opposition.

While Sumulong did not entirely sustain the views of Governor Wood, he was anti-Quezon, and therefore he campaigned
against Fernandez.

Quezon respected Sumulong more than any other member of
the opposition. He challenged Sumulong to a series of debates.
Up and down the island all through the campaign the skillful
antagonists dueled verbally in a series of public debates, Quezon
upholding Fernandez, Sumulong protesting. (As Lincoln had
debated against Douglas a century before.)

Wood sprang to the support of Sumulong in the hope of defeating Quezon. Quezon turned his attack against Wood, campaigning through province after province to portray Wood as
the arch enemy of the Philippines. Wood, entrenched in the
Palace, countervilified Quezon as a tyrant and dictator.

It was a hot struggle with no holds barred and the first campaign I had ever watched from the inside. I lost more sleep than
usual, not wanting to miss any of the excitement. Sometimes

members of the press and Quezon's secretarial staff sat up all
night in Quezon's home in Pasay waiting for word of his latest
foray in the provinces. I remember one morning he came in
about six o'clock, exhausted and begrimed after a night meeting
and a long drive over dusty roads.

He dropped into his chair, then burst out in a passionate
tirade. "How I wish," he fumed, "that the goddam Americans
would tyrannize over us so that I could have stronger issues to
debate against Wood."

How typical of our ironic situation, I thought. Here was
satire, a politician fighting to win an election and complaining
because he could not find enough blame in his opponents! India
had no lack of complaints under the English, Indonesia had long
lists of grievances under the Dutch, and here was Quezon backing a valuable issue and with no useful complaints to launch
against America!

Against the American Wood his protests were legion! But
he was not attacking America.

Now that I knew America I agreed with Quezon. I could not
believe that what Wood was trying to do to us had the support
of the American public. Americans were fair. They simply did
not know the Filipino, his needs and his dreams.

There it was again—my personal motivation. I had to help
make the Philippines understandable to the world. I had to help
somehow with the small might allotted me. Why should one
man, representing his country in another land, be permitted to
misrepresent his nation's ideals as Wood was doing?

Moods of passionate indignation are not rare with me. This
was a situation I felt keenly because I was Filipino. I went to
the *Herald* office, sat down at my typewriter, and launched an
arrow into the air in the shape of an editorial attack against
Governor Wood.

The editorial appeared on the following day and received a
flattering amount of approval within my immediate range.
Since the *Herald* was pro-Quezon everyone on the staff ap-

plauded. On the campus the students, pro-Quezon to a lad, were highly approving. The Senate denizens of course were pleased. Wherever I went on my daily rounds I was told I had done well. I preened in my warrior's plumage and rejoiced in the trophies of victory.

The telephone rang early the next morning. I was having breakfast at home with my mother. General Frank McCoy, chief adviser to the Governor General, asked me to come to Wood's office at once.

As fast as I could get to Wood's office I was there. Everything about the place intimidated me: the glowing wood paneling, the heavy furniture, and most of all the impressive brooding figure of General Wood.

On his desk lay yesterday's *Herald*, folded back to my editorial. How many times have my irrefutable words stared up at me from desks of power? My own fiery opinions accused me and I could not, would not deny them, not even under Wood's accusing glare.

"You wrote that, Romulo?" His pointing finger shook. He was boiling. He had not asked me to be seated but launched his attack in a roar.

Then, with swelling anger, he shouted, "Don't you know what would be happening to you if you'd written an editorial like this under the Spanish regime? You'd be facing a firing squad on the Luneta at this very moment!"

"General," I asked, very softly, "may I sit down?"

My debating experiences had taught me the cutting value of a soft word. He did not answer so I sat down. Then I proceeded to talk, quietly but emphatically. "Certainly I know what would be happening to me under Spanish rule. But when I wrote that article I knew I was under the protection of the American flag and that is why I felt at liberty to write as I did."

He sat back and stared at me. Finally he said in a bitter tone. "Don't you think it's a pity that you should have been educated in the United States and come back here to be led about by a politician like Quezon?"

I pointed to the *Herald*. "Quezon had nothing to do with my writing that editorial. It represents my views as a Filipino and the views of the Filipino people. Quezon is the leader of our people and the editorial concerns him only in that way."

He whipped over to sarcasm. "So," he said cuttingly, "you are a politician as well as a newspaperman!"

I stood up. "If you have sent for me to ask whether or not I am a politician I don't want to waste any more of your time."

Wood slapped his hand on the desk. "I sent for you to tell you, you are in the wrong!" he shouted. "This editorial is not fair to me. As Governor General of the Philippines I deserve better treatment from the *Herald!*"

"The columns of the *Herald* are open to you, Governor," I told him. "Anything you wish published by way of an answer will be published. We will print it in the exact place of this editorial and allow you the exact amount of space. Write whatever you like and send it to me."

Several days later I told Quezon of the meeting.

"What has happened since then?" he asked.

"Nothing. I haven't heard a word from the Governor."

Quezon laughed and said I wouldn't hear again from Wood. He was right. Quezon declared I had won the victory.

Perhaps it went to my head. At any rate I made a serious mistake. I indulged in bitterness.

I have since learned that there is no situation that is not worsened by bitterness. But I was young and hot-headed and could not forgive Wood's incessant attacks on Quezon. In Filipino minds an attack on our leader was a blow to the very heart of our country.

I had our *Herald* cartoonist, Fernando Amorsolo, draw a cartoon of Wood stabbing a Filipino woman, personifying the Philippines at the mercy of a heartless representative of America. Amorsolo put his heart into the drawing and it caused a

great deal of comment in the capital. But the instant I saw it on
the front page of the *Herald* I knew I had committed an ugly
injustice. It was too late to withdraw the cartoon, but I did
run an apology in the next day's edition. It was too late. The
harm was done and I had made my first powerful enemy.

That enmity would last throughout the long-drawn-out contest between Wood and Quezon, which Quezon carried to
Washington, and which would end with Wood's death, and,
ultimately, Quezon's.

We must be fair. General Wood was against Filipino independence because he was honestly convinced that in the long
run the Philippines would be better off under the protection of
America. He was interested in the common man; he always saw
that the national treasury was filled and the national budget
balanced. He was an excellent administrator, and in all matters
except independence he was fair and just. But he did not understand the Filipino dream of running his own country and being
free to do so. Better a dinner of herbs in freedom, than caviar
under a crown.

Again it was carnival time. The pre-Easter festivities were to
climax as always with the series of balls in the auditorium presided over by the carnival queen. This festival is similar to the
Mardi Gras in New Orleans and the queen is chosen for her
beauty by popular vote.

Carnivals had small place in my life. Even in my student days
I had worked on newspapers at night and news stories of a
pressing nature had kept me occupied during this carefree time.
The past four years had been spent in America.

This season, the year after my return from America, found
me celebrating the carnival against my will.

Each Manila newspaper chose its own Filipino beauty to
sponsor for carnival queen. Each ran articles citing the good
looks and accomplishments of their choice, published her pictures, and solicited votes in her behalf. The *Herald's* candidate

was a Miss Virginia Llamas, from the town of Pagsanjan. She was a high-school student in the Philippine Women's College. I did not meet Miss Llamas in person during her campaign, but as I selected pictures from her many publicity shots to fill our daily pages I was struck with the certainty that I had met her before.

Finally I remembered. A picnic had been given by the Columbian Association and among the guests was Miss Llamas. I recalled we had been introduced, without mutual interest. I had thought her beautiful, but my attentions were on the girl I had brought to the picnic, a girl I had met shortly after my return to Manila who had done much to heal the scars left by my broken campus idyl.

So for the *Herald's* sake I was glad that when the contest ended, our candidate had won. Miss Llamas was to be beauty queen of the carnival and reign over all the auditorium balls.

The day after we printed this triumphant announcement Manuel Earnshaw called me into his office. He was general manager of the *Herald*, formerly Resident Commissioner in Washington, and a great friend of Quezon's. Any request he had to make of an assistant editor would be a "must."

He was an enthusiastic man. "Rommy," he began, "I want you to act as prince consort to our queen. Escort her to all the balls and be seen with her everywhere all during the carnival. The *Herald* elected her and everything you two do together will be good publicity."

"Are you kidding?" I demanded.

I didn't like the idea at all. My girl and I had planned to attend the carnival as spectators. She was not going to approve of my acting as escort to the queen.

I protested. "I am in mourning. I cannot possibly attend a ball."

Earnshaw said he realized it was true that my father had recently died. "But this is for the paper," he argued. "It's important. You can mourn your father in private. The *Herald* is entitled to all the publicity the carnival can give us, after all we've done for the carnival, and you're just the lad who can get it for us by escorting the queen."

There was no refusing him. It was true that as prince consort I would have the inside track on all the carnival news. It was a good break for the *Herald*. But how could I explain this to the young lady who had expected to enjoy the carnival with me?

I made one final stand. "How do I know Miss Llamas wants me? I've only met her once."

Earnshaw said he would take care of that.

I went home in a gloomy state of mind. My mother, sisters, and brothers were already at the table. When I announced my rise to royal estate everyone whooped with mirth except my mother, who became unexpectedly indignant.

"You, an editor!" my mother said. "You, a university graduate, who has been to the United States! Acting as prince consort to a Miss Philippines!" Then, suddenly suspicious, she demanded, "Did she ask for you?"

I could see what my mother was thinking. Firmly wedged in her mind was the image of King Cophetua forced to kneel before the maid from the country. It was true, as all her publicity had stressed, that Miss Llamas was from the provinces, but as a matter of fact so were we!

My brothers and sisters had no respect for my feelings. Carlos with a crown on his head! Carlos in ermine! They had never heard anything so funny.

Laughter lightened the gloom that had lain on our home since our father's death. I was almost glad to be in this absurd position since it served to make my family temporarily gay.

But I resented the appointment, and my resentment fastened on Miss Llamas, whose pert, pretty face had won her the crown.

I hoped Earnshaw would forget the entire idea.

Earnshaw never forgot anything. That afternoon he bounced into my office. "Well, it's all arranged. I've just talked things over with our queen and she has no objection to your being her escort."

"Objection!" I howled. I was the one to object. With what little dignity I had left, I snapped, "Perhaps she had better speak to me about it!"

Earnshaw gave me a queer look. "Perhaps you had better speak to her."

There was an edge to his voice. It was the voice of the *Herald*. Meekly I asked where Miss Llamas was staying.

She was at the home of her uncle, Catalino Lavadia, Secretary of Commerce. I had met him in New York with his wife, a charming lady.

He greeted me at his door with an irritating grin. "Well, how is the prince consort?"

At that moment Miss Llamas joined us. Her color was high, her manner imperious. She started right in. "Why are you refusing to be my prince consort?"

I was staring at her. She was so angry and so much prettier than her pictures that I, usually glib of speech, found myself tongue-tied.

"Who says I refused?" I stammered.

"Mr. Earnshaw!"

"I merely suggested . . ."

"Then it's decided!" The ice maiden melted. Miss Llamas smiled. She was beautiful! I stammered out my thanks. It was too late to tell her or anyone else about the other girl.

The night of Virginia's coronation in the auditorium was one of the most humiliating experiences of my life. She was poised, beautiful, triumphant. I was in misery. She was serene; I squirmed.

Some artistic genius had decided that the motif of the coronation ball should be Roman. Virginia wore her flowing imperial robe with ease and grace.

Just before the procession was to start I was crammed into

a short toga and jersey tights that were far too small and made me horribly aware of my knobby knees. My bare feet were laced into Roman sandals which turned out not to be a pair, but in odd sizes. The tight thongs of one cut between my toes while the sole of the other flapped like a Chaplin shoe. My laurel-leaf crown was of cutout tin with jagged edges. I could not adjust it where it did not stab my head, and as I led the glowing queen the long way across the auditorium floor to the clapping of thousands of spectators one shoe slapped loudly over the sound of applause and a tin point in my slipping crown drove into my temple like a dagger.

It was a walk taken in nightmare, but the ridiculous figure I cut need not have worried me for all eyes were on the queen. Virginia's gracious, smiling dignity saved us. Worst of all for me was the glimpse I caught of the girl of my dreams. She was sitting alone in a box viewing my march with amused disdain.

As soon as the Queen was crowned, I left her on the throne surrounded by her court and dashed to the box where the girl was waiting. I danced every dance with her.

There are nine nights of carnival and nine balls. Eight of those evenings I escorted our queen across the auditorium floor to her throne and left her there while I danced with my girl. Miss Llamas never reproved me. She kept her queenly dignity on and off the throne.

That intrigued me. That and her beauty, which seemed to grow with the nights of carnival. Still I have no idea why on the ninth and final night I did not rush from the queen's side as usual but lingered beside the throne.

"Will you dance with me?" I blurted out at last.

It would have served me right if she had turned me down. Instead, she gave me a look of mock concern.

"Are you sure you're not sick?" she asked.

We danced. She thanked me in the sweetest way for having acted as her prince consort. There was no reproof for the nights I had left her to dance with her courtiers. I found myself unable to leave her and we spent dance after dance together. Once I glanced up at the box where I thought the other girl would be waiting. She had gone.

The next day I called on Miss Llamas at her uncle's home, not as a reluctant prince but as an eager and humble suitor. I came with an invitation. I wanted her to visit my home and meet my people. She refused.

But my entire family had fallen in love with her. They sang her praises and only my mother was silent.

I spoke to her privately. "Mother," I said, "I think I am falling in love with Miss Llamas."

My mother spoke in the positive tone she seldom used. "I think she is the right girl for you."

Heretofore the struggle to get ahead had been foremost. Now all that mattered was the winning of a beautiful little girl from the town of Pagsanjan. For once, speech was letting me down. My Tarlac dialect is Pangasinan. Virginia's was Tagalog. She spoke Spanish, the speech of love, far better than I. I had to carry on my siege in English, the language we had spoken together from the first.

Every day I sent her a letter, special delivery; every day a gift of the sort a "nice young girl" could receive. I presented myself at her uncle's door whenever opportunity, or Virginia, would permit. For once, my many jobs and responsibilities were not permitted to interfere.

Miss Llamas had won her contest honestly. She was beautiful and popular. There were other men with more to offer; above all, these others had leisure time. I was willing to work hard, to offer more in the end, but meanwhile time was what I didn't have! I had to spend the mornings in the university classrooms, my afternoons with Quezon, evenings at the *Herald*.

The pursuit of love is a feverish process, and I was not certain mine was getting me anywhere. That cool, aloof dignity of Virginia's left me desperately unsure of myself.

At the height of this war of attrition Quezon upset my life and my love by asking me to go with him to America.

Half of me was wild to go. Such an invitation meant I was singled out from his other secretaries to accompany my hero to Washington, where he was to lead another mission for independence. We would be away three months.

How the honor would have thrilled me a few weeks before! Now it could not have come at a more inopportune time.

Miss Llamas had shown no particular interest in my attentions. She had not encouraged me; on the other hand, she had not been openly discouraging. I had lavished upon her all the romantic technique I had learned in the United States. She was not impressed.

Aside from "love," another word, "independence," lured me. If I could help in that fight in any way I would, even if my heart broke. I took temporary leave of the *Herald*, the university, my hopes of Virginia, and sailed with Quezon.

One resolution I made was that Miss Llamas was not to forget me. I posted burning messages from every port, and once in Washington not a day went by without a letter and gift being sent to the Philippines. Wherever my travels with Quezon carried me, my first hunt was for a suitable gift, my next for the post office.

During those three months in Washington a little more impetus was given to the independence fight. My admiration for Quezon grew. How much at ease he was in Washington, and how well thought of by the Americans on Capitol Hill. I was proud of him, proud to be seen with him, proud of the small victories won.

Our return home was a triumph. Once I had watched Quezon make such an entry into Manila from my perch with other students on the old Spanish wall. Now I was part of his entourage. Part of the glory of his return rubbed off on me.

I hurried home, and was just about to leave for my first call on Miss Llamas when a delivery van stopped at our door. All the gifts I had chosen with such care in the United States were carried into my house. There were boxes of books unopened, boxes of moldy chocolates. I was furious! How dared this little schoolgirl from the provinces do this to me!

I confronted her in her uncle's home with my accusations. She was impersonal, aloof. I tried to sweep her off her feet. She remained firmly rooted to the ground. All my learned-in-America technique failed.

"But why?" I kept insisting. "Why this coldness?"

For a long time she would not explain. Then one day she broke down. "I cannot feel sure of you," she said. "Something tells me you are a most unreliable man."

Another man might have given up. I was filled with boundless hope. She was thinking about me!

I felt I was advancing in my campaign. It has always taken very little to encourage me. My efforts were intensified. I was working against time, as Virginia was about to graduate from high school. Then she would leave her uncle's home in Manila and return to Pagsanjan.

The thought was unendurable. I gathered my forces for a major offensive, do or die. Zero hour was the night of her graduation, with its emotional ceremonies and Virginia sparkling in white. The basket of flowers she received that night from me was, I am certain, the largest floral display ever arranged by a Manila florist. In my pocket, over my heart, was a ring.

In the midst of the festivities I managed to maneuver Virginia to a window. There I poured out all the oratory, all the poetry my heart had been secreting these many anguished months. I brought forth the ring. All my hopes were in that tiny circlet.

She was deeply moved, but she kept her head. "I must consult my family," she said, and that was all she would say, but the look she gave me needed no words to make me feel I had seen heaven itself. I slipped the diamond on her finger. The next day she left for Pagsanjan.

Now, in addition to the crowded, busy weeks, I had Sundays!

Pagsanjan is about a three-hour drive from Manila. I bought a car. Every Saturday night after putting the *Herald* to bed, I would drive out of Manila about three in the morning. I would arrive at Pagsanjan about six, go to the Abella Hotel, bathe and change, and hurry to nine o'clock Mass.

There I would catch a glimpse of Virginia with her head bent demurely under its square of black lace, surrounded by her family.

In those days, in the Philippines, the Spanish rules of courtship were universally preserved. They still are in decorous homes. After Mass I would leave the church and follow Virginia to her door, keeping a respectful distance. Her family knew I was following, Virginia knew, but I might have been an invisible man. On red-letter Sundays her father, seeing me loitering outside their gate, might speak a word of greeting. Then the ladies would bow. I was visible! I might even be asked to lunch!

These invitations became more frequent. After lunch Virginia and I would be permitted to sit and talk in the drawing room. There was nothing private about these tête-à-têtes. Every word was overheard, every movement observed, for all the doors to the room were left open and wherever one looked one would see Virginia's father, her brothers and sisters, her mother, and also her two aunts in their home across the street, sitting in strategic positions and all in full view.

But if the night was to be a moonlight one Virginia would ask me to remain over for the evening. I would hurry through my dinner at the hotel to be in the plaza in time for the promenade. This custom in the Philippines starts at dusk. It is the gathering time for the young people of the community, with a band playing in the plaza and the boys and girls walking to the music, chatting gaily. Every now and then in passing I would touch Virginia's hand for a moment and I would notice that she wore my ring.

Still, she would give me no definite answer.

I was becoming impatient. I was earning a fair income and I

wanted to marry. I wanted to marry Virginia. At the university I was promoted from assistant to associate professor. The *Herald* was doing well and Quezon continued to show his trust in my judgment. I wanted a wife and a home of my own. The only wife I wanted was Miss Virginia Llamas, and she was keeping me in suspense.

It dawned on me that with the conventional Llamas family a formal request would be necessary. I asked Virginia for an appointment with her father. But I wanted to know from her first if she wanted me to ask for her hand. It was then that she gave me her affirmative answer. And she suggested our wedding day—her birthday, July 1. For days I walked on clouds.

I rounded up a family delegation to go with me the next Sunday to Pagsanjan—my mother and my sister Lourdes, with the man she had recently married, Carlos Kipping. The drive had never seemed so long. I was edgy with nerves. The atmosphere in Virginia's home did not help. There was a definite chill in the air.

Virginia's parents and aunts met my family group with ominous reserve. Virginia was in an adjoining room. Something was decidedly wrong. She was, I was told later, fidgeting with a compact, as my mother with her customary dignity made a formal request in my behalf to Virginia's father.

Mr. Llamas shook his head. "I cannot consent to their marriage."

There was a crash. Virginia had dropped the compact.

My tiny mother drew herself up like a tigress about to spring. Her eyes flashed, his flashed, pride struck pride.

"Why?" she demanded.

Mr. Llamas did not weaken. "Because it has come to my ears that your son has already contracted a marriage while in the United States. I am having the charge investigated by Resident Commissioner Pedro Guevara and by Secretary Lavadia, and until I know the truth I will not give my consent."

I had been ordered to remain silent throughout these preliminaries, but now, in a storm of indignation, burst out.

"Marriage?" I shouted. "That is a lie! Everything you have heard is wrong. Sweethearts, yes, I have had those, but all that is over. I swear to you I have never been married. But your refusing us cannot spoil everything because your daughter and I have already decided to get married. We only came today out of deference to you to ask you to agree to the date!"

Virginia had entered the room. She was staring at me. So was her father.

"What date?" he thundered.

"Our wedding day! Virginia's birthday!"

In the stunned silence that followed this pronouncement my mother stepped forward. She was bristling with indignation. "Mr. Llamas, do you think I would be here today with my son if he were already married?"

Before this onslaught Mr. Llamas threw in the sponge. "You have convinced me," he said, and turning to Virginia, "you have my consent."

And then, what emotion was in that home! In a surge of good will and happiness two families became one.

Back in Manila I blissfully set about the happy task of house hunting. A small bungalow in the Malate district seemed perfect, and I would be able to pay for it out of my earnings. When I told my mother that, she said there was no need for me to buy the house on time. Then she gave me a bankbook made out in my name. She had banked every peso I had given her since my first job on the *Cable-News!* Month after month she had accepted a large share of my salary without a word. I thought it was going to the support of our home, instead mother had saved it all for me.

Women amaze me with the skill they show at weddings. In the Philippines, as in all countries that follow Spanish customs, the burden of preparation and all the wedding expenses are assumed by the groom's family, from the bride's and her attendants' gowns to the wedding bouquet and the ring. When I found myself with sons to marry off my wife and I went through this procedure with mixed joy and dismay. Virginia has combed three continents to provide for our sons and their brides.

My widowed mother did not shirk her responsibilities. Actually I think she enjoyed the turmoil and the planning, as many women do. She approved the little house and furnished it for us as her own special gift; then, like a general commanding her troops, she marshaled all our relatives and let them know what gifts would be most acceptable. By this strategy all the linen, glassware, silver, and kitchenware we could possibly need was provided for the new home, all perfectly matched and without duplication.

A friend or relative need only inquire what sort of gift the dear young things would like, and Mother was right there with the answer. She kept lists. Everything was chosen for us down to the last broom. Virginia and I had only to exult in our beautiful wedding and look forward to happiness.

We were married on July 1, 1924, in the Pagsanjan town church and honeymooned in the mountains at Baguio.

When I returned to the university a new success awaited me. There was a demand for certain types of textbooks, and in my spare time, in collaboration with two of my esteemed colleagues, I wrote a book on college composition especially suited to the needs of Filipino students. I also prepared an adaptation of an American textbook, *Better English*, published by The John C. Winston Company for advanced students in the fifth and sixth grades. Both books were published, and with their royalties I bought my bride a piano for our new home.

I had married a young girl of fragile, doll-like beauty. Still I was not surprised when Virginia assumed charge of household and personal accounts and showed such business acumen and common sense that since our marriage I have carried out no plans that were not first discussed with her. My mother had also been dainty and beautiful, but she had cared for her husband and children and home with skill and intelligence, as well as love. I am afraid I took it for granted that a girl like Virginia would be an artist in homemaking and in social living.

She managed with such quiet ease, as my mother had, that I did not appreciate her calm efficiency until the night we gave our first dinner party. I was in a dither for days. Virginia was serene. Our first guests were to be the retiring head of the English Department, Dr. Scott, and his wife. He was my superior and I wanted to show off my beautiful young wife and our new home. It was a farewell party, as he was about to return to the United States and I was to take his place, at his recommendation.

Virginia was working on a budget. She made her plans for the dinner well in advance, choosing every course with care. We had a new cook, hired the week before.

Work kept me in the *Herald* office on the day of our party, and I did not get home until an hour before dinner. Before I entered the house I heard the crash of crockery.

Virginia met me at the door. She was pale but calm. "The cook is drunk. He is smashing all our dishes."

I hurried into the kitchen. The floor was littered with shards of our fine new dishes and glassware. There were no preparations toward dinner. The cook was standing by the cold stove, eyes bloodshot and head lowered. He charged me and offered to fight. I was going to hit him with a golf club I had picked up but Virginia stopped me. She was perfectly at ease.

"Don't worry about him. Go and get dressed. I'll attend to everything."

She was at the garage talking to my driver, Emilio, when I recovered enough to call her. I asked, "Where is the car going?"

"To the Hotel de France," she called back, and the car drove away.

That meant nothing to me. I went back to the kitchen, dismissed the cook, and saw him out of the house. Then I glanced around the kitchen. Dinner was obviously an impossibility, so I decided to follow my bride's advice. I bathed and dressed and met her in the living room.

She was serene and smiled at me sweetly. "Everything is all right," she said. There was no time for further explanation because Dr. and Mrs. Scott were coming up our walk.

Our guests never knew there was anything out of the ordinary about that dinner or that they were the first guests in our new home. Virginia was unruffled and gay so I soon lost my anxiety. The dinner was perfectly cooked and perfectly served, by a servant strange to me. I said nothing, but relaxed completely after the first course. I had forgotten the Hotel de France had a superb catering service.

It was a perfect evening, and after the Scotts left I told Virginia so. She put her hands to her head and moaned.

"Oh that dinner! Our budget! It cost one half of your salary this month. And I have been trying so hard to save!"

I told her it was worth every cent, and it was.

It is understandable that everything I earn is always turned over to her.

After that hectic beginning all our social plans have gone well. Virginia attends to everything.

A few years more, and with the same serene aplomb, Virginia would seat sixty guests at our Manila dinner table at a party in honor of General Douglas MacArthur. At a white-tie dinner and reception honoring John Foster Dulles' appointment as Secretary of State thirty-two guests sat down at our table, and later, at the reception, we welcomed one thousand more. When President Garcia visited Washington we received five thousand guests at a reception and then gave a dinner for President and Mrs. Eisenhower in the Philippine Embassy.

Virginia meets every mammoth social emergency with the same calmness she displayed when she salvaged our first dinner for two guests at the beginning of our marriage.

Her true development has come in Washington, where she

attends personally to all details of our extensive entertaining on ambassadorial levels.

The social season starts in November in Washington. By September she has all our embassy affairs organized, some of them months in advance. Guests of honor are chosen and guest lists gone over with the social secretary, Mrs. Gertrude K. Guevara—called by our boys Nonna—whom we have found a valued addition to our lives. Then Virginia enters upon a course of reading. She studies the biographies of all the guests so she will know who they are and what subjects can be brought up that are certain to spark their interest. None of this is due to any suggestions on my part. She has worked out her own scheme of hostess-ship.

She reads the newspapers I read, the Washington *Post*, the *Evening Star*, and the New York *Times*; she is au courant with world affairs and knows what is transpiring on Capitol Hill. She is the gentlest of women, but her way of thinking is sound. I often say we share one opinion and it is hers.

I sometimes wonder, if I had succeeded in my protests against acting as prince consort to a beauty queen what would have happened to my life?

My mother had been right. Virginia was the wife for me.

She was to be my shrewd and loving adviser in the problems I was shortly to face.

Eleven

A SALARIED man does not set his own course. For the rest of
the twenties—the century's and my own—I rocketed between
jobs, always subject to change. Hard-working and uncertain as
were those years, still they hold for me in memory much of the
deepest happiness I have known.

There has been little time in my life for memories. Time is
too precious to waste in looking back. There are memories at
which my wife and I can laugh together, and at others we weep.

So much to remember! I look back and wonder what has become of that young girl and young man who set out with so
much to offer life and each other.

I remember the many happinesses together or shared with
friends, because we were outgoing and in love. I remember myself as young, always fighting battles against windmills outside
the home, and returning to a resting place and haven tended by
one unfailingly good and kind.

One of the early scenes we remember with laughter is of Virginia, flushed and young and newly married, and tearfully
angry because she had found lipstick on the hem—of all places
—of a Chinese robe I had worn to a Chinese dinner, packing her
suitcases and telling me she was going back to live with her
mother, and then angrier than ever with me when I did not hold
her against her will!

Marriages are built on storms and sorrows and ecstasy buried
in the secret places of the heart. There has been the terrible
wracking grief of irrevocable loss and the love that helps and
heals. I have been a happy man and at times a sad man, but in
the long run I can say life has been good.

The endless climb upward, the falling back and starting again, the building and destruction and building again, the anger and prayers and losses, and the laurels and injustices, and above all the family and the friends—all have been worth-while. A small man from a small country has at times found life too large and beautiful to bear.

One of those moments came when Mike was born. Carlos Llamas Romulo, Junior, was named for me. Virginia would have it that way. Then Gregorio, known as Greg, and named for my father. No laurels can equal those moments when the newly born is placed in one's arms to cherish for life, if God wills.

We were a happy family. We were also a family that could use more income than I was earning. I took on the added duties of the university's debating coach, and the team I trained took all local honors.

Success went to our heads. We sent challenges to leading universities in America and all were accepted. In 1928, leaving Virginia with two baby boys, I brought four student debaters to the United States. The tour was wonderful. We debated at fourteen universities from west to east, from Stanford University in California to Bates College in Maine, which is the outstanding debating college in the United States. Everywhere we went we were royally entertained and warmly welcomed, and we won every debate. Our prize was to continue on our way home via Europe. It was the first of my trips around the world.

We returned to Manila and were given a dazzling reception at the pier. The entire student body from the university turned out along with students of other schools, and we were cheered as heroes and draped with floral necklaces the Hawaiians make of orchids and call leis, but which in Manila are made of sampaguita (the fragrant jasmine), our national flower.

My wife and the babies were in the crowd. How often my sons were to welcome me home to Manila, and always see me depart again, too soon, after too brief a time with them. I have few regrets but this is one.

There was no gloom in my heart that morning as we paraded all the way to the university, under floral arches erected in our honor, to a draped band-stand on the campus where I had to make an impromptu speech.

It was one of the most practical speeches I have ever made, because the debating team's expenses for the American trip had been raised by public contribution. Then and there I rendered a public accounting of every penny we had spent on the tour. The auditor of the university was on the stand, and I presented him with the financial statement I had kept despite my loathing of figures and with all the receipts I had saved.

Every member of that debating team has subsequently made his mark in the world.

I had returned to a situation that was to reshape my life, for this year, 1928, was a year of turmoil and change. Strange currents in America were beginning to affect the world. Newspapers are always barometers of economic change, and at this time the Manila papers were in a constant state of flux. I was personally affected when the *Herald* went into receivership, with Alejandro Roces as receiver.

Benitez promptly resigned. He was for Quezon under any circumstances, and he knew Roces would not permit blind loyalty to any political figure. Roces declared the *Herald* politically independent and offered me the promotion to editor in Benitez' place. I took it. The paper was still in receivership when I became its editor. At the same time I resigned as Quezon's secretary. Man cannot serve two masters, and if the *Herald* was to be an independent paper I had to be free. Resigning as his secretary was the only way I could be independent of political pressure from Quezon.

Almost at once I saw the wisdom of this move. Under Roces the *Herald* began to criticize certain official acts of the Senate President. The first attack was a claim that the clothing allowance given members of Quezon's independence mission was exorbitant. Quezon resented this, and ill will developed between him and Roces.

Quezon began maneuvering to get control of the *Herald*, to get it out of the receivership of Roces. He reorganized the group headed by Vicente Madrigal, a shipping magnate, which had formerly controlled the paper, and started proceedings to bring it back under that control. Madrigal was one of the loyal supporters of Quezon. A shrewd, far-seeing businessman, he had succeeded in building an industrial empire.

I did not like Quezon's move. It looked as though he wanted control of the *Herald* just to stop its attacks on him, and this seemed unworthy of the man we were looking up to as our leader toward democracy. I believed then, and still believe, that freedom of the press and freedom of speech are the very bulwarks of democracy.

What I thought did not matter. Quezon took over the *Herald*. He asked me to remain as its editor. My reaction lacked tact. I resigned.

This was out-and-out revolt against Quezon, and for a time I heard nothing from him. I told myself I was sick of politics and that a teaching job and a growing family were enough to content any man. I told myself I was through with politics.

It was self-imposed exile.

Certainly there was enough in my life to keep me interested and busy. At the university, to offset the sedentary teaching, I took up boxing and fencing. Elino Flores, one of our best boxers, gave me boxing lessons, and in fencing I was under Enrique Penabella, a Cuban former fencing champion. The fencing was fast exercise, and I liked boxing. (I gave up boxing when my sons began growing up. Mike was a southpaw, and when I found I could not parry his left parental dignity drove me from the field.)

The truth was I simply could not get interested in strenuous physical activity for its own sake. I am a strenuous man in that

I enjoy activity. But it must be activity with a purpose. I liked newspaperwork because it was active.

I have mentioned the golf club I had intended to use in driving the drunken cook from our kitchen. It was part of a set friends had given me. I had gone out on the links two or three times, but I did not enjoy playing and the clubs stood unused for a long time in our hall.

The same is true of drinking and smoking. I smoked with my reporters in newspaper days, but I never enjoyed it. I will drink a martini when friends are drinking, but without enjoyment. My vice is action, action of the mind and the errands this requires. I am always busy, always going somewhere and hurrying back. Therefore I do not crave synthetic activity.

These days my only form of exercise is walking, and as a rule my gait is slowed to the pace of small, five-year-old legs trotting alongside and a thousand questions having to be answered: "Lolo, why don't we ride on horseback like cowboys?" or, "Lolo, when can we fly to the moon?"

I continued to keep abreast of political movements in Manila, the Philippines, and the world. So much was going on that needed every citizen's voice of approval or dissent, and here was I, voiceless for the first time since I was fifteen years old. In all those years I had known the power of a newspaper at my back, and no matter how small the voice, I had been able to speak. Now I was only the teacher. And there were burning issues that could use my help. It was every citizen's duty to speak up and support movements that were right.

I discussed with my students the political situations in Manila and all that Quezon was trying to do to prepare our country for self-government. So much needed to be done. I lectured my students on their civic responsibilities but meanwhile I was doing nothing to help.

In all fairness I could see that no matter what errors of judgment might be made by Quezon, he was still heart and soul for the Philippines. He was our future. There were projects of his in which I longed to have voice. And I was voiceless.

I missed being on a newspaper. I longed for the right to express an editorial opinion on subjects close to my heart. Nothing is quite equal to the frustration felt by a newspaperman who finds himself without a paper. The frustration grew, so I was in a receptive mood when Roces sent for me.

I have delayed admitting that Don Alejandro Roces was one of my great admirations. I was an impressionable young man. If, as sometimes happened, my heroes failed to live up to my faith in them I suffered, but retained my faith in their best qualities. Quezon was a case in point. He had minor flaws but he was the best leader we had.

Roces was one who never let me down. He was every inch the blue blood, the Spanish grandee. In appearance he might have stepped from a Goya painting, but his ideas were modern. He was wealthy, courageous, and possessed of a social conscience. His integrity was unimpeachable. As the founder of the TVT newspaper chain he was the father of responsible modern journalism in the Philippines.

I knew him as a man of strong opinions, which he never permitted to interfere with the policy of his papers. Not once in all the years that I was with him did he ever try to make use of his powerful newspaper organization to serve selfish personal ends.

I had great respect for Don Alejandro. I also liked his son Alejandro, Junior, or "Andong," who worked with his father in the publishing office and was my good friend.

And also, I missed newspaper work so profoundly that I was ripe for suggestion.

So, facing the grandee of the press in his office, I asked what he wanted of me.

"How would you like to be the editor of a new newspaper printed in English?" he asked.

That meant a rival sheet to the Quezon-controlled *Herald*. I remembered the bitterness of this man's quarrel with Quezon and shook my head.

"It would never work," I said. "All the power in the government would be against us."

Don Alejandro's look held steel. "Scared?"

That was all I needed.

We brought out the first edition of the new paper, the *Tribune*. As the youngest member of the Roces chain it was well-received by the public. Quezon and the powers around him did not like the paper. I did not like Quezon's not liking it. As editor of the *Tribune* I took umbrage that the leader of a nation should show open antagonism to a newspaper that promised every intention of being fair.

Roces had announced that intention. He was an honorable publisher. He was a patriotic Filipino. And he was the soul of integrity. My loyalty was to him and the *Tribune*.

Quezon was frank in expressing his disapproval of the new paper, which promised stiff competition to his own mouthpiece, the *Herald*. Some of these opinions were expressed during the Senate President's frequent appearances about the city in night clubs and cabarets. I was no lily-souled puritan, but it did seem to me that the leader of our people should set a better example.

I have always believed a man in public office has certain moral responsibilities. After I myself took office I often longed to give way to my temper, which is hair-trigger, but restrained myself because I felt it was up to me to set an example of dignity. Often in hot weather in Washington or Manila I long to leave off my tie and unbutton my shirt collar, but I do not because I believe there are certain standards to be maintained.

And because I had so greatly admired Quezon I was the angrier with him for letting his dignity fall.

So I wrote an indignant editorial in which I expressed my opinion of the night clubbing of our Senate President. I knew I would hear from Senate headquarters and I did.

The summons reached my home at seven the next morning. I was to be in Quezon's office at eleven that morning. When I left for the university I was deeply worried.

Virginia's calm words, as I left her, were a help. "You are in the right," she said.

I conducted my classes in a haze of anxiety. During a study period I went over to the *Tribune* office and told Roces what I was about to face.

"I may be in serious trouble," I warned him, and remembering Quezon's violent temper, "I warn you, if Quezon raises his voice I will raise mine. And if he raises his hand . . ."

Don Alejandro cut in with advice I have never forgotten. "It is only when a man knows reason is not on his side that he uses his fists. Keep in mind that Manuel Quezon is the president of our Senate. Treat him with respect, no matter what happens, and you will have me behind you."

His cool dignity steadied me and I was calm when I confronted Quezon.

It might have been our first meeting. The same man, the same office, the same glistening narra desk, and spread out on its surface this time the accusing editorial page. Only now the paper was the *Tribune* and I was its editor. I was no longer the trembling cub. Outwardly I was calm. Inwardly I shuddered with the trepidation that boy reporter had suffered a dozen years before.

Again the finger pointed, the deep, dark look probed. "What is Roces trying to do?" Quezon demanded hotly. "Get even with me?"

I had seen him often in action. His rage was terrible to watch, worse to endure. Now his anger was at breaking point.

I spoke coolly. "Mr. Roces had absolutely nothing to do with that editorial. He did not see it until it was in print. I wrote it and I assume full responsibility."

His eyebrows met and his slender, beautifully groomed figure trembled with anger. "I don't want to lose my temper," he said. (It was already lost.) "But can't you see what you have done? You have libeled me!"

"There is no libel here," I answered calmly. "There are a thousand witnesses to the fact that you are being seen around town at night in cabarets. What sort of example is that for the leader of the Philippines to set for our young men?"

All this time we had been standing, glaring across the desk at each other.

"Sit down," he said suddenly and more reasonably.

We sat, and leaning forward he was again the charmer, his manner flattering, his voice winning.

"Romulo, let's make a bargain, you and I. I'll promise not to be seen in night clubs any more if you will promise not to write on the subject again."

"I promise," I said.

I was completely won over. All the old boyish idolatry swept back. I wasn't the fighting editor and the university professor but the high-school student looking down at his idol from the Spanish wall.

With a confidential air, so charming and typical of Quezon, he took his wallet from his pocket and opened it to show me a clipping inside the cover. It was a clipping of the editorial. "This is to remind me, Rommy, to keep me straight."

He smiled the warm gentle smile that said, There are covenants between us!

I stammered like a moonstruck boy. "Mr. President, this proves you are the man I have always admired."

Once more I was his wholehearted devotee.

Away from his office and that all-enveloping charm I was assailed by nibblings of doubt. Had he clipped that editorial from his home newspaper before his wife had a chance to read it? It was not a subject to discuss with one's wife. Women, I had learned, are likely to be too clear-visioned for comfort. I had my boyish illusions. At heart I was still one with the Rover boys.

I added a new hero to my galaxy in this same important year, 1928. Although he roused my admiration at first meeting he was not to attain full stature in my personal Hall of Fame until the war in the Pacific, when he became the defender of the Philippines. Douglas MacArthur first came to Manila as a brigadier general of the Philippine Scouts, to help train our young men for military life. Then in 1935 he returned as Quezon's military adviser. This was Quezon's idea, but even he had no idea then how much this defense would mean to the Philippines.

Chief assistant to MacArthur was a young, personable, serious-minded major who was liked by everyone. We called him "Ike," and were delighted when he was made a lieutenant colonel.

My wife and I became close friends of the MacArthurs. They came often to our home and Virginia and I visited in their beautiful apartment in the Manila Hotel. It was a friendship that was to lead me into the tunnel on Corregidor.

Arrows were pointing the way to our freedom. "The Philippines for the Filipinos," Taft had promised. The new American officials in authority being introduced into our country respected that promise. Wood was gone, and in his place came Henry L. Stimson, who as an excellent American Governor General showed respect and encouragement to the Filipinos. He consulted the Filipino leaders on every point; he assisted them in their advance toward independence; and, most appealing of all to national sentiment, he divided invitations to Malacañang equally between Filipinos and Americans.

Stimson was a good friend of Quezon's and he became a friend of mine as well. As the *Tribune* editor I was able to support Stimson in every way, and gladly did so. It was a blow to us when he was recalled to America to become Secretary of State. But he was followed in 1929 by Dwight F. Davis, who was followed in 1933 by Frank Murphy, who like Stimson respected Filipino ideals and aspirations.

Now we could see the advances being made on our national

front. The Philippines was forging ahead. Strong voices were needed to insure freedom. Whatever I had to give that could be of assistance was given. In the *Tribune*'s editorial pages I could trumpet our national ideals and needs, plead for racial equality, the recognition of Filipino rights. Whatever I wrote was endorsed by Roces.

How generous he was in his support of a fiery young editor! His son, Andong, was a true newspaperman himself, having worked from the bottom up on a Denver daily. He and I worked closely together as a team. In return I gave the *Tribune* an increasingly larger share in my daily life. It became the leading newspaper in the city.

There were three Roces papers: the *Tribune*, printed in English; the *Taliba*, in Tagalog; and *La Vanguardia*, in Spanish. Two were evening papers and the *Tribune*, a morning one. All were printed daily.

In 1930, shortly before my thirty-first birthday, Don Alejandro appointed me his editor in chief in full charge of the Roces chain, called the TVT Newspapers. Now, for the first time in my life, I felt I had achieved success. I had a comfortable home, an expanding family, everything a man could desire.

I was head of my department at the university and a member of its Board of Regents. I had a position of value in the community, and above all I had the right to speak forcefully for any cause I felt was just. Don Alejandro permitted me to control the editorial policy of the three papers, subject to his approval which was always fair.

I was still separated from Quezon, and the paper he controlled, the *Herald*, was still the *Tribune*'s enfeebled rival. Still that did not prevent my supporting him in any of the crusades I felt were right. Foremost always among them was the fight for independence, and behind that I gave all the editorial power three leading newspapers could command, with the full approval of Mr. Roces.

It was my good fortune that this editorial power had come to me just as the fight for independence neared its crisis. Its key motivation was the first independence bill, known as the Hare-Hawes-Cutting Act. This was being discussed in the American Congress in the early thirties. Quezon sent Osmeña and Roxas to Washington in 1933 to work on its behalf. Their mission was designated by the first syllable of their surnames, the Osrox Mission.

While the two representatives were waiting in Washington for the bill to be passed a coolness grew between them and Quezon in Manila. I have never known the exact reason but it was rumored that Quezon accused his emissaries of not consulting him often enough. It may be he feared that if the bill passed, Osmeña and Roxas would get all the credit and displace him from the nation's leadership.

At any rate, Quezon in Manila carpetbagged against the bill. While the two leaders in Washington were giving it their fullest support, Quezon at home was working up general resentment against it.

The bill's primary proviso called for American military bases to be established in the Philippines after our country was free. Quezon seized on this clause and used it as a weapon against the bill. He made it an election issue. By submitting the issue in his campaign to the Philippine electorate, he hoped to defeat the bill overwhelmingly.

The Roces papers were at first noncommittal. Don Alejandro sent me to Washington to see for myself how the bill was progressing and to write a series of interpretative articles about the Hare-Hawes-Cutting Act, giving both the Quezon and Osrox points of view. It was my duty to see that our newspapers continued to be fair to both sides.

Actually Don Alejandro and I were united at this time in disapproval of Quezon. We could not condone his undermining the efforts of the two good men in Washington. Roxas was a great liberal and our best economist. Osmeña was one of our greatest statesmen; he had in fact started our struggle for independence. It seemed to me they were being belittled by Quezon's exploitation of the military base clause.

On the other hand I was slowly inclining to the conviction that Quezon was right in protesting American military bases in the Philippines. Once we achieved our independence might not the presence in our country of military bases, manned by representatives of those who had once ruled over us, stir up trouble?

Perhaps it was best, as Quezon urged, to settle this matter in advance before it was too late.

While Quezon was obviously exploiting this issue to its fullest to his own advantage he was also showing his customary foresightedness. American military bases in the Philippines were to be a burning issue in my country years after the Philippines were set free.

Why did it always come down to the one conclusion—that everything Quezon did was done for what he believed to be of future benefit to the Philippines? He would sacrifice anyone and anything that stood in our country's way. I began to see the good in Quezon's attempts to sabotage the Hare-Hawes-Cutting Act, but I regretted the way it was being done.

Perhaps there was no other way. Quezon was at the exact center of Philippine power and saw every side. I had risen to a position above my expectations, but I was still an outsider.

As for Roces, he remained wholeheartedly against Quezon.

I wished I could judge in his fashion, white or black, good or evil. My trouble was that I expected all my heroes to be perfect, and heroes, being human, are seldom that.

I was in the throes of this quandary when a surprising invitation came from Quezon. He was going back to Washington and wanted me to go along as his adviser.

From an editor's point of view this was a splendid opportunity, since it would place me on the inside of the struggle over the bill. Roces was willing, and I went with Quezon.

It soon became obvious in Washington that the American Congressmen and Senators were solidly in favor of the bill as it was. The Osrox Mission to America was a success. Quezon refused to give in. He made up his mind he must fight the military base clause. The bill, as a specific issue, must be put to a general vote in the Philippines. I had nothing to say about this. I had great respect for the opinions of Osmeña and Roxas. Now these men and Quezon—all admirable—were deadlocked in opinion. It was not open enmity, but the coldness grew.

The three of them decided to return to the Philippines by the eastern route, hoping that a long boat trip around the world would serve to settle their differences. We visited Paris, Rome, Singapore, and Hong Kong, and the trip did no good at all. By the time we reached Manila the three contestants were barely speaking.

I managed to stay on good terms with all of them. While I disapproved of their stubbornness I made no attempts to reconcile my three traveling companions. That was not my job. I was along on the world tour as a reporter, and my allegiance was to Don Alejandro Roces.

Nevertheless the trip had been stimulating. It was my second time around the world.

In Manila the fight was renewed in deadly earnest; the rift widened. The Hare-Hawes-Cutting Act was submitted to the electorate, and Quezon and his men, who opposed it, won the election.

Quezon promptly began plans for a new independence bill to be known as the Tydings-McDuffie Act. It was similar to the first and only the provision concerning military bases was changed.

The Osmeña forces raised a great storm against the new bill. They were powerful men. We heard Quezon was deeply worried about the way things were going. That did not bother me, for in a series of articles in the *Tribune* I was carrying on a steady barrage of criticism against Quezon. Four men had gone around the world together; now only two remained friends.

But Quezon never allowed personal resentments to stand in

the way of anything he wanted. He invited me to breakfast in his home. I went braced for a reprimand for having attacked his policies in the *Tribune*. Instead he seemed deeply worried and almost sad.

"Rommy," he began gently, "I have never needed you as much as I need you now. This is going to be the fight of my life. If I lose it I am finished."

Something was coming. I waited. "Yes, Mr. President?"

"I need a newspaper," he said, "a nationalistic paper that will express my views and fight with me. One newspaper chain controls public opinion in this country."

"What have you in mind?" I asked.

He became the enthusiast, keen-eyed, boyish. "I'd like to see the *Herald* reorganized and given a new infusion of blood. That would give new life to public opinion! The country needs a paper with a fresh point of view. I don't know anyone who can run such a paper, Rommy, except you."

I was stunned. I was now in my mid-thirties, when a man should be permanently established. I was established. My future was settled. I was editor in chief of a leading chain of newspapers. For the first time in my life I felt secure. There were my wife and three sons to be considered, for Dick (Ricardo) had been born. Everything was as I had wished it to be, and here was Quezon suggesting that I push over all I had built as if it were a heap of cards.

But what he was offering in exchange, I knew. I muttered something about having to discuss the offer with my wife and left him.

That night I talked with Virginia. Her first reaction, based on affection, was my own. "Don Alejandro has been so good to us," she said. "Everything we have we owe to him. What will he say?"

"He won't like it," I said. But I knew it would be worse than that.

The Roces publishing group was a family affair. The em-

ployees were part of the family. That was the way Don Alejandro wanted us to feel, and we did. Then there was his son,
Andong, my close friend and a loyal one. It would not be easy
to break the news to him.

Yes, my future with the Roces family was safe, but it was an
employee's future. The Roces chain was a closed family corporation. It was not the sort of organization in which I could
eventually own a few shares. I had gone as high in the firm as I
would ever go.

There was another important argument in favor of my leaving. TVT was an all-powerful chain, which shaped the thought
of the Philippines. I felt the country needed a counteracting
influence if we were to achieve a true democracy. I tried to look
ahead over my own small destiny to that of the Philippines, the
way Quezon looked, far ahead always to the country of the
future. If, in this locking of horns between the Osrox faction
and Quezon, the Osrox side should win it would mean Quezon
would be in need of greater support than ever if he was to maintain his leadership. And I believed in him as a leader.

With a new newspaper, the policy of which Quezon had assured me would be in my hands, I could fight on Quezon's side;
I could be free to campaign for him if needed.

Quezon had promised me an independent paper. That would
give my voice more power than ever before. I had to look forward to the country that would be ours. Independence would
not be easy for us. I was convinced that in those first difficult
years of freedom the country would be better off with Quezon
than with Osmeña and Roxas.

Added to this was my hero worship of Quezon. I wanted to
be with him, win or lose.

And we might so easily lose. I might be throwing over all
present and future security.

"But at least," I told Virginia, "whether I make good or fail,
at least I'll be striking out for myself." It is every newsman's
dream to run a paper his way.

Virginia understood. She said, "It's your decision. You must be the judge. Only let me say this, that you'll be starting all over again."

That was true, and with much to lose.

It took me a week to decide. I would make up my mind and then panic. I would start for Quezon's office or Don Alejandro's and get cold feet and turn back. I could not sleep. My poor children, my wife, what would the change do to them?

But once I was certain I pulled myself together for the big break and the new beginning and went to Quezon.

"I've decided," I said. "I'm willing to take the chance."

"Good," he said. But he looked stern and unhappy.

We both knew how much he was asking of me and what I was risking. If he lost his fight he would have little to offer me. But if he won I would share his victory and his future, wherever that might lead.

Now I faced the saddest part, that of telling the Roces family I was leaving. I tried to speak to Don Alejandro but could not, and went instead to Andong. It was even worse than telling the old gentleman. There were tears on both sides. We had been like brothers.

"Rommy," he pleaded, "have you really thought what this will mean to you? Do you realize you are throwing away a great future as the leading editor of the country for the insecurity of a new paper based on a politician's promise? Why, it's only a venture! You know how insecure political promises can be. Think of your family, Rommy!"

"I've thought of them," I said wretchedly. "I have given a great deal of thought to this. I know the risk I am taking. If I fail, I have no one to blame but myself. If I succeed, I hope you will be proud that your father gave me my start and that the finest journalism I'll ever achieve will be due to the training I've had from him. Any newspaper honesty and integrity I show in the future I shall have learned from him. Will you please tell your father that for me, when you tell him?"

Because I could not bring myself to face Don Alejandro just then. I did not have the courage to be the one to let him know.

Andong told me, "This will be a bitter disappointment to my father. In my opinion you are making a terrible mistake. To leave us for something as vague as a political paper that does not exist—I cannot understand you and my father will never be able to."

But he said he would break the news for me. That was at noon.

At four that afternoon I was summoned to Don Alejandro's office in the TVT building. I was very meek as I entered, in fact I had spent the hours since leaving Andong losing most of the confidence Quezon had inspired in me. The old man just sat looking at me sadly. He was very inch the grandee, but I could see he was deeply wounded.

"Romulo," he said, "I don't know how to begin. I need not tell you how disappointed I am. But since this is your decision I wish you the best of fortune, and if I ever can help you in any way I will."

When I walked out of his office I was two inches high.

The entire day was one of mourning. That afternoon I called my staff together, told them what I was doing, and bade them good-bye. They were men I had chosen and gathered together during the past half-dozen years on the TVT. I had trained them and watched them develop into the finest staff in the Islands.

They all wished me well, but every one of them told me later that when they heard my plans and thought of everything I was giving up for what might be no more tangible than a chimera privately they thought I was a damn fool.

But Quezon, to me, was the Philippines. Once more I threw over all I had gained and followed him.

Twelve

THE struggle to build a new paper started all over. We wanted the *Herald* to be the voice of our nation and the support of Quezon and MacArthur in all they hoped to do for the Philippines. I worked hard, but soon found that part of the day was not enough. The *Herald* was truly *my* voice. I could take any side I believed in. I severed my last link with the University of the Philippines, for all my life was to be devoted henceforth, so I believed, to publishing. I resigned as head of my department at the university and as member of the Board of Regents. All was sacrificed to this new venture that deserved everything I had to give.

It was the end of teaching for me. But the editorials I wrote and the causes I sponsored were teaching in a broader sense, or so it seemed to me.

Quezon lived up to every promise he had made me. He helped gather the capital to reorganize the *Herald*. It was a morning paper printed in English, and had been named the *Herald* because it was to be the announcing voice of a new and independent Philippines.

We eventually won the fight. The people were overwhelmingly in support of Quezon. With the *Herald*'s backing, the Tydings-McDuffie Act for Philippine independence got under way, and in this same year of the newspaper's reorganization, 1934, the act was approved by Franklin Delano Roosevelt.

At last a definite date had been set. We would be free men in the Philippines on July 4, 1946. On the day of the signing I thought many times of my father and grandfather. I wished they might have known!

Freedom was still twelve years away, and much was to happen to the world and America and the Philippines in that space of time. And much to me.

The careers of MacArthur and Quezon were in the ascendancy, and the *Herald*'s star rose with them. We were working together against the time when the Filipino would be a first-class citizen in his own land, and there was much for him to learn, many plans to be laid in advance.

For freedom would not be easy. It never is. It would be more difficult for the Philippines than for many countries, because we had to face the fact that the islands, although potentially rich, had not tapped their resources. We were a poor country and a small one, and we could not afford to be hurled unprepared into competition with countries larger and richer and more powerful and far better trained. The Tydings-McDuffie Act meant we could prepare.

So we rejoiced and were anxious on that day, November 15, 1935, that saw the inauguration of the Commonwealth Government of the Philippines. The greatest crowd that had ever gathered in our country massed on the Luneta to see Manuel L. Quezon sworn in as president and Sergio Osmeña as vice-president of our new commonwealth. Frank Murphy, our good friend and America's last Governor General, became the first High Commissioner.

On that day, frankly wiping away tears as were all the others among the thousands gathered in the park, I had much to look forward to and much to remember. I could recall by hearsay the fact that the Philippine Republic and I had been born together. Then had come the years my country had spent as a territorial possession of the United States, and now it was a commonwealth. The advance had been great since the days when my father had crept into our house, gun in hand, in the night after fighting in the hills against the hated Americans. I remembered my grandfather's torture at American hands. I thought back to my childhood, of the patriots whose lives I had studied, the heroes I had worshiped, the martyrs to our country's freedom. Had they died without knowing their deaths were worth the dying, or had they been content to know they died for freedom?

In that solemn moment, when the Stars and Stripes fluttered over the Luneta and then beside it, slowly and grandly, rose the colors of our own Philippine flag—the red, white, and blue in each flag meaning the same truths to two separate peoples, the white for truth, blue for faith, and red for the blood of our martyrs—I felt then and I feel still that no one who dies for freedom dies in vain.

At the close of the last century the Philippine Republic had been born, and now we could look forward to 1946 when it would be born again.

During the wait for freedom we would continue our training in democracy under American tutelage. Gradually Filipinos would supplant Americans in our government, until 1946 when we would be completely under Filipino rule.

It was impossible for contemporary Americans, who had always been free, to understand why so many Filipinos wept that day. Now that Americans know the heavy grief of war and the threat of the loss of freedom, they can perhaps more fully understand.

In the next month, December, my wife and I celebrated with a trip around the world—my third, her first. It was sparked by an invitation from Notre Dame University, offering me an honorary degree of Doctor of Laws. Since then I have received thirty-nine degrees (I tell my sons I am being educated by degrees), but this was my first. I was greatly excited by the honor and so exhilarated by the journey that we decided to continue on around the world.

My first honorary degree—how proud I was of it! Adding to my pride was the fact that at the same time the honor was awarded Franklin Delano Roosevelt. A Filipino editor and the

President of the United States spoke on the same platform at South Bend, Indiana.

To be on the same platform with Roosevelt, to speak with him, and later to be granted an exclusive interview in Washington meant a great deal to me. I was face to face with a hero. In my opinion he had saved the United States from revolution when he took office in 1933. In my eyes he was a great American and a great man.

I make this difference because to me the difference is profound. Churchill, for example, is a great Englishman. He has been first and last for Britain, and his loyalty is laid at the feet of the British lion. He is indeed an English patriot and will be immortal as such. However, he has not looked to the freedom of all nations. In fact, as prime minister he opposed the independence of India, Pakistan, Burma, and Ceylon.

In my speech that day at South Bend I spoke of the relationship between the United States and the Philippines. I spoke of America as "a generous benefactor, a loyal and true friend, and, if we can honor the debt in no other way, we can pay with our lives."

That was December 9, 1935. Another December, only a few years away, we paid that debt with Filipino lives.

My wife and I spent a month of gaiety in New York. Quezon had just been there and had taken lessons at the Arthur Murray dancing school. Nothing would suit Virginia but that we should take lessons. Every morning at ten she dragged me off to the dance studio, where we practiced the tango, waltz, and rhumba, so that in the evenings we could relax on the dance floor. It was a gay restful trip the rest of the way around the world, and we returned to Manila and the family fired with enthusiasm for travel.

In 1940 my wife and I were planning another trip. We wanted to be the first Filipino couple to fly around the world, an innocent ambition nipped in the bud by Pearl Harbor.

Since I had left the TVT chain to fight beside Quezon, he and I had worked closely together and pursued a friendship that often threatened to go on the rocks. Now that he was President of the Commonwealth he lived with his family in Malacañag and the doors of the Palace were never closed to me. I supported him with the *Herald* in all that he did which I felt was right, and as far as our country's future was concerned he was never anything but right. But we were both quick-tempered and there were minor disputes along the way.

Misunderstandings went back over the years. There was the perfectly ridiculous affair of the daylight saving time dispute. I don't know why Quezon took it into his head that a country with the hot climate and long days of Luzon should require daylight saving, but he did, and as president he was able to put the order into effect. As a result we rose in the dark and went to bed in daylight, and it was all very silly.

We received many letters of protest against this nonsense, so I wrote an article stating my views. I knew Quezon would not like it, and the day it appeared I made my appearance at the Los Tamaraos Polo Club with some trepidation. Whenever a controversial article or an editorial attack of any kind appeared, all our friends, and some not so friendly, congregated at the club to note the general effect. I was greeted by all with congratulations. Friends slapped me on the back to say: "Good, Rommy, it's time to tell the old man some truths he should know." That was before the "old man" arrived. A few minutes later he came in with Major Nieto, his handsome aide.

Quezon was in evening clothes and looked very angry. There was sudden silence in the room, and in it his voice could be heard saying fiercely, "Is Romulo here?"

I wished I were anywhere else, but I meekly admitted my presence.

He fixed me with that angry eagle stare that could subdue the bravest of his enemies. Only I was not his enemy. I was not going to be cowed, not even when he started in on me full blast before all our friends.

"Romulo, who gave you the authority to speak for the Filipino people? You have never been elected to public office, yet you dare criticize a man who has been elected by the people!"

He went on into an angry dissertation on the advantages of daylight saving, then, suddenly deepening his fury, he unleashed his wrath on me in personal terms. Every now and then he would turn to his audience, the same audience that a few minutes before had hailed my editorial, and ask, "Don't you think I am right?" And everyone nodded.

"Excuse me, Mr. President," I interrupted, and I walked away from him and joined a group of ladies.

For the rest of the evening I ignored him. He tried to speak several times but I avoided him.

The next morning I was in my *Herald* office when the office boy entered.

"The President is here," he began nervously, as Quezon came in and brushed him aside. Quezon was flushed, he wore riding boots and carried a crop. My first thought was, he is here to beat me! He had once physically attacked another editor who had roused his ire.

I stood up behind my desk. "Mr. President," I began.

But he waved me down with a gesture of the whip. "I came to apologize, Rommy!" Then in the same breath he burst out querulously, "But you were rude to me! You turned your back to me at the club last night!"

I had myself in hand by then. How variable he was, how winning and angry by turns!

"I preferred being rude to being disrespectful," I told him. "If I had stayed with you I would have said something critical, something I would be sure to regret, and to me, Mr. President, you will always be a leader to respect, so I chose to leave you without saying a word. I am sorry, but I had to do it."

And then he was his gay, charming, irresistible self. "Let's forget it Rommy. Why don't you and Virginia come to lunch at the Palace tomorrow? Oh, and about daylight saving, I'm going to repeal the order!"

A final gay flick of the riding crop and he was gone.

How could one analyze such a man! The variations in his mood were mercurial. He changed at a word. He had tuberculosis and I later learned this disease can breed suspicion and jealousy and changing moods. I learned to expect such rifts in the fabric of my idol, but the flaming personality of Quezon was never to fade. He was a great man, one of the greatest I have ever known.

And still there were times when he left me bewildered and a little resentful, not knowing what to think of him. I was a pawn in a game too intricate for me to comprehend.

There was the time he had summoned me from my desk at the *Herald* to his summer palace at Baguio.

"Rommy," he began, in that flattering tone of confidence that is one of the strongest weapons of those in power, "José Avelino (Secretary of Labor) is tendering his resignation. Publish this in the *Herald*. Say you have the report from an authoritative source but don't mention me."

So I published it—a big scoop—and what a hullabaloo resulted!

Avelino was a close friend of José Yulo, Speaker of the House, who telephoned me. "Romulo, who gave you such a story? Avelino is with me and he says it is not true. He has no intention of resigning."

I muttered the usual newspaperman's defense about not betraying my sources.

The next day Quezon called. He sounded so pompous and stern and unlike himself that I knew Avelino and possibly Yulo were with him. "Romulo," he began, formally, "it is the height of irresponsibility for you to print such a story stating that Avelino has resigned when he has not. He has no intention of resigning and why should he? Where could we get a better man? From whom did you get such a canard?"

I stammered something, but he was berating me and did not hear. "You should not have printed that story, Romulo, without consulting Avelino or me. Please deny it and credit the denial to me." And he slammed the receiver down.

I hung up in my turn. Something had fallen from my sky. I had been "had," and would never know why. Apparently Quezon had wanted to ease Avelino out of office or had some advantage to gain by threatening to do so, and then had changed his mind.

This happened when I had been about twenty-seven years old, still ridden by the idealism of youth, and it was a wrench to me to see so close at hand what politics could be and what wiles a man had to use to make himself president of a commonwealth.

And still, no matter what his reasons were for this bewildering maneuver, I can be certain now that in the long run Quezon was right. Politics was a slow-moving and intricate game of chess and he was a champion whose eye was on the play many moves ahead, with no thought for the pawns who fell along the way.

On another occasion he sent for me to visit him at Baguio. Again that flattering charm and confidence was unleashed that can capture the young and trusting and even the old and wary.

"Romulo, you know the Senatorial elections are to be held soon. I want you to be a member of the Senate. Get ready to be a candidate for our party."

This announcement came out of a clear sky. I was speechless. The idea was completely strange to me. I had never thought of myself in a political office. I was the reporter, the observer.

Here was Quezon announcing I was to enter the inner circle. I could be one of the men of power about whom I wrote in the *Herald*. I was completely fascinated, trapped.

But I stammered protests. I was too young, still in my twenties, an editor, nobody knew of me. . . .

Quezon waved my protests back. He never wasted words.
"Listen to me and don't argue. Two of the Manila newspapers
are taking a straw vote on the Senatorial elections and I want
you to win that vote. I will watch these two straw votes closely.
I want you to win so that we can use your victory as a base
for the plans I have for you. I'm going to groom you for your
future, Rommy, and this is the beginning."

And there it was again, the vague glittering plans held ever
ahead of me by Quezon, the carrot dangled before the young
and hopeful donkey. Excited at last, I was fired with energy.
We won both straw votes overwhelmingly. I came out first in
both lists, the *Free Press* and *La Vanguardia*.

I was keyed to fever point with plans. I would be the "boy
Senator," the youngest ever to serve in that august body whose
affairs I had reported so faithfully since I was fifteen. Election
was nearing and my friends worked harder than before.

Then, three days before the convention, Quezon sent word
for me to come to him at once at Malacañang.

My wife had a curious reaction to this call. She said, "I have
an idea he is going to tell you not to run."

I was indignant. "What nonsense! How can he? The idea
came from him. I'm practically in office!"

In the Palace I found the President still in pajamas and still
in bed. He got up and put his arm over my shoulders in a
fatherly gesture. "You know, Rommy, you are very young,"
he said gently. "I've been thinking your future over carefully
and I've decided it is best not to hurry you. You know the old
saying: A man in a rush gets nowhere."

I found myself thinking numbly, Virginia was right! "If you
are speaking of the convention . . . ," I began.

"Yes, I am, Rommy. Governor Daniel Maramba is from the
same district as yours. He came to talk to me yesterday; also the
leaders of Pangasinan and Nueva Ecija. He has been Governor

of Pangasinan and he is getting old. This will be the last chance
he will ever have to be a Senator, and he wants to be a Senator.
We must consider the values."

That warm, beautiful voice which could charm immense
audiences was lulling me into a state of hypnosis.

"Maramba has solid political backing (which I knew I did
not have), and remember, Rommy, he is old and he needs the
job. He does not have the time ahead you have, or your future.
You have a wonderful position as the *Herald's* editor and you
are the highest salaried newspaperman in Manila. You have a
lifetime ahead of you. So why not defer to an old man and let
him run in your place? You won't lose anything by waiting.
Your time will come."

I hunted words through heartbreak. "I never thought of being in the Senate, Mr. President. It was your idea from the
beginning. You remember you sent for me in Baguio. Since you
made the suggestion it's your privilege to cancel it. . . ."

I was speaking with pain, not so much for the loss of a dream
as for the crumbling of an ideal. I had been a decoy pigeon dragging a simulated broken wing through the dust, and now both
wings were broken. Once more I had been used, for what purpose I did not know. To draw votes, perhaps, from a more
powerful opponent of the favored Maramba? I would never
know.

Quezon saw my hurt. His voice was crisp and businesslike as
he said, "Tell your friends you are going to defer in favor of
Maramba and ask them to back him to the hilt."

And then, suddenly gentle, he said softly, "You know I am
always behind you! And honestly, Rommy, I need you more
where you are now than in the Senate. I can take care of the
Senate."

And I believed him. I would always believe him.

I pulled myself together. "Thank you, Mr. President. As
you say, the future is ahead of me. I will stay wherever you
think I can serve our country best."

But I didn't feel that assurance as I walked out of the Palace. I walked like an old man. I was a candidate who had been defeated even before he started to run.

When I went home Virginia took one look at me and knew. "I was right?" she asked.

I said wearily, "You bet you were!"

She stopped looking tragic and became angry. "He can't do this to you! He got you into this! It was all his idea! It isn't fair."

I told her, old in wisdom, "It's politics."

Now I really knew what politics were, and I never wanted to be part of the game again. I told that to Virginia, and stressed the fact that I had entered the race unwillingly in the first place. Quezon had charmed me into running. I told her I had seen and heard enough of politics and politicians to last me the rest of my life.

Virginia agreed with every word. My sheltered bride had shown more insight into political intrigue than I.

Maramba was elected, and died before he could be sworn in as Senator. Another election was held and another candidate elected. I was no longer interested.

My life was active. I had no time to brood over what Quezon had done to me. Slowly my resentment cleared, as I realized I did not know what threads were being drawn in that long pattern for the future being woven by Quezon. I felt that no matter what he did or how greatly I might doubt him, one thing I could never doubt—whatever he did, he did for our country. He was our country. As its leader he has no peer.

I felt that then and the feeling has lasted.

Slowly the hurt died and respect returned. I had been a very small frog in the political puddle, and if I had been stepped on no personal harm had been intended. Quezon remained my leader and adviser. He liked me and he showed it in many ways. If he misled and misused me it was for larger purposes I did not as yet have the political insight to see. And I wanted to know.

I am a curious person. I could not resist trying to find out what was going on in the political realms high over my head.

My wife was less forgiving.

Two days after the convention a party was held at Malacañang. The President danced with Virginia and while dancing she gave him a piece of her mind. She is a logical woman and her arguments were pointed. To the tune of soft music my forthright young wife let our president have it between the eyes.

"I just want you to know," she told Quezon, "that our disappointment is not in my husband's not being nominated, but in you!"

And Quezon answered, "Rommy will be something more than a Senator, you can be sure of that. I'll make this up to him in other ways."

My wife took this with a grain of salt, but she was pleased. She told me, complacently, "I think Quezon's conscience is pinching him!"

She was evidently right again, for the next day he sent for me. He seemed aloof and uneasy.

He said, "I am going to speak to the publisher about doubling your salary. . . ."

I had to control my temper. I wanted to burst out in a furious rage. But my respect for him was my restraint. I wanted to tell him:

Are you trying to buy me off, Mr. President? You don't have to do that! You don't have to talk to Madrigal and get me more money! I'm satisfied with what I'm getting. There are greater values than those made by money and power!

But I didn't. No one should ever speak to the head of a country in such a manner.

I went home and wrote an indignant letter telling him what I thought and carried it back to his office. I handed it over to Jorge B. Vargas, his secretary. No President anywhere could have had a more loyal, honest, and competent secretary than Vargas was to Quezon. He knew the administrative law inside out. He had besides perfect command of the English language.

"Please give this personally to President Quezon," I told him. "Don't put it in your files and forget it. You can read it if you like." I had left the envelope unsealed.

Vargas took out the letter and read it, then gave me a long, curious look. "I'll see that the President gets it," he said.

I waited for an answer, becoming more faint-hearted by the hour as I remembered the violence of my words. But as the days passed and no reply came from Quezon I decided he had forgiven me and the subject was not mentioned again.

Not until after the war, after Quezon's death did I learn he had never received the letter. My friend Vargas had a better temper and more discretion than I.

So things went on as before. The politician was always in Quezon, but he made up for it, and wounds would heal over and we would forget and forgive. And there was his wife, Doña Aurora, a saint of a woman, and his two lovable daughters, Aurora (Baby) and Zenaida (Nini), to help those who were at temporary outs with him to forgive.

I continued to have my small troubles with Quezon, and he continued to be the fatherly adviser. In moments of national stress I would see the true patriot, then love, respect, and reverence would come rushing back.

He was behind me with all the weight of his office when, in 1937, the success of the *Herald* inspired the creation of a new newspaper chain. Again the struggle began. Money was raised and a new combine, the DMHM Newspapers, was formed, with Quezon as its backer. The chain was first organized under Vicente Madrigal—who had headed the group that had reorganized the *Herald*—and then sold to a group led by J. Amado Araneta, a sugar industrialist and one of my best friends. An enterprising, far-seeing entrepreneur, Araneta was never afraid to venture in new fields and he was usually successful. He had built the profitable Araneta Coliseum, the largest of its kind in the world, with a modern shopping center around it, and he also controls a large segment of the sugar industry of the Philippines. This new enterprise, DMHM, was to support Quezon in his fight for the Tydings-McDuffie Act. It consisted of the *Herald*, a morning paper printed in English; and the *Debate*, in Spanish; *Mabuhay*, a morning paper printed in Tagalog; and the *Monday Mail*, a weekly printed in English.

I was publisher-editor, with a share in the stock, of the DMHM chain from 1937 to 1941. They were wonderful years, filled with a sense of achievement and personal happiness. It seemed to me my life held everything one man could wish for, but over this happiness hung the shadow that was the gathering fear of war.

Quezon's promises of mysterious advancements did not end. Several times he said to me, "Rommy, you have a great personality and you can do much for our country and the sooner we get you into politics the better."

I had learned to say nothing.

Just before the war we were in his Pasay home and Quezon turned to me suddenly. "Rommy, just between ourselves, I think it's time you started into politics. Since you're the idol of our English-speaking youth I'm going to make you Secretary of Public Instruction. But don't say anything to anybody about this until I have all my plans laid."

The following day I met Chief Justice José Abad Santos as he was leaving Malacañang Palace. He stopped me to say, "Be ready. The President told me confidentially he plans to appoint you as Secretary of Public Instruction. Congratulations, Rommy."

Once my heart would have been set pounding by such news coming from one as close to the President and as prudent as Justice Santos. But I remembered the Senate fiasco and said nothing. I was not to be left hanging out on a limb again. By this time I had four sons to consider, for Roberto, our Bobby, had been born.

Then a few weeks later the President mentioned the subject

again. We were in his car on our way to the university where he was to speak to the ROTC cadets. As if he had only then brought up the matter Quezon said, "Rommy, if nothing else develops I'm going to make you Secretary of Public Instruction."

But something else did develop. A few weeks later the Philippines was plunged into war.

Thirteen

THEY say the decade between thirty and forty is the age of youth, and that between forty and fifty the youth of age.

The start of the forties—the century's and mine—was the nadir of my life. At this period a man should be close to the summit he has set his eyes upon in youth, and I felt I had arrived there. All I asked was to retain my personal happiness and to use well the power given me as head of a newspaper chain.

But in the next ten years I was to experience the heights and depths of living; many lifetimes would be crowded into this decade.

Why does disaster seem most often to strike when one is sure all is well? Almost overnight all I loved was lost to me, all I had worked for was gone, and I was left without a family or a country or a home.

Still this tragedy was to bring me closer to two who have meant much to me, MacArthur and Quezon.

Of course there were premonitions of war. One week before Pearl Harbor I had toured Indonesia and had prophesied that Japan was getting ready to strike.

I talked in secret session with men who represented seventy-five million Indonesians, and all were ready to stand by America because they felt America was the only white nation they could trust.

What has become of that Asian trust? How has it been lost, and in so brief a time?

At that time wherever I went in the Far East I was questioned eagerly by men longing to be free. "Is it true what they say about America?" they would ask me. "Is it true that America allows Filipinos in the Philippines to vote, and permits Filipinos to represent their countrymen in the Philippines?"

And when I told them, yes, it was true, they would sigh with longing and say, "How lucky you are—under America."

Recently on trips to the Far East I have been queried and the questions are very different. Now they ask, "Is it true, these stories about America? Is it a fact that men of colored skin are not regarded as equals and must take humble work for little wages and not eat at the same tables as whites? Is it true that in some parts of America men of color are more fearful of white men than we have ever been in Asia?"

Before Pearl Harbor the people in Asia blamed the imperialistic press for keeping the truth about them from America. Now they blame a sector of the American press for distorting the truth about their ideals and ridiculing them as men and dreamers of the dream.

This change has come about within the past ten years.

The qualms that assailed me on my prewar tour of the Far East convinced me that Japan was at the boiling point. These experiences were incorporated in the series of articles that won the Pulitzer prize; and later in articles and speeches and books. I shall not repeat them here. Suffice it to say that while one can anticipate disaster one is never fully prepared for it. I forget what I can of the war in the Pacific and the tragedy that swept over the Philippines and my small personal life, but still there are memories, untold before this, that will stay with me as long as I live.

Sometimes I am again overwhelmed by the sickening despair of those days, when we were trapped with MacArthur's forces in the tunnel on Corregidor; and I find myself wondering what would have happened to the Philippines and to America if Quezon had yielded to that despair and left MacArthur's side and surrendered the Philippines to Japan.

These were tense hours, while the trapped President of the Philippines pondered which was best for his country—neutralism (and that was what Quezon really advocated) or the American way.

Quezon had been faithful to America. Japan had offered every inducement to lure him to its side, which the Japanese argued was best for the Philippines and all Asia. Quezon could not be blamed for wondering if perhaps they were not right. Every report that reached our rocky perch in the bay told of disaster and death. Through our telescope we watched Manila being smashed into rubble, while from Bataan came the daily death lists that told us the best of our youth was dying in a cause we knew now was hopeless.

Quezon, from his hospital bed in the tunnel, coughing and weakened by the old lung lesion that had opened in that damp confinement, had ordered me again and again to besieged Bataan to carry his words of courage to our boys. And I, crouching in foxholes under fire, read to starving, sick lads who were to die the promise made by America's president:

The world will long remember what you, the people of the Philippines, are doing and what you have been doing since this war began. I renew my solemn pledge to you that your freedom will be redeemed and your independence established and protected. . . . Stand firm, people of the Philippines, your day is coming.

And they believed, and went on fighting and dying for freedom.

I have another brief memory of a battlefield on Bataan among the dead and dying of hearing an American stretcher bearer call to another, who was about to give aid to a wounded Filipino: "Hey, take this one first. He's *white*."

Strange, sad memory of a bloodied peninsula contested foot by foot by Orientals, who for the first time in the history of Asia were fighting beside white men—against Orientals.

The thoughtless words were spoken under stress, but I remember the hurt in them and the look on the face of the wounded soldier who was left on the ground.

But the message I had read in the foxholes that day—the pledge made by President Roosevelt to our fighters—has also been remembered, and its promise fulfilled by America. The lads who fought for America and lived are now free men.

I remember evenings on Corregidor when Manuel Roxas and I, unable to bear the confinement of the tunnel any longer, sat out on the Rock under stars hidden by gunsmoke and amid the present violence planned a glowing future for the postwar Philippines. Earlier Roxas had been a hero of mine in another way. I had criticized him in my newspapers, but I admired him for his brilliance and his patriotism. When he had founded the "Bagong Katipunan" I toured the provinces with him to explain the purposes of the organization. It was to arouse the spirit of nationalism among our people, principally the youth, and to instill in them the protectionist spirit.

Now we were close again, under fire.

When the war ended and MacArthur came back to the Philippines as its liberator one of the first things he did was to imprison those Filipinos, who with Roxas had served as members of the Japanese puppet cabinet set up during the occupation. He did not, however, include Roxas among them, and Roxas was set free.

I had thought it a mistake at the time for Americans to sentence men to prison for having worked with the Japanese government. The defense of those who were with Roxas was that they served in order to prevent as much ill treatment as possible of their countrymen at Japanese hands.

Evidently the majority of Filipinos agreed with this, for those who had collaborated with the Japanese during the war were elected to high offices in the Philippines after the war.

These men had not taken part in the long fight. They had not been hunted and in hiding and without food. When war ended they were rested and well cared for and they were available. One cannot judge the reactions of men at the mercy of an army of occupation.

No such temptations were put in my way. My job on Corregidor was to broadcast to a captive country and encourage it to keep up the resistance. I was the voice of the Voice of Freedom, the radio station in the tunnel, as the Japanese were aware. That made me a marked man. Rewards were promised to any who would betray the hiding places of my wife and children. This kept me in a state of terror.

Every broadcast that came from the mainland, every message arriving by "bamboo telegraph" increased my fear. I had no idea where my family were hiding or how long they would be safe. How they were living I did not know, nor would I know for three years and a half.

Day after day I broadcast over our makeshift radio the words and courage of the stalwart, indomitable MacArthur and the frail, indomitable Quezon. From captive Manila came word that Filipinos were being executed for listening to the Voice of Freedom and printing the broadcasts for those who had no radios. All reports that came to us from behind the Japanese lines were grim and frightening, like a horror film seen faintly and all the more terrifying because so much was hidden.

We grew more bitter day by day on the Rock, with the daily threat of death, with filth and gangrene and hunger, and above all the tormenting suspicion that we were being let down. Americans and Filipinos fighting together shared that fear. Where were America's planes, which we had been promised, which we had watched and prayed for? What had really happened at Clark Field and Pearl Harbor?

Trapped humans gnaw on conjecture. Questions and suspicions fed the hopeless bitterness of life on the Rock.

Why, at Clark Field near Manila, so we asked one another, had our planes been waiting on the field that day, lined up in formation, ready for the Japanese? Why, after all the warnings, the wrecking of America's fleet at Pearl Harbor? And why, since this evil was done and the planes at Pearl Harbor and Clark Field demolished, why were not other American planes being sent to save some of the young lives being offered up hour after hour on the Rock and at Bataan?

For a long time I was too bitter and too angry to see the truth, and by the time I did the war was over.

Now, across the safe gulf of the years, we know that orders had reached Clark Field to get the planes into the air that morning, and that they did take off and they stayed up until noon. But when lunchtime came the fliers followed their usual custom of grounding their planes and going off to mess hall in a group. This was a habit the Japanese knew only too well, so it was at noon, while the fliers sat at lunch, that the Japanese planes swooped down on Clark Field.

There was a rumor that MacArthur had hoped to send these very planes to attack the Japanese base at Formosa and forestall this attack, which had been expected, but that for some reason his directive had been delayed. Why had this power been withheld from our hero, we wanted to know? And we asked one another, is it true that General MacArthur's directive was delayed intentionally?

But the most frequent question, and the bitterest, was always: Where are our planes?

Later, of course, the actual facts were revealed. In our trap on the Rock we could not know of the tremendous offensive America was concentrating in Europe. Marshall and Eisenhower needed all-out support over there. Enemy submarines were concentrated on the floor of the Atlantic. America's fleet had been destroyed at Pearl Harbor. Washington was desperately building up America's defenses and offensives where they were needed most. America could not spread its offensive across two oceans. The Pacific problem would have to wait.

So there were no planes to spare for the defense of the Philippines.

On our pinpoint in the Pacific we asked questions and were given no answers. Among those who questioned with growing despair was Quezon.

And one day in the tunnel Manuel Roxas came to me. He was one of the important three of our Filipino group in exile with MacArthur; Osmeña, Roxas, and Quezon. I had a feeling then that sometime he would be President of the Philippines. He had all the qualities of a national leader.

Now he spoke to me in confidence and there were tears in his eyes. "Carlitos, something serious has happened. President Quezon wants to go back to Manila."

"To the Japanese?" I could not believe it.

"Yes, he has drafted a letter to President Roosevelt saying he wished the Philippines to take a neutral position. He is asking for a treaty between Japan and the United States to neutralize the Philippines. Since the United States is practically defeated in the Pacific and the American Navy has abandoned us he believes we should surrender. Osmeña and I have tried to argue him out of this, but he is determined. He wants a guarantee from the United States and Japan that neither will molest the Philippines, so that we can return to Manila."

"But why?" was all I could say. "Why?"

"Because Quezon believes this is the only way the Philippines can be saved from total destruction. This war is between Japan and the United States. Let them fight, but not the Filipinos, he keeps saying. Osmeña and I tell him that this means desertion on our part and that in the end it will be bad for our country, but he says he is only concerned with what Filipinos are suffering now."

I asked stupidly, "What does General MacArthur say?"

"The General says, if this is what President Quezon wants he will transmit the message to President Roosevelt. But I tell you, Carlitos, surrender is the worst thing that can happen to the Filipinos. It will brand us as cowards who prefer comfort to freedom. We will be humiliated all over the world, and everything Bataan has meant to us will be lost."

I felt stupid, unable to express an opinion. I could only say, "He is a sick man." But was Quezon's stand once again an indication of his prescience, his sixth political sense, his unquenchable love for his people? I did not know.

We both thought of Quezon, coughing in the foul air of the tunnel, with his frail body hungering for the food and physical comforts of Malacañang Palace just across the bay. No wonder he craved the peace of body and heart that could be won by such a little thing as a few words sent from one president to another. Roxas and I talked the problem over from every angle. Unquestionably this decision was right for the sick man. What was right for the Philippines, the country Quezon had always put ahead of self? We could come to no decision.

A few hours later Vice-President Osmeña sent for me. The tall, slender, studious man who was second in command in our government looked sad and stern.

"Romulo," he said, "get ready to leave. I am taking you and Major Stevenot with me. Quezon is going back to Manila." Major Stevenot was on MacArthur's staff. Before the war he was president and general manager of the Philippine Long Distance Telephone Company, an American business executive well-liked by the Filipinos.

"When he returns to Manila," Osmeña explained, "we will take a submarine and go to the United States and set up our government in exile in Washington. Because I shall never surrender. Quezon thinks the patriotic thing to do is to give up. That is his right. But I think the opposite."

Osmeña, the thoughtful, withdrawn student, was a flashing-eyed warrior I had never seen before.

I told him, "I am with you. But I should like to discuss this with the President."

No suggestion was made concerning an appointment with Quezon. I was not a participant in the discussions. I was on the outside looking in. I retired with this newest worry to my desk in the tunnel and prepared my broadcast for the evening.

It was a blockbuster of a broadcast, if I may say so. I was desperate and pulled no punches. I declared the Filipinos were fighting as never before, determined to hold on and keep faith in America.

Certain Filipinos, I hinted, were beginning to have cold feet. That was not true of the fighters, I said. We were going to fight Japan to the end, to the last man.

Quezon sent for me directly the broadcast ended. He had been listening and he was very angry.

"Romulo," he began furiously, his feeble voice interrupted by coughing, "what are you trying to do?"

I told him. "I feel I am expressing the way the soldiers feel on Bataan when they are risking their lives to keep their faith in freedom."

He interrupted. "Don't you know the only thing we can do is to go back to Manila? What have we left to fight for? Do you remember when I was urging the National Defense Act and the Americans were all against it? Do you remember how their newspapers have ridiculed MacArthur and our army? They promised us that as long as the United States flag flew over the Philippines we would be safe, that nobody would dare attack us. Well, that flag is down now and the Japanese flag is over Manila and where are we? Left with no one on our side anymore, with no help from America; left in a hole, in a trap . . . ridiculed and deserted. . . . It is true our boys are fighting on Bataan and with what? Inadequate arms, rice doled out by handfuls . . . they are dying. . . ."

His voice broke. He went on. The patriot who loved the Philippines first and foremost was talking.

"I tell you our boys are dying. Our country is being destroyed. Do you expect me to continue this sacrifice? The fight between the United States and Japan is not our fight. I want to stop this murder. I want to go back to Manila and try to protect the Filipinos, our people, our own people, Romulo, not America."

I said, "But this is against everything you said before the war."

"Of course it is," Quezon said fiercely. There were high spots of red on his cheeks; he was a sick man. "Because now we are dying. Now we are in defeat. And why? Because we are not getting protection from those who promised us protection. America is not sending help. We must try to save ourselves and to hell with America."

What arguments were left? Quezon had been the idol of our young Filipinos, and now that youth was being butchered with no defenses given them, nothing but unfulfilled promises. His illness was aggravated by the growing death lists. When on the Rock Americans in uniform were openly bitter, it is not to be wondered that the head of a nation in exile exceeded them in despair. There was not a man in uniform who was not certain by this time that the fight to hold the Philippines was hopeless.

And still, Americans and Filipinos were fighting on, and together.

"Sir," I said, "what of the long-distance viewpoint you are always citing? It is true that this is a fight between America and Japan, but it is also true that America is fighting for ideals that are also our ideals. We are not fighting for America but for ourselves."

I cannot forget his anger. "What good are ideals to boys who are dying? Don't you realize, Romulo, that every single drop of blood shed by every Filipino boy there on Bataan is on my conscience, that it is I, their president, who sent them there? No, I am determined to go back to Manila. I am writing to President Roosevelt; Chief Justice Santos is helping me. I want President Roosevelt to know how I feel, as the leader of boys without arms or defenses." Then, suddenly, he turned on me. "What do you think?"

It was a surprise question but my answer was ready. "Mr.

President, you may be right. I understand why you feel as you do. But as I said before, I think you should first consider the long-range view. I still believe America is fighting for freedom, and that in behalf of a distant tomorrow we can't back out now."

"But why?" Quezon spoke nervously, like a man close to panic. "When neutrality for the Philippines will keep both America and Japan away from us and insure peace for us, when it will stop this butchery of our youth?"

"No, Mr. President." On this point I was positive. "If Japan wins, we will be under Japan. You know the tactics of the Co-Prosperity Sphere."

But Quezon seemed unable to consider this. "I still think surrender is best. It will stop the destruction, stop the dying. I can't sleep thinking of those boys across the bay. I ordered them there. I kept them on Bataan. Their lives are my responsibility. No, I cannot sleep." His soul was in agony.

His look was haunted. He was a sick man, ridden with guilt. He looked very ill. I heard his coughing and looked at the damp stone walls, and could not wonder that his dream of peace lay far outside of the tunnel. I could not argue against such despair. Nobody could question that it was the patriot in him talking.

I went to MacArthur. I told him I felt we were facing a crisis. He and Quezon had been close, and I hoped he would be able to control the situation. He refused to try to influence Quezon.

"I have my own views, Carlos," MacArthur told me, "but I think Manuel is entitled to his. He wants to correspond with the President of the United States in this matter, and I have promised to transmit anything he has to say."

"But what do you personally. . . ?" I began.

MacArthur's answer was crisp. "You want to know what to expect of me, Carlos. I will continue fighting. Manuel can do as he chooses. He is your people's leader. I stay here."

There were dark days after that for Roxas and the others close to Quezon. I belonged in MacArthur's department, but

I was kept informed of the situation. MacArthur refused to discuss the matter. He continued his policy of hands off, determined not to influence Quezon one way or the other. He knew his friend. He knew the best policy to follow with Quezon was to permit him to make up his own mind.

Quezon's message was written and sent to Roosevelt. An answer was received and decoded. Quezon read the decoded cable.

Roxas told me the contents. The message ran like this: "If that is the way you feel you have a perfect right to surrender, but I shall give the United States Army orders to continue fighting."

"And Quezon's reaction?" I asked.

Roxas smiled. "Quezon is a fighting man and Roosevelt's was a fighting reply. Quezon has said nothing, but I do not think he will surrender now. He isn't the kind to let Americans do our fighting for us."

Next morning, stepping out of the tunnel for a breath of fresh air, I met Osmeña on the same errand. As we stood sniffing the salty, cordite-scented air of the bay it seemed to me Osmeña looked more at peace than he had for days.

He said gravely, "I believe our President has changed his mind."

I knew then the crisis was over. If Quezon had surrendered and Osmeña had carried out his threat to go to Washington as head of our government in exile I would have gone with him. By now we would be on our way, under the Pacific in a submarine, seeking the western coast of America and dodging enemy submarines. I shivered at the thought. Even bomb-blasted Corregidor was better than that.

Since then I have thought often of this struggle between Roosevelt and Quezon, of Quezon's willingness to yield and Roosevelt's telling him to go ahead, American soldiers would fight on. Would the Filipino soldiers have stayed with the American fighters or would they have given up?

It is my opinion that if Quezon had capitulated, the Filipino soldiers would have continued to fight beside the Americans. They did not stop fighting even after Bataan fell and the Rock was turned over to the Japanese.

When I was born, the Filipinos were fighting America and the fight for freedom continued for three years. Now they were fighting again, for and with America. The American flag was down in the Philippines, but even after the country was captured the Filipinos kept fighting and helping to prepare for MacArthur's promised return.

Quezon, his family, and staff were rescued from the Rock and set up our government in exile in America.

MacArthur was ordered from the Rock to direct strategy from the safer headquarters at Melbourne, for of what use is a captured commander? He went with reluctance and after twice refusing, the true commander who hated leaving his men. I stayed on the Rock with General Wainwright, broadcasting over the Voice of Freedom and hoping against hope that somewhere, somehow my wife and children would hear my voice and my promises that help would come. I still believed. I still urged all my fellow Filipinos to believe that despite death and delay freedom would come to the Philippines.

My wife and sons remained lost to me. No word came. Luzon was held by the enemy. I could only hope my family was safely hidden somewhere in the Luzon hills. I had no knowledge of where they were living or how or even if they were living through those more than three long years of war.

I was taken off the Rock the day Bataan fell. By MacArthur's orders, at Quezon's request I was flown in a rickety, patched-together crate under fire over Manila Bay to arrive at Mac-Arthur's headquarters in Australia, and finally in America, as "the last man off Bataan."

So little was I the soldier that at the risk of a belated court-martial I must relate how in San Francisco I read the dispatches

given me by General MacArthur to present to Secretary of
War Stimson and President Quezon in Washington. It did not
occur to me military dispatches were to remain unread until
they reached their destination. I knew the information contained within concerned me, and I was curious.

The contents were balm to my troubled state. With pleased
surprise I read I had been promoted from lieutenant colonel to
full colonel. I rushed off to a San Francisco tailor specializing
in military wear and bought out his modest supply of lapel insignia, the four-starred shield I was entitled to wear as Mac-
Arthur's aide-de-camp.

Evidently my purchase led the tailor to expect a rush of
similar orders, for the following year when I was once more
in San Francisco and dropped into his shop he informed me
ruefully that after my visit he had ordered dozens of this insignia and none had sold!

How many four-star generals did he think there were? At
that time there were only two: MacArthur and Eisenhower!

I have written often of this sad return to America and my
subsequent career as a lecturer and writer on the subject of
Bataan. From this time on, my life would be written in headlines, but I am not concerned with them. It was the marginal
notations of the heart that were most important to the man
within. That man put on a flamboyant front to America, but
under the showy façade was a homeless, pauperized, thoroughly
frightened human being.

For the first time I was afraid of America. I feared its wealth
and its security and its lack of interest in the war. I had experienced that lack at first hand. I was at the point of physical and
emotional exhaustion, and my personal fears for my lost family,
which I felt by leaving the scene of war I was deserting, were
part of the nightmare.

For their sake and our country's I could not yield to these
fears.

I would learn later my wife was sharing them with me.

Hiding with our boys in the hills, creeping from one hiding place to another always under the very noses of the enemy, she was nevertheless kept informed of all I was doing on Corregidor and in America. She had her sources of information. I had none concerning her. And because once, during a period of nervous stress when I was working overtime, I had collapsed at my desk in my newspaper office and found myself temporarily paralyzed she now feared that for me. She knew whatever I did would be done to the limit of my strength. Others would comment upon my inexhaustible energy. She knew the truth.

America demanded the last limits of that energy.

Arriving in Washington in July, 1942, under directions from General MacArthur, I was officially assigned by President Quezon and Secretary Stimson to give the Philippine side of the story.

It seemed to me this was the opportunity I had been awaiting all my life. At last I had the chance to try to promote the Philippines internationally. For I found that in America everyone I met knew of the part America had played in the defense of the Philippines and of the last brave stand made there by American boys, but few knew of the part the Filipinos had played.

Through the good offices of my agent and friend, Harold Matson, and W. Colston Leigh of the well-known Fifth Avenue lecture bureau I was launched with the velocity of a projectile on a lecture tour that was to carry me to 466 cities in every state of the United States.

Into thousands of willing American ears I poured out the heroic saga of Filipino resistance. The American newspapers had given the American side of the struggle. Little had been written of the seventy-five thousand Filipinos who had fought with the Americans in the tragic attempt to hold Bataan and Corregidor. Much had been printed and spoken of the assault to American pride in the Pacific; little of the Filipinos' part in the last brave stand and their humiliation.

I lectured until I was hoarse. I wrote of fighting and of loyalty until my hand ached. I traveled in trains and planes and cars to every corner of the United States, to and fro, from icy north to sun-drenched south. It was a grand tour, unequaled since, I am told. After every speaking trip I returned to the Waldorf in New York, which had become my only home.

Living in the Waldorf was part of the façade. Living there helped give me courage. For the same reason my first act upon arriving in New York was to go to the best tailor I knew and order the finest suits to be made. I was building a shell around the man within, a man I had never been before.

For the first time in my life, from my standards, I was a pauper. I had arrived in America with a lieutenant colonel's salary and the uniform I wore, which was much too large. I went to the Waldorf because it was a hotel I knew and where I had friends. My friend Cugat was playing in the Starlight Roof and the manager, F. Dell'Agnesse, was also an old friend of prewar days. In the lobby there were always faces of old acquaintances. That was why I chose to live at the Waldorf instead of going, as I might have, to a cheaper hotel.

That was why I chose my uniforms with care. The first I ordered cost $175, and it was a uniform such as was worn by generals at the Pentagon. I might have ordered a cheaper suit, but I did not. I was wearing the four stars of a general's aide and my own colors of combat and I was in America as a representative of MacArthur.

Clothes are important, as I have said before, in that they give you self-confidence. You are at ease in a suit made for you by a good tailor. If you are badly dressed you are uncertain and ill at ease.

I dressed as well as possible that I might be a credit to my country and to MacArthur. That eye of his could go over a uniform and never miss a button. Even separated from him by the Pacific I was aware of his scrutiny. I was here on his duty;

I was here to give his side, the Pacific side, the Philippine side, to America.

"Six months of speaking in America, Carlos," MacArthur had said to me before I left his headquarters in Australia, "and we will be ready here for the offensive. Then you can return to the Philippines with me."

President Quezon appointed me Secretary of Information and Public Relations in his war cabinet. When he sent for me to give me this appointment I was lecturing in Boston.

In his room at the Shoreham Hotel he greeted me: "Romulo, you remember how I promised you in Manila that I would make you Secretary of Public Instruction? I am now giving you an equivalent cabinet position here in Washington. I am appointing you today as Secretary of Information and Public Relations. You have earned it and I am happy I can do it now." I served from 1943 to 1944.

It was during this period of speechmaking, traveling, and mental and physical strain that I underwent with President Quezon an experience I was to refer to as "my second Bataan."

Fourteen

GENERAL MacArthur at the outbreak of the trouble in the Pacific had inducted me into the United States Army as a major in charge of press relations for the Filipino side. I had left my desk on the Philippines *Herald* to assume this responsibility in the American headquarters on the old Spanish wall. Quezon knew nothing of this until he arrived in headquarters one morning to see MacArthur. He insisted upon calling in Roxas, and the three of us had our pictures taken together. He was pleased to see me there, in uniform, beside MacArthur.

Then came the flight to Corregidor. Quezon took his government group with him, but I remained in headquarters; I was Army. I remained in Manila with MacArthur's rear echelon. MacArthur was with Quezon on Corregidor. Then I was ordered to the tunnel, just ahead of Homma's advancing men, and Quezon greeted me there with enthusiasm interrupted by fits of coughing.

Then in America, in Washington, he had welcomed me. I had been appointed MacArthur's aide-de-camp upon my arrival in Australia. Quezon had agreed with MacArthur that I could be of more service to the Fil-American cause as a lecturer and writer than I could be in the headquarters at Melbourne. His first words of greeting upon my arrival at the Shoreham were a hearty, "I am glad you are here, Rommy. You are just in time to help me write my book. I have agreed with Morgan Shuster to write the story of my life for his publishing firm."

I was taken aback. "But, Mr. President, I have just signed a contract in San Francisco to write the story of my escape from Bataan."

"That will be all right," he said. "Your experiences are very different from mine. We (by this he meant his family and staff) are going down to the Homestead, so come along."

Uncertain as to what was the best thing to do, I went with him to the beautiful resort in Virginia. Nothing more was said about his book, so I seized every opportunity to work on my own. He seemed tired and very frail and in no mood to discuss what had happened in the Philippines. I told him that Secretary of War Stimson had suggested I go on a lecture tour around the United States and tell of the Pacific front, a plan MacArthur approved. Quezon agreed it was a good suggestion, so I carried out my plans and started on the tour.

For several months I saw little of him; meantime I completed my book. One manuscript copy was in the publisher's hands ready for press, but we would need Quezon's approval as head of the Philippines before releasing the book.

Returning to the Shoreham in Washington I left a copy of my manuscript in the President's suite with a message stating it awaited his approval; so did I.

I had to leave Washington again and again, still waiting. Each time I returned I inquired with growing anxiety of friendly members of his family or staff if the President had read my manuscript. Each time he sent word to me or even told me face to face that he was anxious to read it but had not as yet found time.

We were on the best of terms. There was always a speech or article he wanted me to write for him, or a request that I accompany Mrs. Quezon and the children to church or some place of amusement. To all appearances our little group in exile at the Shoreham was a united group.

But publication day was drawing near and my manuscript was still unread.

Advance copies of the printed book were sent to me. It could not be released without Quezon's approval. I could take no pride in it with this shadow hanging over me. I took a gift copy to him, duly signed. He had to approve it! He was still the chief of my country, even if that country was captive. Books had been distributed all over America, ready for sale, and a cocktail party had been arranged in my honor in New York on publication day.

But the book now stayed unread by his sick bed; he was too ill to read it and it could not be published without his permission.

Friends close to the President were pleading in my behalf. Serapio Canceran, his very friendly secretary; Colonel Nieto, his aide; his sweet daughters, Baby and Nini; and his wife, Doña Aurora; all my good friends were doing their best to help the book along. These days are remembered as among the most harrowing of my life.

I thought constantly of all I had lost. My family was missing and my life ruined, and all I had left was a suitcase full of uniforms and my speaking voice and my book. Never in my life had I felt sorrier for myself than during those days of waiting.

I tried to keep a bold face to the world, and went ahead with my lecturing with an anxious heart. On these lecture tours I wore the uniform of the United States Army. I was not trading on my war record, but as a United States officer, speaking with special permission from MacArthur, I felt myself on official detail and the uniforms a must.

Suddenly, in the midst of one of the trips, Quezon summoned me to Washington to his bedroom at the Shoreham. The peevish invalid was gone; in his place was the hero of my boyhood.

"How is your book, Rommy?" he asked me in the kindliest way.

I managed to stammer, "Still awaiting your okay, Mr. President!"

"Then go ahead! Publish it!" He scolded as if I had been negligent in the matter.

I rushed to the phone.

I Saw the Fall of the Philippines was not delayed in publishing, but, I have been told, the delay did cost me its sale to Hollywood.

After it was published Quezon seemed highly approving of its contents and often joked with me about its sales. "Well, and how is my friend the millionaire?" he would ask.

He did not live to see his own book published, nor the Philippines he loved set free. He died in exile on August 1, 1944, in Saranac Lake, and half my life seemed to die with him. He remains my hero, the finest type of true leader I shall ever know. In the history of the Philippines he will remain the prototype of political greatness, a man with human faults, but always the leader whose foremost concern was the Philippines and peace.

The last time I saw him was at Saranac three months before he died. Colonel Nieto had phoned me in Washington at the President's request. When I saw him propped up against his pillows, his cavernous eyes still blazing with the old fierce flame, his voice firm and strong, but his coughing so persistent it seemed to sap his strength, I could see the fighter was still undaunted, but I feared he did not have long to live.

"Romulo, I have sent for you to decorate you," he greeted me. At his bedside was Colonel Egmidio Cruz, one of the real heroes of the war, who had been sent by President Quezon to the Philippines by submarine to get first-hand information of conditions under Japanese occupation. Using several disguises he went from province to province at the risk of his life. He had recently returned safely to Washington to give our leader the first complete report of the sufferings of our people. Colonel Cruz had been awarded the Medal of Valor, the equivalent of the United States Congressional Medal. Also with him that morning was Major Benvenuto Diño, one of the assistant physicians to the President.

"Major Diño, please read the citation," the President ordered.

I was touched as the citation was read commending me for my wartime service, for my work as Secretary of Information and Public Relations, for my lectures and my writings, for my "dedication and devotion to the best interests of the Filipino people." I was awarded the Distinguished Service Star, one of the highest Philippine decorations. The President then ordered a bottle of champagne, and as he had a coughing spell he asked Major Diño to make the toast in his behalf.

As I thanked him, he handed me a Manila envelope. In it was his picture on which he had written: "To Carlos P. Romulo—a patriot. Manuel L. Quezon."

I was too full for words. I said in a bare whisper, "Thank you, Mr. President, thank you, sir." My eyes were misty and my throat dry.

I could not have asked for a higher accolade from him who will ever be to me and to our people the embodiment of unalloyed patriotism.

Like a gray shadow the figure of Osmeña took Quezon's place in our government in exile. Osmeña the statesman, the gentle of spirit had always been willing to sacrifice his personal interests to stand in the shadow of Quezon. Studious and far-thinking, he had stood beside Quezon to advise, support, or restrain.

In time others would assume leadership, but Quezon cannot be forgotten. Quezon once said, "I would rather see the Philippines run like hell by Filipinos than run like heaven by the Americans."

I had shaped my life upon his ideals.

After Quezon's death I tried in every way to carry out his ideals and if possible broaden their concept. His life had been given to the Philippines. He had seen its future always as the dream to be worked toward. I saw it as a free nation and as part of the free world. The Philippines in itself was no longer enough. It was part of our world. It had a large stake in the future of that world.

I was a small man from a small captive country in a world embroiled by war. The American invasion of the Philippines was imminent, but no one could be certain what the end would be. Even so, I dared dream largely, even then.

I told those close to me: "Before long, the entire world will have to sit down at one table and map out a common peace. When that day comes I want a seat at that table and I want to help write the peace."

Only a year after I escaped from Bataan I wrote an outline for my pattern of that future world, a pattern which "to the majority of mankind is still considered to be the inviolable sanctity of the human soul."

In my book, *Mother America*, in 1943, I gave that outline, and I wrote: "The future pattern established in the Pacific will determine the future of the world."

The end of colonialism was to start in the Pacific after the defeat of Japan. In the Far East was the beginning—the dawn of the new free world.

All the 'forties were kaleidoscopic, lived with such intensity that in memory they resemble momentary impressions on a TV screen, so rapidly flashed before the eye that one can scarcely believe they have been seen. From the hour the Philippines was attacked until the end of this decade I would not know a day that did not contain killing tension. These were nightmare years, and still they hold wonderful memories.

Among these stand out unforgettable incidents that are proof of the steadfast kindness of America. The years of writing and lecturing in the United States are ever to be cherished because of the friends made and the kindness shown. I was a man without a country, but everywhere I traveled, from New York to California and back again and again, I was made to feel at home.

There were incidents that touched the heart, laughable incidents, and ridiculous ones. There were moments of sheer terror, such as the time a girl I had never seen before was found dead outside my door in a leading hotel; and again when, in another famous caravansary, a mysterious little man with his hand on a small satchel crept into my room and FBI men—whom I had not known were keeping a twenty-four-hour watch over me—materialized in an instant, as if they had sprung from the floor. With all their watchfulness the little man got away, and I never have known what that was all about.

There was the day of days, my birthday in Miami, when word reached me from MacArthur—my first news of them—that my wife and sons were alive, guarded by guerrillas somewhere behind Japanese lines. I dared speak of this to no one, knowing the reprisals being carried out in the Philippines.

At this time all my thoughts were centered on the coming invasion. When I dared dream it was in hope of a time to come when war would be ended and I would have my family again and build another home for them in a free Philippines. I wanted to get back to Manila and rebuild my newspapers in such a way that they would serve to influence not only my country but all Asia. Because I had fought for freedom in war did not mean I would not continue the fight in peace. Quezon had died for that freedom. I would live for it.

All my hopes were based on the coming struggle in the Pacific. During this period of my life I was a soldier, nothing more.

My bags were packed. I had secret orders. I was to rejoin General MacArthur in Hollandia and with him take part in the siege of the Philippines. My watch was clocked to Pacific time in those days and my thoughts were always on the great offensive piling up in the Pacific—the troop ships, the carriers, the planes, and the young men, the thousands and thousands of young men—all from America, all readying to set my country free. I was in a state of high tension, waiting.

In Washington Osmeña, taking Quezon's place, was to be sworn in as President in Exile of the Commonwealth of the Philippines. I delayed my journey to the Pacific for this important event and accompanied him to the oath-taking in the

Department of the Interior. After the ceremony we drove back together to the Commonwealth office on Massachusetts Avenue.

As I settled into the car beside my new president I was oppressed by the sadness of this ceremony of a nation in exile and the fact that Quezon had not lived to see his country's liberation, although he had kept in close touch to the end with the powerful offensive building up in the Pacific. I was thinking of Quezon when I realized Osmeña was speaking to me in his slow, scholarly voice.

"I will appoint you Resident Commissioner in place of the one we have now, this afternoon, as soon as I ask for his resignation."

I had to ask him to repeat his words. I was certain I had misunderstood him. I had known Vice-President Osmeña never favored the appointment of the then incumbent Resident Commissioner, but this sudden reversal of my planned future was overwhelming.

"Surely you heard me," he said, a bit peevishly. "I need someone here in Washington who is well-known in America and who can be articulate about Philippine ideals."

I was not articulate at that moment. I was stammering, uncertain how to react or what to say. "But my bags are packed," I said. "You know I am under orders to rejoin MacArthur. I am leaving day after tomorrow."

But Osmeña went on with the deadly assurance of a gentle man whose mind is made up. "I will appoint you this afternoon, Romulo, and you can make your first speech on the floor of the House, make your connections with the members, and then you can rejoin the General."

So that was the way it happened. My ambitions since the war had not been political, not for myself. In my wildest dreams I had no such thoughts as this. I was a soldier, an officer preparing to return to the battlefront. Now a few low, dignified words had stripped me of uniform and made me into a person of politics and power. I was completely dazed.

I did not fully grasp what was happening to me until the next day, when I found myself repeating the oath after Sam Rayburn, Speaker of the House, with Congressman C. Jasper Bell of Missouri and Majority Floor Leader John W. McCormack as my sponsors. Minority Leader Joseph W. Martin was present, also Congressman Karl Stefan of Nebraska, Congressman John D. Dingell of Michigan, and several others.

After taking my oath Speaker Rayburn said: "We are proud to welcome a great Filipino whose loyalty to freedom and democracy has been proved in Bataan. We are happy to number you among us. The Philippines has chosen well in having you as its representative here."

Then a great burst of happiness grew in me and a prayerful hope that wherever my wife might be she would hear my broadcast in this proud hour.

Virginia told me later she had heard my voice over the radio she kept hidden in the stove in her Luzon refuge. I think in that moment our prayers touched.

I had no time to worry as to whether I was fit to be Resident Commissioner or not. The hour was set for my first speech in the House, and I made it the very next day after taking my oath.

I made another speech, made my connections among the Congressmen, then set out to rejoin MacArthur.

I have written at length of the tense days preceding liberation and the day when beside General MacArthur and President Osmeña I waded ashore on the invaded beach at Leyte and felt again under my feet the firm warmth of Philippine earth. MacArthur had returned, and with him I had come home.

It was D-Day on Leyte, October 20, 1944. On that day, on that beach under fire, I broadcast over the Voice of Freedom. Somewhere in our islands I could only hope my wife and children would be listening.

I spoke to them and to all in the Philippines:

. . . this is liberation that brings us home.

Freedom returns to us by way of America.

Two years ago I said to you when our forces were trapped in Bataan that America would not let us down. I can now tell you what you know yourselves: America did not let us down.

For two years I have lived close to its war-stirred heart. I have seen America swing into action. In thousands of miles of travel, in hundreds of cities, I have seen Americans give of themselves without stint to avenge Bataan. . . .

You must continue keeping faith with them.

The Filipinos kept that faith.

I returned to America to the floor of Congress and gave my report on the reconquest of the Philippines by MacArthur's returning forces and the invaluable help given them by our guerrillas.

Then I was back in liberated Manila, a ruined city where thousands were hungry, where families were living in caves dug out of the ruins, with disease spreading due to a general breaking down in health and medical care, and for the first time in Philippine history a rising evil of juvenile delinquency, the inevitable aftermath of war.

According to figures collected at this time our beautiful city of Manila had been eighty per cent destroyed. General Eisenhower has stated that only Warsaw suffered such complete annihilation.

I wrote to a friend in America, "I saw my 'home' yesterday. Ashes and ruins. It was razed to the ground. Have not found Virginia nor the boys. My eldest is with the guerrillas again in the Sierra Mountains. I am broken-hearted."

Fifteen

ASK the average man for the happiest day of his life and he will have to think a moment before replying. Not I. I know.

Before 1945 I would have answered that my happiest was the day of Virginia's high-school graduation, when I persuaded her to let me slip on her finger the ring I had brought with such nervous trepidation. That moment remains unequaled for ecstasy. It was the triumph of youth.

But the happiest of my days was the morning I crossed the airfield outside Manila and saw standing, in front of three tiny Piper cubs that had somehow escaped over the melting but still dangerous Japanese lines, my wife and our two youngest sons. They had landed on Grace Field outside Manila, while I was with General MacArthur raising the American colors on reconquered Corregidor.

We had been separated for three years. Dick, our third son, was so grown I took him to be Greg.

Bobby, the baby, had turned into a little man, wary of the uniformed stranger who kissed his mother, whose companion and cavalier he had been through all the life he remembered. At first he refused to speak to me, as he had been warned never to talk to strangers.

Our two oldest sons joined us soon after and we were a family again, but it took all the political astuteness I possessed to rewin Bobby! Once when I lost all patience and spanked him with a rolled newspaper his eyes filled with angry tears.

"Not even the Japanese did that to me!" he stormed, and any father will know how I felt then.

I brought my family to Washington and Virginia began organizing a home, not easy in wartime.

There was so much for a reunited family to talk over. I was amazed to find that the most intimate details of my years in America were known to them. The bamboo telegraph had been kept busy with my exploits, and while I had been kept in darkness as to their war years every trip I had made, every speech I had given on the floor of the United States Congress, and almost every important person I had met were well-known to my family behind the enemy lines.

Mike and Gregorio, high schoolers, little more than children in our eyes, had fought with the ragged army of resistance. My wife and the two younger children had spent the three war years constantly on the move, protected always by friends. Once she had hidden in an orphanage, and General Lim, one of our heroes on Bataan, had come to warn her to get out. She left that night, and the next morning Japanese soldiers entered the place, took into custody a Filipino officer, General Simeon de Jesus, who had also been hiding there, and executed him.

Another time she returned to Manila, then suddenly decided to leave for the province, and the following day the city was bombarded by American planes. She had gone to her home town then, to Pagsanjan, but the war followed her there also, and at last she took to the hills, protected always by guerrillas who kept her on the move, always ahead of danger.

It was Mike who started the move for her rescue. He reached MacArthur on Leyte, who arranged with General Walter Krueger for the Piper cubs to pick her up with our two small sons, and then, with all plans made, Mike could not locate his mother! In rags, with a beard, he hunted her from *barrio* to *barrio*, but no one would tell him where she was hiding.

"But I'm her son, General Romulo's son," Mike would protest.

His mother's defenders would regard him with suspicion and say, "What proof have you?"

And he had no proof.

In Washington my wife and I, reunited, faced life as if for the first time together. My life was more than half over, and I had to begin in a new field to win a place for my family and myself. The truth was that I had looked forward to war's ending as a resting place, but there was no time to rest.

From the day of liberation to the present day history was to move very fast for the Philippines and the rest of the world. And for me.

General MacArthur had returned me from the Philippines to report to Congress on the conditions in recaptured Manila. It was a sad and terrible report. My narration, accompanied by motion pictures taken in the ruined city by the Signal Corps, became a documentary that was shown all over the United States.

And this, although I did not realize it then, was my final work with General MacArthur. From now on I had to devote myself to the civil welfare of my country. Military life was behind me. The fourragère and colors were laid away, to be worn only on special occasions, and the uniforms were supplanted by the formal attire required by protocol on Capitol Hill.

But the friendship, the respect, the hero worship—for I can think of it now as that—I held for General MacArthur is still there. I hold for him the greatest admiration and my personal gratitude. I think of him as the military genius whose interest in the Philippines before the war, when he organized our army and favored our independence, has enshrined him forever in Filipino hearts; and, above all, he is the liberator of the Philippines.

To me, personally, on Corregidor and Bataan and later in Australia, he was always a rock of salvation, always ready to give me support when it was needed.

I felt very bad when he was recalled. It was, I suppose, an inevitable reaction to the General's having written a letter to Minority Leader Joseph Martin, which was interpreted as being anti-administration, a letter President Truman resented. But was there need to swing the ax in just that fashion?

MacArthur is a keen analyst of world affairs. His mind, razor sharp, knew the situation in Asia better than any other person in military life. If he had been permitted to carry out his plans Korea would have been a victory and not a stalemate.

I like him best for his humanity. MacArthur thinks of world questions in human terms. Before any military movement his greatest concern was always: How can we save lives?

The MacArthur I knew was and is a builder of human unity, an exponent of human dignities. He might have been of incalculable value in Asia where he will always be revered as one of America's great heroes.

I walked beside a great hero on the beach at Leyte.

The two years I was to serve in Washington as Resident Commissioner of the Philippines would contain the most revealing experiences of my life. Before my appointment in 1944 I am afraid that although I was a seasoned journalist and soldier in his mid-forties who had seen much of the world and its work, there still lurked somewhere within me a starry-eyed young dreamer. Two years in Washington did much to finish the dream and dim many of the stars.

I had come to America lonely and broken in spirit, and America had opened its wide and wonderful heart to me. Now it welcomed my family. My sons resumed their interrupted schooling and made new friends. My wife and I made friends also; we went out a great deal and entertained at our home. Life became adjusted in Washington to a semblance of what it had been for us before the war.

The atom bomb exploded over the world, and when the smoke cleared Japan had fallen. An unsteady peace was established in the Pacific. In the Philippines the struggle against the war-borne encroachment of communism began. My country needed help.

As Resident Commissioner my days were spent in placing one vital issue after another before the American Congress. There was no more thought of returning to the Philippines. My place in behalf of my broken country was beside the Potomac. Osmeña and Roxas were carrying on the fight for the presidency of the Philippines in Manila and I was alone.

One after another I fought for the acts that were to save my country from complete postwar ruin. In rapid succession they came, the Filipino Naturalization Act, the Philippine Trade Act, the Philippine Rehabilitation Act, the Recision Act. At first I was distressed to find that in Philippine negotiations with America big business played a leading role. In my coast-to-coast wartime speaking tours I had met many American businessmen, friends from prewar Manila. I am not averse to big business, which is the backbone of any country, but now I could see that those friendships had been on a purely social level. This was different. Now I was asking for financial aid for a country that had given of its best—its youth.

"Remember Bataan!" I had exhorted, up and down and across America, in chilling weather and in southern heat. But who now remembered Bataan? The faith given at risk of life, the bloodshed and the dying, the torture and the hunger—who remembered these? Who in America remembered the shining example of loyalty to democracy? War was so short a time behind us, but memories are shorter.

In the Philippines we remembered.

The talk was starting on Capitol Hill. "We must rebuild Japan. We must bolster Germany."

And when I asked, Why? the answer was firmly given: "To make these countries oppose and fight communism."

"But in the Philippines we are already fighting communism," I would argue, "and this attitude on America's part is giving communism a head start in the Far East."

But some Americans were already forgetting the Philippines. In time loyalty and idealism would be forgotten with Bataan.

Washington offered a peephole into an America I had not known existed. I was seeing American business interests at work at close range, and unhappily I was the target.

Good friends of mine in Congress, who were fighting for justice and fair play, were forced to listen to some powerful business interests. They dared not turn their backs or they would have found themselves off Capitol Hill. So they tried to compromise.

There was work to do for the Philippines in Washington. There was a fight to be waged but a fight of another type. War was over. America became a world leader. She had to shoulder obligations she never thought she would have. We in the Philippines believed—and we had a right to so believe—that we had first claim on America's interest and attention.

Philippine independence would be proclaimed on July 4, 1946. Our country was prostrate; a devastating war and a cruel enemy occupation had destroyed our industries, sapped our national strength, and wrecked our economy. The Philippine Trade Act and the Philippine Rehabilitation Act had to be passed by the American Congress, and time was of the essence. We needed the Trade Act to help cushion the effects of independence on our economy; we had to have the Rehabilitation Act to rebuild the Philippines from the rubble of war.

Some of my friends in Manila urged me to return. "This is the time for you to come back," I was told by one of our Senators. "You are one of the war's heroes and you must enter politics now. We must rally our people and prevent them from being misled by those who tried to mislead them during the war."

But I happened to be in Washington and I knew, more than anyone, the fight that had to be fought on Capitol Hill for the Philippines. All attention in my homeland was concentrated on the national elections. Someone had to be the watchdog for Philippine interests in the United States. I decided to remain as Resident Commissioner.

We had only a few months in which to fight for the Philippine Trade Act and the Philippine Rehabilitation Act. There was also the Filipino Naturalization Act and, later, the Recision Act.

The Filipino Naturalization Act that had failed of passage several times had to be enacted into law. Thousands of Filipinos in the United States were being discriminated against. The Chinese, the Japanese, and other Orientals could be naturalized, but not the Filipinos. I could not tolerate such injustice. I did not want my fellow countrymen to change their citizenship from Filipino to American. Personally I feel that my citizenship as a Filipino is my most cherished possession and I would not exchange it for that of any country in the world. Still I felt that the Filipino, who for reasons of his own wanted to be an American citizen should be entitled to the same legal privileges as the Chinese, the Japanese, the Indians, the Greeks, or the Spaniards.

When in 1945 as Resident Commissioner I visited all the Filipino communities on the Pacific Coast from Seattle down to California and New Mexico I saw that a Filipino naturalization act was needed by these hard-working, thrifty, law-abiding countrymen of mine as an act of justice. I therefore took all the necessary steps to have a bill passed by Congress, and waited for action to be taken on it on the floor of the House.

After my return from Leyte, immediately after my speech reporting on the reconquest of the Philippines, the naturalization bill was taken up and passed by voice vote. The Senate followed suit and a few days later it was signed into law by President Truman.

Then came the Recision Act, which I consider a grave injustice against our Filipino veterans.

World War II was over. The world was outwardly at peace, but in the Philippines the war against Communist infiltration had started. The Red propagandists fed their bitterness to veterans who had given their all to the fight beside America. The Filipino soldiers, who fought as members of the Army of the

United States, and the guerrillas had been praised by top American military authorities for the delaying action that had cut months of fighting from the Pacific struggle and saved thousands of young American lives. Yes, war's end found us covered with laurels; we were heroes.

But the Recision Act withdrew from our Filipino servicemen many of their rights as veterans under the American flag. I went several times to see Secretary of War Stimson to argue against those injustices. For example, the Filipino veteran who had been promised a dollar would be given only one peso instead. But a peso is worth only half a dollar in the Philippines, and the cost of living was on the rise.

And the argument returned to me was always, "Not to abide by this would upset your economy in the Philippines. Your cost of living is not as high as in the United States."

Then I would answer, "Isn't it important to you, more important than our economy, not to upset the world's opinion that America always stands for fair play? Besides, it is not true that it would upset our economy."

That argument was waved back.

I would continue. "Why, if this is being done to Filipinos, why is it not being done to Puerto Ricans, Cubans. Italians, and other foreign soldiers who fought for the United States?"

That was never answered in definite terms.

Other rights to which we felt our Filipino soldiers entitled were given to other veterans, but not to ours. It was ironic that funeral rights were given us; a man had to die to prove he had fought for America.

I knew the discontent this was causing in a troubled Philippines. When Quezon and MacArthur were in Corregidor a bill was introduced in the United States Congress federalizing the Philippine Army. This was passed by the Senate. Why it was not passed in the House or why joint action was not taken by the House and Senate is a question that has never been answered. In the post-Bataan heydey of our accepted heroism this decision had been approved by the Senate. We should have pressed vigorously for similar action in the House when the iron was hot. When we were less important the act did not get through the House. If our army had been federalized, we would have had no veterans' problems after the war, and we would have avoided all the resentment directed against the United States by veterans who felt they had been unjustly treated.

Then the Recision Act took back what had been given.

In addition to the stress I was under in Washington was the annoyance of a whispering campaign started against me by a few individuals in the Philippines, that I was not fighting hard enough for the Philippines but was only building up myself. This slander, Communist-inspired in the beginning, was whipped up by a vociferous minority. I tried to ignore the reports coming to me from Manila and to keep my mind on the fight in Washington, but from certain unmistakable physical signs I knew it was only a matter of time and pressure before, in one way or another, I would not be able to go on.

Physical and mental strain can be borne, but the persistent gnawing of detractors trying to undermine all one attempts to build is hard to bear. There were many times during these years when I wanted to quit. My wife begged me to withdraw, to retire from public office and its pressures and live a life of privacy and leisure, the sort of life I had never known.

I could not give up. Others could forget Bataan, but not I.

Never shall I forget the bitterly cold morning in Washington when I went to make one final plea to Secretary Stimson. I was trembling with nervousness and cold when I faced him. He opened the conversation before I had a chance to speak.

"I know why you are here," Stimson said. "That Recision Act again. Well, it's no use. I told you nothing can be done. You're wasting your time. It's a closed matter."

I could not yield. I knew the embittered despair this would spread in the Philippines. "Mr. Secretary, do you realize what this will do to Fil-American friendship?" I asked. "Do you want

the Filipino veteran to believe that a Filipino leg or eye lost in
battle is of less importance than the leg or eye of an American
soldier? What has our national economy to do with a man who
died fighting under your flag? In fact, I think the Filipino veteran should get twice as much as the American veteran, instead
of half, because the American fought out of duty and the Filipino out of loyalty."

But Stimson kept shaking his head. "The matter is closed."

"It cannot be closed to us, Mr. Secretary," I replied. "I am
leaving with you this memorandum of protest that at least we
are on record as having protested against it." And I handed him
a three-page memorandum with my arguments against the Recision Act.

I went to Senate Majority Leader Alben Barkley in the Senate. I talked to him as I had to Secretary Stimson. He said he
would study the matter and see what could be done. I conferred
with Speaker Rayburn, with Congressional leaders. With each
of them I left copies of my memorandum, which I know must
be in their official files.

Nothing was done.

I went to everyone I knew in Washington, down through
the lists of the administration, from Pontius Pilate to Caiaphas.
. . . And everywhere I was given the same stubborn answer: "It
is an administration measure. The matter is closed."

This slogan was set up against me like a wall.

And I looked back to my starry-eyed youth when I had believed in America as the land of equality and freedom and I
understood the bitterness growing in a Philippines that had also
believed. I had to keep on believing that somehow the faith was
justified, or leave America. Now I understood the campaign
against me in the Philippines, which stated that I was not fighting hard enough for them. I had to keep on believing in America
and its democratic idealism or all the blood and tears of the war
years were wasted.

While there are such Americans as John W. McCormack,

Walter H. Judd, Clement Zablocki, Olin Teague, William Fulbright, "Mike" Mansfield, George Miller, John D. Dingell, Jr., Alexander Wiley, Arthur Hays Sulzberger, Roy Howard, Phillip Graham, and many others who make every effort to be fair and square I cannot lose my faith in America. In the particular case of our Filipino veterans "Tiger" Teague of Texas has been fighting all these years to correct some of the injustices in the Recision Act. To my mind he typifies true Americanism. And I am certain, sooner or later, we will win the fight.

But it is difficult to keep the faith in Washington. There were times in these affable, smiling, well-dressed, and beautifully-mannered administrative groups, meeting at cocktail parties and dinners, when I knew myself to be surrounded by men who were thinking only of themselves, oblivious of the world around them, forgetful of their friends who sacrificed for them and their country. The injustices and inequalities of the Philippine Trade Act, which I opposed in committees and on the floor of the House, exposed this morass of selfishness coated so thinly with patriotic zeal. I accepted the provisions of the act in behalf of the Philippines because they had to be accepted or we would have had nothing. And far worse they would have been if we had not fought vigorously.

As an example of the onerous provisions of the bill which I failed to eliminate is that which provides that we must amend the Philippine Constitution to give equal rights in the Philippines to American citizens. In the committee hearings I vigorously fought the inclusion of this section in the bill. But I failed to convince Congress and the provision that we must amend our constitution remained in the law as enacted.

Still I believed, and I believe it still, that ultimate world justice lies with America. And this is because I have faith in the American people, in their innate sense of justice and fair play. All my youth was lived in that belief and I could not desert it in my mid-forties. So I continued to fight, and accepted defeat only when I felt it was best to take what was being offered, that this would be better for us in the long run when independence came.

For if I had persisted in fighting for the Trade Act that I wanted, I knew we would have had no law at all and we would not have had the Rehabilitation Act either. Time was pressing. We had scarcely three months to get the legislation through. As I said in part in my speech when the Trade Act was in final debate on the floor:

This bill, Mr. Speaker, is not the kind I would have written in the best of all possible worlds. In such a world, the Philippines would be standing firmly on its own feet, depending on its own resources, producing a diverse and useful variety of products for domestic consumption as for export, freed of feudalism and archaic economic policies, independent in its economy as well as in its politics. In such a world, the Philippines would share in that larger dream—the dream written into the Atlantic Charter, the dream of an economic system wherein all the peoples of the world would truly have free access to the raw materials of our earth.

In such a world, if I had written this bill as I would have wished, it would provide for perpetual free trade between the United States and the Philippines, amid a global community of perpetual free trade. It would provide for no graduated tariffs, no quotas, no limitations on commerce.

If I had written it, the rights assured to the United States would not appear in the bill at all. They would be assured by a treaty entered into on a basis of complete equality between our two sovereign nations. . . .

From the time of our liberation, which began in October, 1944, with the first landings on Leyte, until December, 1945, our total exports to the United States amounted to less than one million dollars. One million dollars! That is the productiveness of our economy today. In an average prewar year, we were producing exports averaging more than 155 million dollars. Our economic fruits of victory, Mr. Speaker, can therefore be put into a ratio of one to one hundred and fifty-five. That ratio spells disaster—not in some distant future, but right now. . . .

This bill, as you know, provides for a period of only eight years of free trade between our two countries. After that, it provides for a twenty-year period during which duties are gradually increased at a rate of five per cent a year. We are therefore inclined to speak of it as legislation providing for twenty-eight years of full or partial free trade.

In point of fact, it is not full free trade at any time, because it establishes quotas which limit the amount of sugar, cordage, rice, cigars, tobacco, coconut oil, and buttons which may be exported from the Philippines to the United States. Neither it is altogether a matter of twenty-eight years of such preferential treatment, since the gradual increase in duties will begin to be felt long before the period is ended. I am not raising objections to these points. I am merely making them clear.

What this period of preference will do is quite simple. It will provide businessmen in the Philippines with some incentive to go back into business. It will banish the dreadful inertia that beclouds our islands. . . .

During these twenty-eight years, we shall be able to plan our economy with a view to the true economic independence which is the right of every sovereign people.

After the founding of the United Nations and just before independence was granted the Philippines, in this same vital year of 1946, there was sandwiched in between these nerve-shattering events one of the most exhausting of all struggles, that of the UNRRA—the United Nations Rehabilitation and Reconstruction Act.

Conditions grew worse in the Philippines. We had to have funds. We were fighting for our sugar quota, for the right to stay alive. As I have already said, in the Philippines our leaders were fighting out the election and I had no one to assist me in America. I felt completely alone, lost between two countries.

The UNRRA conference was held in Atlantic City. As the Chief Philippine delegate I appeared before the leaders of many nations and the futility of my attempt was clear. Outwardly all was good will and respect for the Filipinos. But ranging in the background were the men from Washington and from other

nations, who publicly were all friendliness to the Philippines but
who were maneuvering from behind the scenes to get all they
could for their respective countries. It was a free for all.

What did I have to offer to win their consideration? Only a
handful of statistics compiled by the USAFFE Veterans of the
Philippines as follows:

(a) USAFFE personnel killed
     or died in line of duty,
     including those who died in
     prison camps   over   36,000

(b) USAFFE personnel separated
     from the service because
     of service-connected injury
     or illness   over   9,000

(c) Guerrillas killed, died of
     wounds, or sickness,
     missing after combat operations   over   29,000

(d) Missing   over   15,131
              Total   over   89,131

Estimated Physical loss:

Private property $526,107,000
Public property   259,527,000
Small private property   75,238,000
              Total $860,872,000

To America this was a brief list of numerals. To the Philippines these were our sons and our hard-earned property.

I gave the last of my strength to the meeting at Atlantic City,
returned to my home in Washington, and collapsed. The sum
of $12,000,000 was allotted to the Philippines for relief. I was
completely exhausted, emotionally and physically. I was put
into Walter Reed Hospital and forbidden newspapers, TV,
radio, and all visitors save Virginia. I remained in bed for weeks,

content to stare into space, thoughtless, untroubled. I had as my physician a famous Filipino diagnostician, Dr. Gonzalo Austria, who happened to be in Washington.

Then word reached me of fresh problems of vital interest to the Philippines. The first was a hearing held in the Senate by the Finance Committee to discuss the Philippine Rehabilitation Act. I had to appear. Roused from lethargy and a deathly inertia I summoned enough strength to go in a wheel chair and make one last appeal for justice, accompanied by my economic adviser, Dr. Urbano Zafra, and my physician, Dr. Austria.

It was not my last effort, however. Again and again, while my illness lasted, I appeared in my wheel chair in the halls of Congress and pleaded for justice for the Philippines.

It was not only this struggle for understanding that exhausted me. Between these efforts had occurred what was to be the greatest event in my life and perhaps in the entire world's—the formation in San Francisco of the United Nations.

Sixteen

IN 1945 the first rumors of plans for a United Nations organization were heard. The world had not adjusted to its precarious peace. Every nation, with the probable exception of Russia, felt that the only insurance against further mass murder would be the formation of a world organization that would represent and protect all the peoples of the earth.

This had been a private dream of mine for many years. It had started during student days at Columbia when I took such passionate interest in Wilson and the League of Nations. My youthful ideals were pinned to that organization. Later I had made a study of the League, trying to discover why it had failed, and if a new League were formed what could prevent its failure. I read up on Clemenceau of France, Venizelos of Greece, Orlando of Italy.

As early as 1942, newly returned from Bataan, I had drawn plans for a world organization based on a blueprint of peace in the Pacific. I had definite ideas concerning the formation and operation of such an organization, and had confided to trusted intimates that when it was organized I hoped to be one of those who would be asked to sit at the peace table.

In my own mind I had years before sketched the dream building in which these meetings of the international powers would be held. But of the actuality, the formation of the United Nations, I first heard rumors early in 1945. I was still in uniform and still Resident Commissioner. I had nothing to do officially with the United Nations beginnings. I learned along with the rest of the reading world that preliminary meetings were to be held at Dumbarton Oaks. My days were crowded with duties, but any plan for world peace seemed so important to me that I succeeded in attending some of the meetings as an observer.

I reread every word I could find on the tragic failure of the League of Nations. I became convinced that it had collapsed because the United States had not joined. But if a new organization was formed, with the United States in it to support and lead, how could it fail?

So my hopes and excitement grew when my life-long fantasy appeared as a definite plan. A conference of world powers was called in April in San Francisco. I read avidly every word that appeared concerning the proposed conference, with no idea how soon this interest would act to my advantage.

One night I was in my bed at the Shoreham, trying to lull an overly active mind to rest, when President Osmeña telephoned from Florida. He had been operated on in Jacksonville and was still weak.

"Romulo, I'm sending you to San Francisco," he said in his gentle but decisive way. "I'm appointing you chairman of our Philippine delegation to the United Nations organization conference."

Again, in a moment, my entire world whipped over. My tired brain tried to grasp all his words held for me.

I had never thought of myself as a diplomat. I was unprepared for leadership. I had no experience in international matters. I had been newspaperman, soldier, and lecturer, and was no more ready for a diplomatic career than I had been for military life when MacArthur summoned me to his headquarters on the Spanish Wall. And there were personal reasons that made me hesitate.

My wife and children and I had just been reunited after more than three years of separation. They were newly arrived in Washington. We were estranged at first and were just beginning to be a family again. The barrier between Bobby and myself was breaking down and I was enjoying him. I could not bear the thought of leaving my family again and setting off on a new career as a peacemaker.

But had it not been peace I had prayed for all these years?

Then the thought came to me that this was the opportunity I had been waiting for all my life—the chance to speak for my country, to make the Philippines known.

I discussed the problem with my wife and boys and they decided with me: I should go to San Francisco.

Osmeña had said it was of the utmost importance that the Philippines be properly represented at the meeting. This was a large order for a small country that was still not a sovereign nation. America had not yet granted our independence. We were still a commonwealth.

As the representative of a small, still dependent country at an international conference I would certainly be on the outside looking in.

How was I to insure a hearing in San Francisco? I had heard of some Filipino delegates who had gone to international meetings and were completely ignored.

The next morning I telephoned a friend in the State Department, and asked that he arrange a meeting for me with Secretary of State Edward Stettinius.

"Would no one else do?" he queried.

I told him, "No, I must see the Secretary himself."

Stettinius was to be chairman of the host nation at San Francisco. He met me in the friendliest way, said he had heard about me, and inquired after General MacArthur. Then he said, "And now, what can I do for the Philippines?"

I told him promptly. "A great deal. President Osmeña has appointed me to lead the Philippine delegation to San Francisco and I have come to offer you my help."

I had his startled attention, which was exactly what I had hoped for in suggesting that a small country like the Philippines could be of any use to a powerful country like America. This was possible, I hastened to explain, because our countries shared the same ideals.

"We Filipinos can speak for the small nations better than the United States can," I argued, "and in a way that will be more understandable to the other small countries. But, Mr. Secretary, to be effective I must be on the inside in San Francisco. In the past the small nations have always been left out of everything that is going on in meetings of world powers, and only if I am 'in the know' will I be able to understand and help."

"In what way?" he asked. "What do you mean?"

"I mean," I said boldly, "that I should like to be kept informed during the conference in all matters not pertaining to American security."

He made up his mind at once. "Good! We'll do that! I'll appoint a liaison between my delegation and yours and he will report to you everything that goes on. And you can see me personally any time." He gave me the name of the State Department official who was to be the liaison officer and wished me well, repeating, "Don't forget, General, you can call on me at any time."

I said, "Mr. Secretary, you can be sure I will, whenever necessary."

My weariness was forgotten. I telephoned Osmeña and he was delighted. Stettinius as chairman would know everything that was going on in San Francisco and now that I was in his confidence I would too.

From that day on this has been my line of conduct in any new undertaking. I go to the man at the top and ask to be taken in "on the know." It always works to mutual advantage.

I went to San Francisco determined to do what I thought was right, and in a sanguine mood as to what could be accomplished in the city by the Golden Gate. I felt certain that this time we were going to settle all the problems of the world and I was angered by articles suggesting the conference might not bring about all we hoped for.

So I found myself that April of 1945 in San Francisco, as the chief delegate of the Philippines to the embryonic United Nations. I was the barefoot boy of politics at the august meeting. I had never before attended an international conference. I knew nothing at all of the art of diplomacy, which I have since diagnosed as the ability to make the nastiest possible comment in the nicest possible way. I was an untrained, untested greenhorn, and I had been thrust into the most serious international situation existing at that time in the world.

There were other handicaps.

Fifty sovereign nations were represented in San Francisco. Among the representatives were the exponents of vast wealth and power. They were the long-established, experienced overlords of the earth. Some of these men had sat in on the League of Nations.

In the gathering were those who regarded Asian members as upstarts. Worst of all for me was the fact that I represented an Asian nation that was not yet independent. I was made aware of detractors who felt I had no right to speak. Almost at once I sensed the intrigue and conniving that was to keep the United Nations in a state of turmoil.

Add to these handicaps the fact that for the first time in my life I had stage fright on a scale to match the vastness of our enterprise.

In San Francisco I made errors and enemies and lasting friends. I floundered in diplomatic eddies that I could not understand. I was a very small mite in that great world, but I was determined to make the name of the Philippines known and to make it known in a dignified, effective way.

It was what I had been asking for all my life, and I was going to take full advantage.

A great deal has been written about the first speech I made in San Francisco before that world organization. My opening sentence, "Let us make this floor the last battlefield," has been often described as followed by a standing ovation, the only one given to any speaker before that first General Assembly. Pierre J. Huss, writing for the Hearst Newspapers, said in that moment I made a name for myself and my country. I deny that. The name of the Philippines has stood for national integrity for centuries. It was my privilege, on this day, to voice its precepts to the world.

Into that speech had gone my own prayers and tears; my life had been dedicated to its meaning. I did not speak alone. With me was the Asia I knew—all the troubled, despairing, inarticulate, dependent six hundred million people who prayed to be set free. I had seen their faces. I knew their dreams. I spoke for them.

I must confess the reception given my opening words staggered me. For a moment I stood silent, wondering, and almost afraid. Was this thunder of applause some sort of attack? Then I knew that those who applauded were with me all of freedom's way.

Some others were not, but I was to find that out later.

From that hour on I would be publicized as "the big voice of the small nations."

The speech launched me at once into the debates. It also set the representatives of the colonial powers solidly against me. This became most apparent during the discussions in the Trusteeship Committee.

As soon as I learned that the colonial powers wanted the trusteeship system over trust territories to promote the advancement of the peoples under them only toward self-government and not toward independence I braced myself for the fight of my life.

"Independence" was the only word that could give true meaning to the Charter. That word meant more to me and to all non-self-governing peoples than any other nation could know. My delegation and I were shocked to find it was not included in the original draft and even more shocked when we learned that any attempt to include the word "independence" would be bitterly opposed by the leading powers.

But the word had to be there!

I found out what an uphill fight mine would be during the general debate, when I stood alone against the massed opposition of powers. All the colonial powers were lined up against my stand. A small, brash newcomer to the international arena, I was competing against men backed by centuries of domination. All Europe—all history—was behind them.

Lord Cranborne led the opposition for the United Kingdom, flanked by the delegates of France, Belgium, and the Netherlands. On the debating floor, and by private pressure brought against me from every side, the colonial powers sought to wear me down. All were against me and my one little word.

We argued and came to no conclusion.

It was only a word, they said. "Independence!" What difference between it and the word they asked for, "self-government"?

Impossible to explain to these assured men who represented the great powers how much the word meant to dependent people. How could they know? They were born free.

Why was I fighting so hard, they asked, for a single word?

I was put on the defensive. They said I was delaying the signing of the Charter.

I would not give in.

The general debate ended. The real struggle was to start in the Trusteeship Committee. I had twenty-four hours in which to prepare, not to defend, but to attack.

The delegates went to their respective committees—there were six—to discuss the Charter draft, article by article. My delegation stood by me. They agreed that the word independence must be included in a charter that held full meaning for all people.

Far into that night I continued my fight for the precious word. I went first to the United States delegate. Governor

Harold Stassen was the American delegate in the Trusteeship Committee. I had perfect faith that America would understand. "We are not against you, but we cannot take the initiative," was as far as he would commit himself.

I took this to mean that if I did make a final stand in the matter America would support me. I had to be content with that.

I had expected full-hearted support from all Asia. I did not get it. This was one of the biggest shocks I received during the conference. Sir Ramaswami Mudaliar was the the Indian delegate. I could get no help from him. Madame Pandit was in San Francisco. But because her country was still under the British and she and her brother Nehru were fighting for independence she found herself decidedly on the outside looking in and could offer no help.

I hunted up the Latin-American delegates one after another. Some were for me. Others seemed merely willing to listen.

I spoke to Ambassador Wellington Koo of China and he promised to support me. His chief, T. V. Soong, who was the foreign minister and whom I had met and interviewed in Hong Kong and Chungking, acted as if he had never seen me before.

The hours were passing and I was frantic. Knocking on doors, prowling the corridors of the St. Francis Hotel, and buttonholing delegates at lunch, dinner, and between time I presented my cause. Independence was the only goal.

I argued. It was difficult to argue with people who had always been free. Again and again I was asked, "But what does it matter what word is used when the meaning is the same?" The arguments, the pressure, went on day and night until I felt myself nearing the breaking point. But I would not break.

Independence and self-government are not the same. Independence is the only goal for a people to achieve the genius of its race. The United Nations had to make it the goal.

I was tired out, sleepless, exhausted by the word. I went to bed leaving the matter in God's hand, and snatched a few hours of sleep before the crucial debate in the Trusteeship Committee. Much has been written about that debate. Lord Cranborne and Chairman Peter Frazier, prime minister of New Zealand, spoke for self-government. I demanded independence.

Harold Stassen, representing the United States and acting as middleman at the proceedings, sent a personal note written in pencil after the debate.

"Congratulations. We are proud of you," was all it said.

Then we had to go through it all over again on the floor of the General Assembly.

As finally approved and as adopted by the plenary session of the Assembly, Section (b) of Article 76 in the chapter on International Trusteeship System reads:

"to promote the political, economic, social, and educational advancement of the inhabitants of the trust territories, and their progressive development towards self-government or independence. . . ."

The Philippines won its battle. One word—but how meaningful to voiceless millions in Asia and Africa.

Former Premier Paul-Henri Spaak of Belgium, a finished diplomat and an excellent speaker, one of the real world statesmen at the conference, had opposed me violently in two or three of these acrimonious debates. Then we found ourselves lunching together in the auditorium cafeteria.

"Romulo, I like you," he said suddenly, "but when I am listening to you speak on that podium I hate you!"

I saw then that politics without personal contact can wreak havoc. After several of our luncheon meetings Spaak's attitude toward me softened, and in subsequent discussions in the United Nations he was less belligerent. We still lacked a meeting of minds, but perhaps a meeting of souls must precede understanding. I have learned to respect and admire the Belgian statesman and I consider him one of my heroes, one of the world's greatest men. He and I are now co-chairmen of the World Brotherhood movement, together with Konrad Adenauer of Germany, Madame Pandit of India, and Dr. Arthur Compton of the United States.

This proved to me that no matter how diametrically opposed your views may be from another's if you can succeed in knowing him as a human being you can understand each other. If, as we are told, we are made in the image of our Lord the spark of divinity in you can light the spark of divinity in me, and a light forms by which we can see each other's problems and know we are brothers under the skin.

After the incident with Spaak I have made it a rule to look for the spark of divinity in each man. In some it would be buried too deep for my poor powers to uncover. Certain delegates to the United Nations showed me the purest malevolence, but I persevered and sometimes won the way to understanding. For no matter how deep the spark is buried, one can be certain it is there.

The matter of the veto came up early in San Francisco. I was one of its determined opponents. It provided that any of the great powers could veto any matter involving world security. I feared that such a ruling, if abused by one of the great powers, would paralyze the United Nations, and this is exactly what has happened. In major issues the United Nations has been immobilized by that all-powerful Russian *Nyet*.

I teamed up with Minister for External Affairs Herbert Evatt of Australia, who led the fight against the veto, and we began a spirited series of debates.

I was giving my all to the issue when Stettinius met me in the aisle one day and asked me to have breakfast with him the next morning in his apartment hotel on Nob Hill. A distinguished, gray, courteous host, he put his arm around me in welcome and led me to the breakfast table. The atmosphere quivered with affability.

As we ate, he reminded me of how I had gone to him in Washington after my appointment as chief of the Philippine delegation and asked to be put "in the know" in San Francisco.

"We've done as you wished, haven't we?" he asked. "Haven't we taken you into our confidence?"

I assured him that was true.

He had indeed been kind. The liaison officer had carried good will and information between us, and the members of his delegation had been most helpful.

Still on that happy plane I thanked him, and said I had been kept well-informed of the behind-the-scenes activities.

Stettinius beamed. "That is exactly what I wanted to hear. And you have done a wonderful job, General. Senators Vandenberg and Tom Connally have spoken to me many times about you and we are very proud of what you have done. But at times . . ."

"Yes?" I prompted.

He shook his distinguished gray head. "The veto power," he said sadly.

"I know you favor it," I said. "But I can differ with you honestly."

"Oh yes," he agreed readily. "You can differ. But I want to ask you a question. Do you really want the United States in the United Nations?"

Did I want it? Did the world need it? I thought back to Wilson and his sickness of heart when he knew the League had failed. I knew then how he had felt. Was I to be responsible for another world tragedy?

"Without the United States," I said, "the United Nations will be another League of Nations. Another failure."

And I reviewed for him briefly that sad history of a hope that had risen and fallen to permit a world to plunge again into war.

Stettinius listened gravely. "I'm glad you know all that," he said, "because, as Senators Vandenberg and Connally will tell you, the United States will never ratify the United Nations Charter unless it contains the proviso of the veto power."

"I didn't know," I said, "that the American people were determined to have that power."

"They are," Stettinius assured me. "Can't you see that there should be unanimity among the big powers? If you really want the United States in the United Nations you should know that the United States will never enter the United Nations without that proviso. As a friend I think you should realize how fixed our intentions are."

What could I say? I protested feebly. "But I have taken a definite stand."

"I know. That is why I asked for this talk with you."

We talked for an hour and it was time to leave for the meeting.

"In other words, Mr. Secretary," I said finally, "those of us who are opposing the veto power are to pipe down."

He gave me his friendly smile. "Exactly, my dear General, if you want America in the organization."

I told him that I would have to confer with my delegation. And I did confer, especially with Senator Carlos P. Garcia, now President of the Philippines, who had made a special study of the veto. I also discussed it with Vandenberg. But the decision had to be mine.

Was the United States to come in or stay out?

In the end, while the Philippine delegation went on record as being against the veto, I opposed it no longer. I still say it was wrong.

There were other issues at San Francisco, but to me the veto was most vital. As to the inclusion of the word "independence" in the Charter, that is my cenotaph. It is the Philippine contribution to the world Magna Charta. In my mind, achieving the acceptance of that word is the most satisfying accomplishment of my career in the United Nations.

Pierre J. Huss pleased me with his comment: "Thanks to him (Romulo) the United Nations has 'independence' in its Charter, one of the most important contributions for the evolution of humanity to dignity and freedom."

Among the minor issues debated during the San Francisco conference was the choice of a site for the future United Nations. I waged a hopeless struggle to have San Francisco chosen, although it was against my private interests to do so since my home was in Washington and if the meetings were in New York I would be able to commute.

I favored San Francisco because I believed the future of the world lies in the Pacific. The Atlantic's era is finished. The Old World is truly old.

A suggested San Francisco site was on the hills overlooking the Presidio, a lovely parklike military encampment, in the hills by the Golden Gate. In it is a cemetery for the military dead.

A British delegate in protesting this site made the objection, "If we build the United Nations there we will look down on the graves of all those soldiers."

I answered, "All the better; it will keep us reminded that war is inevitable death. It will not make us forget that our purpose is peace."

It was in San Francisco that I first proposed that a conference of non-self-governing peoples be called under the auspices of the United Nations. For a time this was held in abeyance and I had to push it through in 1948 in the General Assembly. Strange to say, although it has been voted on and approved, nothing further has been done in this matter. Still such proposals have their value in that by our ability to gain approval of them we show their need.

San Francisco added three to my roll call of heroes. They were Paul-Henri Spaak of Belgium, Jan Masaryk of Czechoslovakia, and Field Marshal Jan Smuts of South Africa. Some day I shall write at length of these truly great men. I came to know them well and all I learned served to feed my respect for them as patriots and men of good will.

In San Francisco with a firm hand I signed the United Nations Charter for the Philippines. It was an actuality. The dream of a lifetime had come true for me. How many men are so blessed!

In my library are many shelves of books written about the San Francisco meeting. Of all those written and spoken concerning me nothing has pleased me more than words spoken by one who was in San Francisco and closely followed the conference proceedings—President Hamilton Holt of Rollins College in Florida. A former magazine editor, a great scholar and educator, Dr. Holt had been chief adviser to Woodrow Wilson in the preparation of the Versailles Treaty, and for that reason I cherished the words he spoke when he awarded me a Doctor of Literature degree some months after the signing of the Charter:

Carlos P. Romulo, educator, editor, author, playwright, lecturer, soldier, patriot, I heard you at San Francisco last spring speak with unmatched eloquence for the six hundred million inarticulate and dependent peoples of the world. I saw you stand before the delegates of fifty sovereign nations as the chief champion of liberty and freedom of the world. I witnessed your statesmanship force into the Charter the adoption of the statement that backward peoples of the world "held as a sacred trust of civilization," had the right to aspire to full "independence," while the American delegation (shades of the signers of the American Declaration of Independence) went slavishly along with the empires on this issue until you turned the tide. You emerged from the conference with a moral grandeur which your imperialistic opponents could not fail to recognize. . . . Thus, General Romulo, because you have so nobly fought for the freedom of the Philippines and because, by voice and pen, you have constantly fought for the liberty of mankind, Rollins College confers upon you the degree of Doctor of Literature and admits you to all its rights and privileges.

I would remember the kindness of this tribute in a time near at hand, when calumny too harsh to bear would be heaped upon my weary head.

In San Francisco I felt the presence of Woodrow Wilson. Somehow the signing of the Charter seemed to make some atonement for his tragic betrayal.

A country is as great as its great men. America has been fortunate in its presidents.

Franklin D. Roosevelt did not live to see the creation of the United Nations. He died two months before the meeting in San Francisco. He was the first American president I knew as a public official, and as Resident Commissioner I met him several times in the White House. In my mind he made articulate the ideals of the free world as Wilson did in his day. No other since has expressed such ideals.

I also believe Roosevelt saved the United States from possible revolution in 1933. There are two kinds of revolution: the bloody kind that starts from below and the peaceful kind that starts from above. Roosevelt started the peaceful kind with his social reforms.

So he was hated. So was Lincoln hated. All who make crucial decisions are hated. The ones who hated Roosevelt most were the ones who would have suffered most if what he prevented had come to pass.

I recall a crucial meeting with Roosevelt. The funeral of President Quezon was attended by members of President Roosevelt's cabinet and the President himself was represented by Admiral Leahy and Chief of Staff General George C. Marshall. Quezon's remains were temporarily placed at the mausoleum for the heroes of the Spanish-American War and later transferred to Manila. After the service President Osmaña called on President Roosevelt at the White House and asked me to accompany him.

It was a different Roosevelt from the one I had seen at Notre Dame in 1935 and a different one also from the amiable President who had received President Osmeña and me in the White House the following year. The burdens of state had weighed on him. His hair was gray and I thought I noticed a slight tremor in his hand as he lighted his cigarette.

But his voice was the same, as enthralling as it was when we received degrees together at Notre Dame. He greeted President Osmeña with a cordial, "Congratulations, Mr. President. We Americans suffered a great loss with the death of my good friend, President Quezon. But we are fortunate that his successor is here with us and is a man of your experience."

The two presidents talked a long time. President Roosevelt led the conversation, and only at intervals was the quieter Osmeña heard. The American President was fired with the energy and nervous tension of war. We were on our way back to the Philippines, he said. We were showing the Japanese the Americans were really angry, and our splendid commander, General MacArthur, would have us back before the world would suspect it could be done.

He spoke of the "superb loyalty" of the Filipinos and the guerrilla warfare still being carried out on the Pacific line and the lessons such loyalty had given our allies.

"I have told Churchill," he said, "that because of this he must change his views and set a date for the independence of India as we have in the Philippines. This war should change many of our fossilized views about peoples. It is practically won; our worry now is how to win the peace."

Osmeña pointed out the Philippines would need America's help after liberation. It was promised, with a large heart-warming Roosevelt smile.

"No people has earned its freedom as you have," the American President told us. "Your country was destroyed fighting for us. It is our duty to help you rebuild." And he added, thoughtfully, "I may go to Manila to proclaim your independence." He would have been the first American president to visit there while in office.

He talked to us of his ancestors who had traded in that part of the world. Then he said, "The Far East will be the center of world developments after this war. Freedom will come to many of the countries there sooner or later. Did you know that I have advocated a sort of trusteeship for Indochina preparatory to their independence, and that I have proposed that the Philippines be one of the trustees? Your experience there with us will be valuable as a pattern for that entire section."

Press Secretary Steve Early came in with some photographers and I stepped aside. After some shots of the two presidents had been taken, Roosevelt beckoned me into the picture, saying, "We cannot leave out my fellow alumnus of Notre Dame."

President Osmeña was to see Roosevelt again, for the last time in Warm Springs, Georgia. They discussed Philippine rehabilitation. The day after their conference President Roosevelt died. A giant among men, he left an indelible imprint in the history of humanity's advance toward freedom and human dignity.

Osmeña was the only head of state in Washington on the day of Roosevelt's funeral, so in the mourning procession we rode directly behind the hearse.

That was a sad, a terrible procession. Sad for America, sad for the Philippines. The Filipinos lost a good friend in Franklin D. Roosevelt and no people mourned him more.

Truman will live in Philippine memory as the American president who signed the Proclamation of our Independence.

These American presidents have been the articulate exponents of freedom.

However strongly I disagree with Khrushchev I must admit that he is making Communist ideals articulate today. He is doing what the democracies are failing to do—he is giving voice.

The United Nations came into formal existence.

As Philippine delegate my visits to my home in Washington became briefer and more uncertain, and my sons were growing into men without the companionship I had looked forward to sharing with them. There was little time for the rich, personal family life that might have been ours.

I found myself being whipped through the air over three continents, always going somewhere, catching planes, trying to catch up on sleep. There was the signing of the Bretton Woods agreement for the Philippines, the UNRRA Conference in Atlantic City, the heading of the Philippine Delegation to the first session of the United Nations General Assembly in London in January and February, 1946, and all succeeding sessions.

It was between these sessions I suffered my temporary collapse. Shortly after my recovery I found myself facing the need to make an important decision that would mark a turning point in my life.

Midway in my forties this crisis rose and left me shaken with the knowledge that I had met with and by-passed my chance for national leadership and power.

Seventeen

A MESSAGE from President Osmeña in Manila, late in 1945, interrupted my already hectic life with the force of an earthquake.

A few more months and the Philippines would no longer be a commonwealth. It would be a republic, and the campaign for its presidency was already under way. Osmeña was up for election, and Osmeña the statesman and scholar was far too dignified to run for office in the usual sense of the word. He refused to campaign, refused to leave the Palace. If the people wanted him, he said, let them vote for him without fanfare. He would accept the nomination, but make no personal effort to win.

And so, Osmeña told me, because I was young as politicians go, because I had a war record, and because I was a speaker he wanted me to run with him as vice-president.

It was a decision I could not make alone. I called a family council. My oldest sons were young, but they were like men in their powers of judgment. They had been through war.

We knew this was a fork in the road. Whichever way I chose life would not be the same for any of us again.

Which way? To remain in America or return to the Philippines? Should I return to serve my country in national politics or remain in America and continue to serve it on an international scale? I was torn with indecision. I wanted to go back, to be home. We all longed to be home. My family understood. They gave their thoughts, their advice. Whatever choice was made had to be clear cut.

To serve nationally meant going back to grass roots, begin-

272

ning anew in the old and familiar, severing all the new outside ties, and living for and within the Philippines.

The Philippines was just starting out as a nation. It did not have men trained in foreign service that more seasoned nations have. The government had invested a great deal in me by placing me in Washington. I wanted to pay back that investment.

I studied the list of Filipinos prepared for foreign service. Modesty aside, not one had been trained as I had been for work abroad. I had been schooled by great men—Quezon, MacArthur, Osmeña. I had made important links for the Philippines in Washington and in international politics. There were friendships formed by years of exhausting travel; making speeches in America, Asia, Europe; serving in the United Nations. Backing me always had been the defense of Bataan and the fight to hold the Philippines. I had lived through much and the struggle had paid off in friendship and respect.

I knew I was not indispensable. Someone else could be trained to take my place. But whoever took over would need time, time in which to develop contacts and make friends in America. Beyond those of the war years I had the friendships formed long before, during my school days in America and just before World War II. For the development of friendship time is needed, and now time was of the essence.

There were more immediate considerations. We were engaged in fighting two important issues in the United States Congress—the Philippine Trade Act, which was to be the Magna Charta of Philippine economic life in our relations with America, and the Philippine Rehabilitation Act, upon which the rebuilding of the Philippines depended. These bills had been my responsibility since their beginning, and now, with our leaders occupied with the campaign in Manila, I was carrying on the fight.

If I dropped out the bills might be approved and passed, but I knew no one else who could get the advantages I could. The

Trade Act with its admittedly many faults would be faultier still.

There was another, personal, selfish consideration. My family had spent three-and-a-half years of war behind enemy lines. In Washington I could give them the comforts and schooling Manila could not provide. Manila was rebuilding out of the ruins, and I wanted to spare my wife and children the rigors of a reconstruction era.

I realized that if I chose the international road, I would have to pay the price one pays for being better known abroad than at home, perhaps being less honored in one's homeland, possibly have detractors who would take advantage of one's absence to misrepresent the person and his work. Such a choice would mean losing the closeness and trust of many tender ties.

I decided that all this would have to be risked. My friends in the Philippines would understand in time what it was I had to do. Posterity must give the final verdict. So we reached our decision.

It hurt to turn Osmeña down. The Philippines had need of such a man and I knew I could assist in his campaign. I owed him so much, and above all, gratitude. He had made me Resident Commissioner. The good living my family enjoyed was due to him. But I was sincerely convinced, and my sons agreed, that I could give my best value to my country on a world-wide scale. Osmeña would have to run for the presidency without me.

It was with reluctance that I came to this decision, for the temptation was great to return where I belonged, to rear my family there, and enjoy the love and prestige I could know as vice-president of the Philippines.

No sooner was the decision made than temptation reared from another corner. Another decision had to be made at once—would they never end for me?

This time the challenge came from Roxas. He had decided to run for the presidency against Osmeña.

Osmeña was standing firm in his refusal to campaign. He

still would not leave Malacañang or make any effort to insure his continuance as president. Roxas was certain of victory; I could win along with him, if I chose. He sent a personal emissary to Washington to convey this message. Then he called me over trans-Pacific telephone.

This was temptation of a kind to match Osmeña's offer. In Osmeña's case I had been pretty certain, judging by reports given me, that his refusal to campaign was going to cost him the presidency but that I could be sure of my own election as vice-president.

Again I was promised certain victory. Roxas and I, running together, would sweep the Philippines. Osmeña's followers were the old and established and settled in mind. Roxas and I had behind us the youth of the Philippines. We were sure to win.

And still I turned Roxas down. I was frank with him. I told him I would be a cad indeed if after all Osmeña had done for me I refused Osmeña's offer and accepted his.

So much for history.

If I had run with Osmeña, even if he had lost, I was told I would have won the vice-presidency. So even if Roxas won, I would still have been vice-president. Roxas did win and in two more brief years he was dead; I would have been head of state of my country. Either way, I could have been president of the Philippines.

I was held back by loyalties. This was my shining opportunity and I turned it down. It was my closest brush with power.

I am happy that I made the decision that I made. I had a duty as a Filipino to fulfill in Washington, and I did not fail in that. Can there be greater satisfaction for any man?

On July 4, 1946, on the Luneta in Manila, with my family around me, I watched the swearing in of Manuel Roxas as the first president of the independent Republic of the Philippines. It was a day for which we Filipinos had been waiting for almost fifty years; for which I had waited my entire lifetime.

Hope rode high over that vast gathering, so many of whom were in mourning. Their sons had died beside America's sons, for democracy, and this day was their posthumous award. This was freedom, men and women told one another, wiping away tears. Better a crust of bread at one's own board than a feast at another's table.

Recently in New York at a great fair devoted to world trade I saw an entire floor given over to produce from a thriving Japan, while a single small booth held all the Philippines had to offer. Everywhere in America new Japanese stores and restaurants are doing a brisk business. Japanese products are in every American store. When I see Japanese trade being nourished and reactivated in America while the Philippines has to fight for everything it gets from this country can I be blamed for indulging in bitterness?

There was no bitterness in Filipino hearts that day in 1946. We are a happy, hopeful, cheerful people, quick to anger, quick to believe in the best. We hoped for the best on that July morning, in the heart of our ruined city where so many were bereaved, maimed, or malnourished. We were a poor people and had suffered much, but our dreams were strong within us and our faith was high.

Love and hope for my country was strong within me, and remembered too was a touching farewell from America spoken by Speaker Sam Rayburn and engraved in a silver plaque now among my cherished possessions in my "Kasiyahan" home in Manila:

To Brigadier General Carlos P. Romulo, Resident Commissioner of the Philippines to the United States ... worthy spokesman of a heroic people. ... You leave with us ... the memory of your matchless eloquence ... the example of your sterling character, the inspiration of your unswerving devotion to your country's cause ... you take with you ... our friendship and that of our people ... and the admiration of your colleagues of the Seventy Ninth Congress ... House of Representatives.

I had brought home with me the Philippine Trade Act and the Rehabilitation Act, which had at last been adopted by Congress. I had given years of effort to their winning, and considered them, with all their inadequacies, hard-won victories for my people. It had never occurred to me that they would serve to nourish my detractors. Whatever I did was not enough. Whatever I hoped to do was discredited in advance.

For I found I had returned to the love of thousands but the envy of the few. These last were eloquent and vociferous and I had to face calumny and backbiting that was nonetheless bitter because it was undeserved. I had given the best I had for my country.

Some who sneered at my efforts were men who during the war had openly sided with Japan. Others may have been Communists, I really do not know. They had large mouths and bitter tongues and were the first to heap upon me the sneering charges that I was pro-American, as if, in a postwar world, to retain any admiration or faith in America was a form of betrayal. Falsehoods were spread such as the downright lie that I had applied for American citizenship.

I had long before learned to bear hurt. I could have accepted any sort of attack in any other country. But this was my birthland, and these were my people who were attacking me. Just the same I still feel close to them and I bear them no ill will.

I had to remember that in other lands, such as America, many who were in the public eye were wounded by scorn in their day. Wilson, Lincoln, Roosevelt had suffered. I am far from what they were; I am only my country's envoy abroad. Such arrows may leave their poison in the heart, but they are only of today. And:

> Beyond the shadows is tomorrow's wisdom,
> Today is going to be long, long ago.

Now that Roxas was president the horizon of my world widened. I was no longer Commissioner; my new appointment

fulfilled a dream begun on Bataan. It carried out a promise made
me long before by Roxas.

The appointment came about in a curious way. After his
election to the presidency and before taking office Roxas had
paid a visit to the United States. A suspicion was started by his
enemies in the Philippines and fostered in Washington that he
had served as a collaborator under the Japanese. This was untrue; he had, as a matter of fact, feigned illness to prevent their
enlisting his services. Before his arrival his close friend and
press relations officer, Julius Edlestein, had done a good job
of helping to thaw the frosty point of view in Washington.
Edlestein, formerly of the United States Naval Reserve and
Paul V. McNutt's naval aide and press attaché, was devoted to
Roxas, whom he had known when as a reporter for the *United
Press* he had covered the Osrox Mission in Washington. Apparently the way was smoothed for a good reception for Roxas.

One congressman, however, Karl Stefan of Nebraska, remained unconvinced. He announced his intention of making a
speech on the floor of the House in which he would "expose"
Roxas as a wartime collaborator.

As Resident Commissioner I thought it my duty to protest.
I called on the Congressman and pleaded with him not to make
the speech. I told him I had been on Corregidor with Roxas,
and that if Roxas had stayed in the Philippines instead of escap-
ing with Quezon and Osmeña when the chance was given him
it was because he had hoped to help protect his people.

"You know me," I said, "you have faith in my word. I beg
you not to make such a charge."

He agreed not to make the speech.

When Roxas arrived in Washington I did not mention the
matter to him. His attitude toward me was a little reserved because I had turned down his offer to run as his vice-president.
As we drove from the airport to Blair House he seemed to have
something on his mind.

"Carlitos, I will be very frank," he said suddenly. "I would like to make you our Ambassador in Washington, but I can't because I have promised it to a friend. However, I am going to make you our permanent delegate to the United Nations."

No other appointment could have meant so much to me. It was possible Roxas did not share my faith in the United Nations and that he thought he was offering me second or third best in the way of appointment. But I left Blair House a proud and happy man. One reason I had hesitated in returning to the Philippines was because I had wanted to see what the United Nations was going to do about settling the equilibrium of a troubled world. I had dreamed of it, hoped for it, and believed in it. To actually find myself a permanent part of it was an answer to my most heartfelt prayer.

Obviously Roxas had no inkling of the way I felt. He was actually apologizing for not offering me the ambassadorship.

Before Roxas left, I gave a reception in his honor, and as we stood side by side in the receiving line Congressman Stefan shook Roxas' hand and to my surprise said, "Mr. President, I want you to know I planned to attack you. I was ready to speak against you on the floor, but your Resident Commissioner persuaded me not to."

Roxas turned to me. "Why didn't you tell me?"

I answered, "I felt it was part of my job."

Later in the evening he sought out the Congressman, asked about the nature of the attack and why he had felt that way, and wound up by asking him for a copy of the speech that had never been delivered.

The day Roxas left Blair House he put his arm over my shoulder. "Carlitos, I have been unfair. I thought because you were not with us in Manila you have been against those of us who stayed. I'm keeping this copy of the speech because it will remind me not to pass judgment."

I was glad he had not received the copy before he informed me of his plan to appoint me to the United Nations!

Sometime later, during one of my visits to Manila, he told

me the rest of the story. When he told the directorate of his party that he would appoint me permanent delegate to the United Nations one of the Senators in his group, still resentful because I had refused to run with Roxas, expressed wholehearted approval.

"Good!" he said. "Put Romulo in the United Nations, he can't do anything there."

In other words I was being "kicked upstairs."

My critic was not alone in regarding the United Nations as a futile dream. From its inception it had its enemies. They did not seem to realize their enmity would help to weaken the world's hopes for a lasting peace. And what could one Filipino do in a world organization composed of big and small nations, with the Philippines a fledgling just beginning to test its wings?

Eighteen

THERE came the January morning when I awoke to the fact that this was another birthday and I was fifty years old. For some reason this surprised but did not shock me. I suppose I knew it must happen all along. But I had been accustomed to thinking of myself as one of the young men of the Philippines. So I was startled to find myself fifty, which is the halfway mark for any life.

It is the time when I assume the average man must take pause, evaluate his past, and make plans for a lessening future; a time to give thanks for achievements, and regrets for opportunities missed.

I had time for none of this. My days were crammed with activities, and the fact that I was fifty only served to promise a more fulsome day. There was no time to look on more than the recent past, in which much had been happening to me that would have sufficed for any ordinary lifetime. Actually I felt no older than at forty or thirty and, on occasion, twenty!

There was no time for vain regrets.

Lurking in mind, perhaps, was a memory that nagged: At this time I would have been president of the Philippines if I had accepted Osmeña's offer or Roxas' to run for the vice-presidency. It had come so close, that brush with power.

Many had told me what a fool I had been to turn down that chance. I had done what I thought was right. Still the thought stayed in my mind, and if ever I had regretted any act of my public life, it would have been that.

And still, if I had accepted that opportunity and been pres-

281

ident of the Philippines I would never have arrived at the place where I found myself on this overworked, overcrowded, and thoroughly satisfactory fiftieth birthday.

I was President of the General Assembly of the United Nations.

As President I would have served my country within the Philippines, and I pray served it well.

As president of the fourth General Assembly of the United Nations I was serving my country on an international scale. I had helped to make the Philippines recognized and respected by all the world. I was the first Asian in the United Nations to represent Asia on the rostrum as president of the Assembly.

I believe with Emerson that there is a law of compensation. I gave way before the greatest chance ever offered me, and won more than ever I had dared hope for. And I had hoped, since my student days, to serve my country as I was serving it now.

What time did I have to think about growing old? An active man is timeless. There were indications that I was not eternally destined for this earth, but I was too busy to notice them. A nap snatched in any free five minutes, a game of ping-pong, a relaxing chat over coffee or cocktails with the family or a circle of friends, and I was again youthful and filled with hope.

Many consider the fifties the nearing of the end of the road. For me they were the beginning of the most exciting period of my life. They would be crammed with excitement and wonder and accomplishment and with tragedy. They launched me into what I consider my true career. Of the decades I have lived, the fifties were the most hard-working and the years in which I take my greatest pride.

These crowded fifties would be spent serving in turn as Chief of the Philippine Mission to the United Nations under Presidents Manuel Roxas and Elpidio Quirino, as Secretary of Foreign Affairs, as Ambassador from the Philippines to the United States, and, under President Ramón Magsaysay, as Special Personal Envoy to the United States, with the rank

of Ambassador Extraordinary and Plenipotentiary, as chief
delegate to the Afro-Asian Conference in Bandung, and as Philippine representative to the United Nations Security Council
and twice its president. During these years I served as Ambassador under Presidents Quirino, Magsaysay, and Garcia, and
during the Garcia administration was concurrently Philippine
Ambassador to Brazil and Cuba.

I do not know how many thousands of miles I traveled in this
decade. Titles, decorations, degrees, and the honors heaped on
my astonished and grateful head confused me. Our social life,
Virginia's and mine, had ranged far from the carnival ball where
we had been a gay, young, untroubled queen and consort. We
built our new home in Manila in 1950, the dream home we had
always wanted—we call it "Kasiyahan," which is the Tagalog
word for contentment—but found little time for enjoying it.

Perhaps someday I shall have time to pause and look back
over those wonderful fifties and sort out the events of most
importance to the world and to me.

The presidency of the United Nations was not thrust upon
me overnight. I had to grow up to the measurements it demanded of a proponent of peace. This was done session by session, step by step. It entailed trips halfway around the world,
again and again. It demanded nights without sleep, studying,
writing, poring over documents; days without rest; and always
the curb on the temper and the willingness to give and to receive.

I was like a juggler spinning a dozen plates in the air at once,
with each plate in need of extra caution and a careful eye.

For example, I look back to the year 1948 as one crowded
with projects and responsibilities. Everything I was trying to
do seemed almost impossible. New ideas and projects kept
coming along, piling one on another.

The World Freedom of Information Conference was one of
my ideas. I tried to work up interest in this plan to open channels of information for peoples all over the world so that a fair

press coverage would be given to all. At first no one would discuss it with me. We proposed it for the first time in London in 1946.

After two years of struggle the idea seemed to take fire everywhere at once. Once launched, it was received with enthusiasm, and even nations that were not members of the United Nations attended when the conference was held in Geneva in 1948.

Instead of the fifty members of the United Nations, sixty-four nations gathered. Outstanding Americans came as members of the American delegation, among them Oveta Hobby and Erwin Canham. Their chairman was Assistant Secretary of State William Benton, who was to become chairman of the board of *The Encyclopaedia Britannica*.

The fight for the presidency was three-cornered. My rivals were Sir Ramaswami Mudaliar of India and Dr. G. J. van Heuven Goedhart of the Netherlands. (Goedhart later won the Nobel Prize for his work among refugees.) We were all three good friends.

On the day of election there was a lot of good-natured kidding among us. "Have you prepared your inaugural address?" we asked one another, and of course we all had.

I was elected by the sixty-four nations, and appointed both my rivals chairmen of important committees.

In that conference we saw Russian diplomacy at its keenest. There was no virulence, as in San Francisco and London and Paris. This was one of their peace offensives, and it proved that if they felt the occasion required finesse they could pour on the charm.

France, all the Latin-American delegates, and the delegates of the small nations were insistent upon the right of correction. This, I believe, was instigated to protect themselves against what they believed were injustices committed by some members of the American press. Certain American magazines and newspapers, it was charged, were given to printing scurrilous attacks calculated to make a foreign people appear sinister or ridiculous and objections or corrections were never heeded. The idea projected was to make a covenant, giving the right to demand correction after publication. Such a proviso was considered by the United States as an abridgement of the freedom of the press.

Peoples of small and backward nations are still sometimes held up to ridicule and scorn by the power press. But although the idea was not approved, it was projected, and that very fact served to show the need for a curb against unbridled angling of news.

Also in 1948 the third regular session of the General Assembly was held in Paris, and I found myself elected chairman of the Ad Hoc Political and Security Committee. Abba Eban, a fine and brilliant man, was the able representative of Israel. Certain Arab delegates tried several times to prevent him from taking the floor, and I protected him with all the rules of procedure. He came to me later and said he wanted to thank me for the impartiality I had shown.

He added, "I want to assure you that if you run for the presidency of the General Assembly you will have my vote."

I did run, he did give me his vote, and so did the Arab delegates!

The project for the partitioning of Israel came up when I was in New York the year before. The problem of Israel was of major importance and had to be submitted to the highest authority.

I asked for instructions from President Roxas.

Because a great deal has been written and conjectured as to the role played by my country in the partitioning of Israel, I would like to tell here for the first time what actually happened.

Roxas told me he felt that the partitioning would mean potential danger to the peace of the world. He said, "I'm afraid the Arabs will never accept it. It will cause friction in the Middle East and also establish a dangerous precedent."

He cited a similar situation that had come up in the Philippines. Congressman Robert Low Bacon had presented a bill in
the United States Congress to segregate the island of Mindanao
from the rest of the Philippines. In Mindanao we have our
Moslem population, about 750,000 of them, if not more. They
are called Moros. They were never conquered either by the
Spaniards or by the Americans. Some Americans had the mis-
taken idea that the Moros were against Philippine independence. The Bacon bill was finally squashed, but only after it had
caused a great deal of resentment.

I discussed this thoroughly with Roxas in Manila, and, after
learning that the Israel problem would come up before the
United Nations at Lake Success, I discussed it with him again
over transoceanic telephone. He decided I was to vote against
the partitioning.

In New York I wrote a speech detailing my specific instructions. I telephoned Roxas again and read the speech to him. He
said it was fine, but why hadn't I used the Bacon bill by way of
an analogy? I had forgotten to put it in.

I promised to make the correction and call him back in a couple of days.

During that time I heard from Jewish friends who had
learned the Philippines was planning to oppose the partitioning.

I called Roxas again and told him of the pressure put upon me
by friends, some of whom were very insistent that we change
our position. I said, "I want you to know of this."

But Roxas said I should maintain the position as he had explained it to me. Then I read the corrected speech and he approved it.

"Fine," he said heartily, "deliver it just as it is."

This was just before the conference of the Commission on
Human Rights in Geneva. The Philippines was a member of
the Commission. I had asked for permission to leave the General
Assembly and go to Geneva. In the morning of the day we were

to sail I made the speech at Lake Success, explaining why the Philippines would vote against Israel.

Several hours after that we went aboard the *Queen Mary*. In my party were my wife and I; our son Bobby; my secretary, Anne Dragon; my aide, Lieutenant Teofilo Benitez; and Major Salvador Lopez, my political adviser. Major Lopez was with me on Corregidor; a profound thinker and writer, he had earlier been a columnist on my newspaper, the *Herald*.

Also on board was Mrs. Eleanor Roosevelt, who was to serve as chairman on the Commission; Charles Malik, representative of Lebanon for the Commission; and Jan Masaryk of Czechoslovakia.

The next morning an overseas call summoned me to the radio room, and there I spent the rest of the morning receiving messages on my stand against the division of Israel.

The first telephone call was from Congressman Sol Bloom, Chairman of the House Foreign Affairs Committee and my good friend. We had worked closely together in San Francisco. He was also a friend of President Roxas and of the Philippines. Bloom protested the speech on Israel.

"Is there no way of changing the stand you have taken?" he pleaded.

It was difficult to refuse this friend, but I frankly explained that I had acted under specific instructions from Roxas and he was the only one who could change the decision. Bloom understood.

Other Jewish friends telephoned and I explained to all as I had to Bloom that the Philippines had the greatest respect for the Jews, but that this was the position we thought best.

It is strange to remember that while I have many Arab as well as Jewish friends no word of advice or approval came from any Arab. Nor did any member of the Senate exert pressure. No politically influential Americans tried to influence me either way. Charges that I was directly approached via Washington are untrue.

There were two Jewish parties, for and against Israel, and I had friends on both sides. To all I laid my cards face up, explaining again and again that anti-partitioning was my stand and why it had to be so. President Roxas had given me my instructions; I was but a voice.

A fine restful sea journey this was turning out to be!

I have read fantastic "true" accounts of what happened next. One writer has asserted in a book that the "Jewish bloc" brought pressure to bear against me and threatened me with dire curtailment of any further American aid to the Philippines if I did not yield. This is sheer nonsense. I repeat, I was under no pressure from any official source, with the exception of Sol Bloom, and his was on a purely personal basis.

Actually I have no idea what happened while I was on the high seas, but an unexpected radiogram came from President Roxas, saying that for the sake of our higher national interests he was giving instructions to our Philippine delegate at Lake Success to vote in favor of the partitioning. Roxas hoped I would understand the situation and realize that his reversal of policy was dictated only by his desire to serve our people best.

I felt this public reversal of a stand I had taken was a slight. My pride was stung. I wired Roxas my resignation from the United Nations.

In my wire I stated that having made the speech he had approved and then having had my vote reversed made me feel I had lost his confidence and I was therefore resigning. I said I would continue to serve on the Commission on Human Rights if he wished, but not as permanent delegate to the United Nations.

His answer was a three-page telegram. Roxas hastened to explain that he had done what he thought was best for the Philippines, that his confidence in me was steadfast, his respect for me was what it had always been, and he asked me not to resign.

I withdrew my resignation.

No further explanation was given me nor did I ask what actually took place in Washington and Manila.

What happened I am sure is this: Some of Roxas' good friends informed him or our Ambassador in Washington of the resentment in New York and Washington over the Philippine attitude on the partitioning of Israel. Because of these friendships reappraisal was made. I had made up my mind to do what our president thought was right. Then my alternate delegate was told to change and our position was changed. That was all there was to it.

After the General Assembly and the United Nations had decided upon such a partitioning Israel became a separate nation, a creation of the United Nations. We, its members, were in duty bound to support it, otherwise of what use is the United Nations?

But as to the way it actually happened, I shall probably never know. I did not question President Roxas or anyone else. This particular chapter in history had been exceedingly unpleasant to me and the chapter was closed.

All in all, the year 1948 was for me a year to remember.

So we come to 1949, my fiftieth year and the peak of my diplomatic life.

All I had done in that half-century seemed to merge and grow in purpose during this year. I had been teacher, reporter, editor, publisher, soldier, lecturer, writer, and diplomat. All branches had run together into diplomacy. Nothing had been wasted. I have used it all.

The big moment of this year and of my life found me perched atop the New York telephone books so that I might see and be seen from my perch in the president's chair of the United Nations. This is one change in my destiny that did not come as a total surprise. I had planned and hoped for it.

It had been a long, difficult journey to that chair. It had been bitterly contested all the way by the Russian delegates, headed by my arch antagonist Andrei Vishinsky. The Russians had shown their hatred of America, and of the Philippines for its friendship with America, when the United Nations was first projected in San Francisco. Foreign Minister Molotov had protested my presence there as a representative of a still not fully independent nation.

The way had led from California to Lake Success, to London, Paris, and Geneva, and back to New York, and the Russians never ceased their sniping.

Molotov, Vishinsky, Gromyko, Kutznetsov were to single me out in turn. They were skillful antagonists.

The Russians never had an abler debater than Vishinsky. He was razor-keen. Our debates at the Palais de Chaillot in Paris were vitriolic. I turned the other cheek, and then delivered my wallop.

One day during the conference when we were arguing the Soviet-sponsored proposal to abolish the United Nations Balkan Commission I was mad clear through at the insolence of this proposal. The Communists were infiltrating Greece and hoping to foment civil war there to make it another prisoner country.

When Vishinsky said the Balkan Commission was interfering in the domestic affairs of Greece and should be abolished, I was furious. I was one of the sponsors of the Balkan Commission. His proposal showed once again only too clearly the brazen treachery of the Soviets, and no one knew better than I by this time how treacherous they were. So, on the night before the resolution was to come up, we, the sponsors of the Commission, held a caucus and decided on the list of our speakers. It was agreed I was to be the first speaker.

The Russians kept trying to interrupt me, but President Spaak of Belgium, who was presiding, paid no attention to them.

The instant I stopped, Vishinsky was on his feet. His face was red and rage churned in his words. He began without preamble and without waiting for the chair to recognize him: "This small man Romulo with the big voice who spreads noise wherever he goes . . . who represents an insignificant country like the Philippines and dares attack Russia . . . he reminds me of a Russian proverb . . . his ambition is worth a ruble while his ammunition is only worth a cent."

I was thinking if I answer bitterness with bitterness I will win support for him. But if I answer in a humble manner I will get sympathy for my side. Best to make a joke of this, for no bombast can survive under ridicule.

So when Vishinsky paused for breath I was on my feet. "Mr. President?" I was very meek.

Spaak recognized me with a twinkle in his eye, and as I made my way to the podium I felt the stillness of the audience.

"Mr. President," I began, still meekly, "since boyhood I have known the story of David and Goliath. We have been treated to his usual personal vitriolics by the distinguished Foreign Minister of Soviet Russia, Mr. Vishinsky. As I know none of us in the Assembly are interested in personalities I am not concerned with his personal references, because in this august assemblage we are not present as persons but as representatives of governments. But, Mr. President, I am concerned with what has been said about my country, because while my country occupies what may be only a humble place in the United Nations I believe it to be a place of honor."

At this point I was interrupted by applause from many of my fellow delegates. I paused, and looked hard at Vishinsky.

"And I would like to remind Mr. Vishinsky," I went on, "that we—the small Davids—are here to fling our pebbles of truth between the eyes of all the blustering Goliaths and make them behave!"

I chanced to glance at Spaak. He was grinning from ear to ear.

I added, "And as to my ambition being worth a ruble while my ammunition is worth only a cent, may I also remind Mr. Vishinsky that with the present rate of exchange the cent is worth more than the ruble?"

From that time on Mr. Vishinsky never opened his mouth in

the United Nations against the "insignificant" nations nor against me.

The Balkan Commission was given a vote of confidence and it continued. But the icy, inhuman Russian ruthlessness in the United Nations did not lessen. A book could be written on their attempts to sabotage efforts made in behalf of the freedom and peace of the world.

There was the time when the Philippines was fighting for a seat in the Security Council. Thirty-six ballots had to be taken and the Philippines, although always in the lead, could not muster the two-thirds majority needed to elect. A gentlemen's agreement was arrived at that we would draw lots. Vassili Kutznetsov, Deputy Foreign Minister and chairman of the delegation of Soviet Russia, meeting with me in the delegates' lounge, agreed on the compact and said it would be respected. We drew lots in the presence of President José Maza, with the Russian delegates present. The opponent of the Philippines, Yugoslavia, was the lucky one. Yugoslavia was to serve the first year, the Philippines the second year.

Then, when the first year was about to end, Russia denied the agreement and put up Czechoslovakia as a candidate.

Until then the angriest I had ever been was when I stood on the balcony of the *Herald* building and watched the Japanese planes drop their first bombs on Manila. But this was my maddest hour. We won overwhelmingly against Czechoslovakia. I was appointed the Philippine representative in the Security Council.

In Paris, as chairman of the Ad Hoc Political and Security Committee, I appointed a subcommittee to study the admission of Ceylon. The representative of the Russian group agreed to this and signed the report. But when the report was submitted to the full committee the following day he refused to vote in favor of the report.

"Yes," he said, "I signed it, but I now withdraw my signature."

I was president of the Security Council in January, 1958, when the Kashmir question came up. This was the long-standing quarrel between India and Pakistan. Krishna Menon, representing India, opened his talk by stating that since there were new members of the Security Council he thought they should be given more time to study the subject of Kashmir before taking it up.

In the belief that this was launched against me, I lost no time in setting him straight. I have always believed in preparedness and I always try to prime myself with the facts well in advance.

In the United Nations I did not want to be confused on points of order. At Geneva, before the world press conference opened, I learned the rules and how to apply them and was able to make the Russians toe the line.

As president of the Security Council I actually made the Russians admit I was fair.

Then I became president of the fourth Assembly.

I had no doubts of my election. We had canvassed all the different nations and had the support of an overwhelming majority of the chief delegates. All were for me except the satellite countries.

My name was read, and while I had expected it the thrill was there. Now I would have no more regrets over having sacrificed the presidency of the Philippines. The representative of a small country was being led up by the Chief of Protocol to take his place on the rostrum, and I was that man, the first Asian to head the General Assembly.

As I took my seat in the president's chair I realized my small stature precluded my seeing or being seen; no time to think of that.

I shook hands with the outgoing president, Herbert Evatt of Australia; I made my address, and then declared the meeting open.

In that moment my mind went back to the days in San Francisco before the signing of the Charter, when Stettinius had asked for concord and harmony and did not want me to press for an opening prayer because the Russians were against it. Was there no room at the peace table, I had asked then, for the Prince of Peace? After the Charter was signed, I had said that the hand of the Man of Galilee was in the finished work.

The Russians had fought strenuously against a minute of prayer in 1947. They succeeded in amending our proposal by adding "or meditation," so that the rule as finally adopted reads as follows: "At the opening day of each General Assembly there shall be a minute of silence for prayer or meditation."

I remembered this as I sat for the first time in the president's chair of the General Assembly. Here was my opportunity.

After my inaugural address I concluded: "Let us *pray* the Almighty to give us the vision and the courage to face our awesome responsibilities."

And I banged the gavel for the minute of silence. There was no need to ask that it be spent in prayer. All understood.

In that minute I asked for enlightenment and others there asked, "each in his own tongue."

So, after a two-year struggle I was able to circumvent the Russians' veto against God.

I do not know if the Russian delegates meditated but I know I prayed, and I hope all of those who voted for me prayed.

The meeting then opened and Vishinsky was first to take the floor. As usual he began inveighing against the United States for the nonadmittance of Red China. I called him to order, but he went right on talking as was his wont in the past. I ordered the interpreter to stop working. Vishinsky kept talking. He ignored my gavel completely; I was no authority in his eyes.

But I was president. The loud speaker is connected to the president's table. I grabbed the wire connected to his microphone and gave it a yank. When he saw he was talking into a dead mike he stopped and sat down.

That was my first act of decision as president. I stopped Mr. Vishinsky in mid-air on my first day in the chair.

The score was more than evened on my second day as president. There had been complaints that I could not be seen by the delegates below the podium, so it was then the New York telephone books were given me to sit on. Perched on this eminence I heard Vishinsky make his chilling announcement that Russia had the atom bomb.

It came as a complete shock to me and to all of us present, apart from the Russian delegation. It had been my creed since working in the United Nations to watch for the spark of humanity in each man. I looked on Vishinsky's arrogant, intelligent face, as cold and pure as reason it seemed to me, and wondered, where was the spark in him, then?

Russia should rear monuments to the Rosenburgs and Fuchs —the traitors who presented them with America's atom bomb.

I persisted in hunting for the glimmer of humanity in the Russian delegates. Somewhere, dimmed by totalitarian concept, it had to be. It occurred to me that the Russians knew nothing of America, living as they did their segregated lives between Lake Success and Glen Cove on Long Island. I recalled having heard that all Russians respond to music.

I went before the Metropolitan Opera Guild. A good friend of mine, Mrs. Francis Paine, made the arrangements for me. The guardian angel of the Metropolitan Opera is Mrs. August Belmont, a great lady and a true American.

"I know you hate the Communist Russians, and I hate them too," I said, "but why not try to soften their hearts with music? Cannot some of you invite a few members of the Soviet delegation to the opera, because, even if they could afford them, they couldn't get tickets, since your performances are always sold out in advance?"

Under Mrs. Belmont's leadership, the Metropolitan Opera Guild responded with enthusiasm. They not only invited the Russian delegates to share their boxes at the opera, but invited them to dinner at their homes, along with many other delegates to the United Nations. I was given the Diamond Horseshoe box. The performance was dedicated to the United Nations, and this practice has been followed every opera season since then.

At the United Nations I spoke to Mr. Vishinsky. "Do you like opera?" I asked.

"There is nothing I like better."

This, through an interpreter. I told him I wanted him to be my guest at the Metropolitan. He accepted the invitation.

On the morning of the date set I was presiding over the General Assembly when a note was handed me. Mr. Vishinsky was cancelling his engagement for that night. I called one of my fourteen vice-presidents to the chair and went to my office to telephone Vishinsky's secretary.

"Mr. Vishinsky believes it is too much of an imposition, as he must have four bodyguards," was the explanation. "That will be too many for your box."

"That can be arranged," I said. "And now, please tell me the real reason."

The truth was that the Shah of Iran was in New York. If he was to be present in the opera house that night the national anthem of Iran might be played. Mr. Vishinsky did not want to embarrass me by refusing to stand up.

"Absurd!" I said loudly. "That cannot happen, as I have the presidential box. Now no more excuses, please."

There were no more. Vishinsky entered my box that night bringing only two guards to stand at attention at the door.

No sooner did the opening notes of La Boheme begin than a humming sounded at my ear. Vishinsky, at my side, knew every note of the opera and sang it through along with the performers.

At the end of the first act my wife turned to him. "You love music, don't you?"

He smiled. He actually smiled. Then he leaned over to her and whispered, "Don't tell anyone, but I play the violin."

At that time it was impossible to get tickets to South Pacific. I was godfather to Ezio Pinza's grandson, the firstborn of his daughter, Claudia, and I am a friend also of Mary Martin's. I gave a reception and ball at the Waldorf in honor of the delegations to the General Assembly and invited these two great artists. They went through the highlights of their *South Pacific* repertoire. Among my guests were Vishinsky and his group and the delegates of all his satellite countries. They all came; there was no question of not accepting this time. When the songs ended they all turned to me, "How can we get tickets to this wonderful show? We want to bring some of our friends."

As Van Cliburn has shown us, there is a democracy of music. I was beginning to see Vishinsky as less of an enemy and more of a fellow human.

In the General Assembly we were discussing a resolution sponsored by the United States, but amended in the committee by Soviet Russia. Warren Austin, Ambassador from the United States to the United Nations and chief delegate, was supposed to be the first speaker and came to my office to verify the fact. The Russian Assistant Secretary General was with me. I told Austin I was very sorry but Vishinsky had already registered as the first speaker.

Senator Austin became excited. "But I am the first speaker."

"Vishinsky has signed in before you," I told him. "Much as I would like to give you first place I must be fair."

Austin was furious. "As chief delegate of the United States I demand the right to speak first."

In a low voice I told him, "Please, don't make me tell you what I am thinking, Senator."

"What is that?"

"Go to . . ." I did not continue.

I marched out of the office and to the General Assembly, where I opened the meeting and announced the resolution and the first speaker, the representative of the Soviet Union.

After the meeting Vishinsky came to my office. The Russian Assistant Secretary General had told him all. "I think you are a fair man," he said, and we shook hands.

But I explained firmly, "Don't think there was anything un-usual in what I did! When I was elected president I determined to be fair to everybody."

Then Austin came in. Gallantly, he apologized to me. I apologized to him for my rudeness and curt retort. I regretted the incident all the more because I had real affection for the Ambassador. Senator Austin was a worthy representative of the United States. He won the respect and admiration of the delegates. He was studious, fair, and a perfect gentleman. His record in the United Nations is one of which every American can be proud. He was loved and admired because of his humility and because he was always genial and openhearted. I recall distinctly when he resigned there was an expression of keen regret in the United Nations, because everyone knew he left a void that was not easy to fill. He was truly a great statesman.

Before the ending of the Assembly Russia introduced a resolution on Greece, which brought forth a series of tirades from various sources. I asked Vishinsky to my office after the meeting and begged him to withdraw the resolution. I had been told that a Russian resolution once offered would never be withdrawn.

He said he was sorry but he could not. Then he said that he would have to let me know.

I knew what that meant. He would have to communicate with Moscow. I was amazed when word was sent to me that he had come to a decision; he would withdraw the resolution. It was the first crack in the stone façade.

When the Assembly ended and we were breaking up Vishinsky put his arm over my shoulder and said, "I did what I had to do."

Yes, the spark *was* there.

But while my heart warmed to Vishinsky, the man, my mind could not see clearly through the intent behind him. Backing the Russian delegates to the United Nations was a power I feared and could not understand. I had good reason to fear the government they served. I had seen the lethal Communist machine at work in the Philippines and in America.

When Secretary-General Trygve Lie had to leave the United Nations it was decided by unanimous vote of the Eisenhower cabinet that I should be nominated in his place. I was therefore nominated by United States Delegate Lodge.

The Russian veto defeated me. Vishinsky said no matter how often my name was submitted to the Council he had his orders from Moscow to vote me down. The United States could not win over the Russian veto.

Dag Hammarskjöld was nominated instead, and elected. It was an excellent choice, as subsequent events happily proved. Hammarskjöld, in his unobtrusive way, has given the office of Secretary-General both dignity and effectiveness. He is a diplomat of the first water and he has shown it time and again when he had to untangle the most delicate and complicated international problems.

"I did what I had to do," Vishinsky had told me.

I had no quarrel with the Russians as men. But when they spoke for Moscow, they were no longer men but robots. Vishinsky did everything he could, with the great power given him, to sabotage the work of the United Nations.

He did all he could to win me, as an Asian, over to the Party line. While I was president of the United Nations he invited me three times to dine with him, and twice I talked with him alone, through an interpreter. He urged the uniting of the smaller nations to take steps against the larger "tyrant nations." It was effective argument to the uninitiated.

"Who is encircling whom?" he demanded. "America has bases all around the world. The Americans are trying to encircle Russia because they are afraid of us."

"But Russia has been swallowing up the smaller nations," I argued.

And in an instant I saw the cold, aggressor face of Russia. "If we want to swallow, the American bases will not deter us," Vishinsky boasted.

Russia has had no debater in the United Nations of Vishinsky's stature since his death. Khrushchev and Vishinsky were cut from the same mold, clever and sly and capable of every kind of trickery. Mark the craftiness of Khrushchev when he rages, "Feudalism had to give way to capitalism and capitalism must give way to communism."

When the Russians speak of capitalism they do not mean the capitalism that progresses and develops for all. They use it as another term for feudalism, and in applying that word to America they lie.

I believe nothing served to make communism more respected all over the world than the red-carpeted visit of Khrushchev to the United States, followed by the insulting reception of President Eisenhower at the Summit. Some of the uncommitted countries, seeing the American reception given the Russian leader, probably regarded it as an indication of a sudden leap to power, and may have thought that there was nothing left to do but clamber aboard the Russian band wagon. I am always in favor of step-by-step cultural exchanges, but Mr. Khrushchev's sudden leap upward into American acclaim was a great Russian victory.

However, the Summit debacle and the scenes in Tokyo protesting the American President's visit served to point up the honest esteem the Filipinos showed President Eisenhower when he visited Manila. It was gratifying to me because it showed that everything I have said about my people being loyal not fair-weather friends of America is true.

Among the lessons learned in my lifetime is the ease with which corruption can enter high places in the mask of friendship. Sometimes the recipient is not aware of the barbed hook under the gift; often he who gives may not know, but be the unwitting agent of a craftier mind.

When I was president of the General Assembly I gave some advice to an American friend who was representing a firm in a foreign country which was at the time not a member of the United Nations. The advice evidently worked, for one day he visited me at Walter Reed Hospital where I was confined. He came beaming with gratitude and brought a large check plus an offer of membership on the firm's board of trustees in token of its gratitude.

I told him I could not accept the check or the offer.

"But it's in token of our gratitude," he kept saying. "You didn't ask for it. We've done the same for . . . (And he named two political leaders, fellow countrymen of mine, both of whom I respect.) They accepted and they are members of the board."

"That may be," I told him, "but I am president of the General Assembly. If I take your gifts and if at any time in the future a question concerning your country comes up in the United Nations (as its application for membership later came up) and I take any stand in your favor the finger of suspicion would point at me and justly so."

In lighter vein let me say I did not mind in the least the merriment caused by my being obliged to preside over the United Nations seated upon the three telephone books. I deny the theory that men of small stature are overly ambitious. My lack of height has always been an asset to me and one of which I have taken scrupulous advantage. Lack of size is magnified in the common concept and I was always the little guy. Americans are almost always on the defensive side where the little guy is concerned. When I was a student debating with tall American students at Columbia the audiences wanted to see me win. When I was aide to General MacArthur his being so tall and I so short called forth a great deal of kidding, which we both enjoyed.

At Fort Worth, Texas, I found myself at a banquet table flanked by tall Texans. Someone called to the presiding officer, "Ask the General how he feels being among giants."

I answered, "Like a dime among nickels."

Still my height has given me a few embarrassing moments. A university was awarding honorary degrees to a half-dozen men, among them John Foster Dulles and myself. Mr. Dulles was ahead of me and put his cap on, which fitted him, and then the gown, which was as short as a smock. This surprised me, but there was no time to mention it as he was already going up the steps. I put on the gown next in line, which was obviously his— the hem hit the floor. There was no time to exchange, as by this time Dulles was on the platform. Clutching my clouds of glory around me, I went sweeping up after him. As I did I heard a voice behind me saying, "The General looks like the Archbishop of Canterbury."

Mr. Dulles watched me advance with a perplexed air. As I sat down he whispered, "I have a suspicion they've switched our gowns."

I whispered back, "Not a suspicion. A certainty."

But my favorite episode along these lines took place in Peoria, Illinois. In the lobby of my hotel I noticed a man with a newspaper keeping a sharp eye on me. I decided he was an FBI man watching me for security reasons; such things had happened before.

Suddenly he stepped before me. "Are you General Romulo?"

"Yes."

"You are the president of the United Nations?"

"I am."

"You were aide to General MacArthur?"

"Yes."

He looked me over from head to feet—it did not take long. His look held utter disbelief. Finally he said slowly, "Well I'll be goddamned!"

Several days after the adjournment of the General Assembly I received two radiograms, one from President Quirino and the other from Manuel de la Fuente, Mayor of Manila, both inviting me and my wife to return to the Philippines for a visit. I had accepted an invitation of the new Republic of Indonesia to be its official guest, and so I decided to stop in Manila on my way to Jakarta.

As our plane entered Philippine territory two squadrons of Philippine air force planes escorted us, on arrival thousands of our fellow countrymen gave us a tumultuous welcome at the airport, the city of Manila had a medal struck for me and awarded it to me at a mammoth banquet, and the Philippine Congress received me in a joint session. For the first time it approved a joint resolution by which I was awarded a Congressional Medal of Honor for "placing the Philippines on the international map and for constructive service to world peace." President Quirino during a state banquet at Malacañang Palace conferred on me—the first to receive it—the highest Philippine decoration, Rajah of the Order of Sikatuna, the same decoration given to President Eisenhower when he visited the Philippines in 1960.

But the most affectionate tribute I received was when I visited my home town, Camiling, to visit my parents' graves and I was greeted by one of the town policemen with, "Hey, Carlos, you haven't changed. Tell me," he said as he laughed heartily, "can you now multiply seven times eight?"

He was one of my former classmates in the Camiling primary school, in the one-story brick building still standing near the church in one corner of the Plaza.

Nineteen

THE glass pinnacle that is the United Nations in New York is the finger of hope pointing the way. It has its detractors and its flaws. But who can see the hopeful, interested faces of its visitors—often as many as nine thousand in a single day—who come from all over the world to it as to the shrine of hope and not believe it is worth-while?

I have mentioned intrigue in the United Nations. It is there. It is in every institution created by man. I saw it first in San Francisco and watched it operate while president of the General Assembly, and know that in the main it is used as an expedient that works toward the greater good.

Agreements in the organizations of world power are never reached on the floor. They are made in the delegates' lounges and corridors long before the voting begins. I had known the night before I was made president that the honor was mine.

But the decisions in the United Nations are not made in the corridors. They are made in Washington and Paris and Rome and Manila and Mexico City. The delegates act upon instructions given by their governments, after discussions with their superiors at home.

A delegate in that sense is like an ambassador. In Washington the ambassador can act without specific instructions on matters within the broad policy of his government by using his judgment. As I said in a speech before the American Public Relations Association at White Sulphur Springs when an award was presented to me (the first they have given in sixteen years) "for having successfully interpreted Filipino ideals to the American

304

people," a successful ambassador has to bring the bacon home without spilling the beans.

The same is true of a delegate to the United Nations. His government has instructed him how to vote, but to win support for that vote he must exercise his personality and his persuasive powers, his skill in bargaining and his powers for bargaining on his fellow delegates. So he is not a robot. He has studied the field and reported all to his government and offered his advice, and when the time for action comes he goes out into the lounges and corridors to see what his vote can bring in the open market.

When a country has a proposition to make and wants a resolution drafted the procedure follows certain unwritten rules. The delegation first gets the approval of its home government on the general idea to be sponsored. Once given the green light they discuss the problem between themselves, draft it, consider it from all sides, and get it into the shape in which they want it, knowing full well it will never be accepted in that form.

So, to allow for the trimming it is sure to get on its way through the millrace, they ask for more than they ever hope to receive. As in all parliaments, there must be give and take, and one never expects to get all that is asked for in the beginning. The seasoned chairman of a delegation pads the original resolution with nonessentials, hoping that once the bargaining is over and the trimming accomplished the stark outlines of the resolution are still there.

Then the delegation ponders the lists for like-minded delegates, who may be counted upon to support its resolution. They have to build world favor for it. They must woo and convince and win.

Actually the chairman consults no one except his government, his secretary of foreign affairs, and his president or head of state. The construction of the resolution is his and his delegation's.

The chairman goes among the delegates, handing out copies of his resolution and asking their support of it. They in turn sound out their delegations for approval or disapproval. A friendly delegate, after conferring with his group, may be able to assure the sponsoring chairman of his support, but it is not that easy. No delegation is going to support another's resolution without exacting its own pound of flesh in return.

The friendly delegation makes an x-ray study of the resolution. Is it in line with the national policy of their delegation's government? And if so, and they favor it, will the sponsoring delegation look kindly upon a project of theirs?

Or, the friendly delegation decides, this paragraph must be changed, this suggestion canceled.

So the resolution travels on and on through the various delegations, suffering criticism and sees change and substitutions and suggestions at every halting place, and when its gamut is run all that has been done to it must be approved by all the nations together. Only after this is done may the resolution make its appearance upon the floor.

And by that time the votes have been counted on the outside. Whether the resolution is out or in, we already know.

Where has this resolution been approved and passed? Over coffee or stronger drink in the comfortable delegates' lounge, over breakfast and lunch and dinner tables in restaurants and hotels.

You will see, in the comfortable upholstered chairs in the lounge of the United Nations, groups of three or four or a half-dozen people together, and you may know world issues are under discussion. Even in these subconferences he who calls them together must be careful, because, sad as it may seem in such a building, there are those who cannot be asked to sit down together. Even in the Asian group one cannot ask the Indian and Pakistani delegates together, or Pakistan and Afghanistan, or Israel and Saudi Arabia. If you want them to support your resolution they have to be spoken to separately.

But because each will sit down with other delegates and confer and because all are willing to gather behind these glass walls an uncertain peace has been maintained.

The weary chairman who has gone to each of the delegations and brought these groups together learns now how the voting will go. "If it does not go against our country's policies," or "we will consult our government," is the first stipulation always. And to the question, "How do you feel about this suggestion," there is usually a, "Well, perhaps an adjustment can be made." Then there is the payment exacted in, "And if we do vote on your side, we have a candidate coming up for such and such a position or for such and such a council, can we count on you?" So the delegates bargain and this is the balancing of power.

But the point is, this discussion is going on, not behind the boundary lines of individual countries, but here in this glass tower on the East River. Here men are grouped to settle differences which, settled one by one, leads to many an important understanding.

So the talk goes until the cups and glasses are empty and the exhausted chairman is content with a job well done.

No, it is not ideal. But it is the best plan we have worked out so far. Without personal contact there is no hope.

Beyond Russia, Red China is the country to be watched. I cannot forget a trip I made, just before war broke in the Pacific, from Rangoon to Chungking. For eleven days and ten nights I rode in a jalopy over the Burma Road, which is an incredible accomplishment literally scratched from the living rock by Chinese hands. Without trucks or bulldozers, nothing but the power of sheer numbers, the Chinese built the Burma Road. That is a sample of what those always swelling Red masses can do when they are harnessed for industrial purposes, or for war, under the lash of a dictator.

Russia is intelligent. It must know it is building a Frankenstein's monster in Red China.

Nothing indicates the future of the world more clearly than the evidence of these hungry, dangerous masses rising in the

Far East. Remember Japan reached its industrial height and struck. Germany reached its industrial height and struck. But these countries were limited in space and breeding capacity. Red China is limitless in both. No other country in the world has its potential for danger—or for good.

And next to China is India, with its seething masses of man power that may also be harnessed in the near future.

Remember, China will shortly have the nuclear bomb. We must keep in mind what has happened in Africa. We must review and remember all that has happened to the world within the past half-century in a turn from the stabilized old to the dangerous new.

In the United Nations I took the stand for the Philippines against Russia and, in turn, Red China. I was against its admission.

One argument hurled against me was, "But if Red China is admitted to the United Nations it may behave better."

To which I answered, "The United Nations is not a reformatory."

An overwhelming United Nations majority condemned Red China as an aggressor nation.

In writing the United Nations Charter we stated it to be an agreement among human beings, not among governments but the people of those governments, the peoples of the world, and the United Nations must be based upon an unassailable moral principle.

If we admit a nation recognized to be an aggressor nation, such as Red China, we are killing the faith of the people. We are killing the United Nations, if we admit a bandit nation to that group committed to peace.

Red China is still holding Tibet and North Korea in her bloody grasp.

I made many speeches against the apartheid policies of South Africa. The United Nations endorsed resolutions condemning

South Africa, but could only condemn, since it cannot interfere in a domestic matter.

Perhaps I am proudest of the fact that in 1949, as president of the General Assembly, I was the first to recommend the channeling of atomic power into the controlled uses of peace. Four years later President Eisenhower made that recommendation in a formal proposal.

The United Nations has grown in stature since we saw it born at San Francisco. I had hoped to see it attain universality and it has. In San Francisco there were fifty-one nations, now there are ninety-nine, and Dag Hammarskjöld has asked an architect to see how the assembly rooms can be enlarged for a possible one hundred or more member nations.

I had hoped the economic and social side would assume an importance that would equal the political. The work of the Economic and Social Council as well as of the Trusteeship Council have assured more and more the importance of the United Nations.

I had hoped it would be the conscience of the world and it is.

I had hoped it would help erase the racial barriers and it has.

The intangible, invisible power it wields, not seen by ordinary eyes, has given Asians and Africans the sense of belonging to the human family, where before they were the stepchildren of the world.

There would have been war in the Suez, in Indonesia, Iran, Greece, and Turkey were it not for the United Nations.

There would have been war in Laos.

Soviet Russia would have conquered Asia if the United Nations had not interfered. It has had a restraining influence on Moscow.

India and Pakistan would have fought over Kashmir.

Africa would have been in chaos if we did not have the United Nations and Dag Hammarskjöld.

If Adolph Hitler or Kaiser Wilhelm had known before their invasions of other Continental nations that their acts of aggression would stir into action forty-five armed nations banded together and prepared to fight—as notice was served against Russia when we met in 1948 in Paris regarding the Berlin crisis—two tyrants would have been stopped in their tracks. There would have been no World War I or World War II. There we were in Paris, nations of every race banded together and prepared to fight, and critics of the United Nations should remember that!

United Nations intervention saved Korea. If the Communists had won there all the Far Eastern world would now be in Red hands.

Among the intangible values of the United Nations are its great undertakings: the Children's Emergency Fund, the refugees' relief, as well as economic aid and the experts sent out to underprivileged areas.

If the world is going to evaluate what we believe to be the gradual evolvement toward world brotherhood the United Nations must be accepted as having done essential spade work for that future. That is why I am a firm believer in world brotherhood and why I am working with Lester B. Pearson, the Nobel Peace Prize laureate, and Dr. Everett Clinchy in the Council on World Tensions.

My mind dwells upon the kindness shown to me as president of the General Assembly by the world press. Honors poured in from all over the world; receptions were given me as an official guest of the heads of nations, and honorary degrees were awarded from universities in Asia, Europe, and America, starting with Harvard.

I shall always remember riding through New York, seated in an official car between President Harry S. Truman and Mayor William O'Dwyer. There was confetti and the affectionate cheering of American crowds in the streets and office windows, cheers for the President of the United States and the Mayor of its greatest city, and an occasional, "Hey, there's Romulo!" I remember saying to my two companions, "See, they see me in spite of my size."

And President Truman, in fine humor that day, saying to the Mayor, "Bill, you are mayor of the greatest city in the world, and I'm president of the greatest country in the world, but the General here, he's president of the entire world!"

When we came to where we were to lay the cornerstone of the United Nations building all the flags were flying. An impressive ceremony followed, and again President Truman gave me precedence, insisting I was president of the world.

I remembered our dead boys on Bataan on that day. I was those beloved dead and I was Asia. And I would never again feel twinges of regret that I had sacrificed my chance to be president of the Philippines.

When I was secretary of foreign affairs and still president of the General Assembly, in 1950, I laid the foundation of my policy of nationalism for the Philippines. It is important to underscore this now, because six years after I enunciated these principles Nationalism was brought forth in Manila as if it were something new, a policy that was being inaugurated for the first time. In my home province, Tarlac, before those close to me, because they have known me since childhood, I laid down the fundamentals of my program as secretary of foreign affairs. In this I stressed my faith in youth and in heroes.

In part, I urged:

Let us teach our people again to be proud that they are Filipinos. Let us teach them to realize anew that being a Filipino means having as rich and noble a heritage of language, culture, patriotism and heroic deeds as any nation on earth. Let us teach a steadfast faith in Divine Providence, a stable family institution, the unhampered enjoyment of civil liberties, the advantages of constitutional government, the potentialities of a rich and spacious land. A strengthened national spirit can provide the motive power to raise our people from the depths and . . . pour new life and vigor into the national system. . . .

We have suggested the enshrinement of the Filipino Unknown Soldier on whose tomb in Fort Santiago now burns the Eternal Flame as symbol of our devotion to the cause for which he died and as beaconlight for our people in any national crisis that may come.

But the reinvigoration of the national spirit must take place in the grass roots, in every city, town and *barrio* in the Philippines, and it must start among our own people. . . .

Let the school teacher in the *barrio*, the principal teacher in the town, and the division superintendent of schools in the city or province assume the leadership in the campaign of nationalism by organizing appropriate programs honoring our heroes and asking the youth organizations to take full charge. Let us organize community assemblies . . . and let these assemblies share responsibility with the government officials for the maintenance of peace and order in the locality and for such other worth-while civic purposes as the food production campaign.

I repeat that we must bestir ourselves—in work and production, yes, but no less actively in mind and will. . . .

You might wonder that I who have served you in the field of diplomacy should set so much store by the power of nationalism. This is because I know from personal experience that in order to become an effective internationalist, one must first strive to be a good nationalist. To be a worthy citizen of the world one must first prove himself to be a good Filipino.

I return to Washington and my small grandsons greet me: "We have been good boys, Lolo."

"And what does that mean?" I ask.

"That means you will bring us toys when you come home."

The same theory applies to the international scene. The time has come when all the children of the world must be good children or the results will be too terrible to contemplate.

The world has changed since I was born. One nation can no longer afford to subjugate another. One race dare not look down upon another. Economics and mutual safety have built laws where the precepts of decency have failed. We have learned that we must show courtesy, that we must share.

"A cup of water to drink in my name . . ." Jesus laid down the principle of human survival two thousand years ago. If only we had listened then!

Twenty

TIME does not move rapidly and life is not short. My fifties were crammed with activity and honors, but it seems to me, looking back, they extended over half my lifetime. I was well and active, still cat napped as I had all my life, and only on occasion felt all energy vanish. But interest, never. At heart I was and am still the eager boy reporter, interested in all that moves on the face of the earth.

"Don't you ever get tired of people?" someone asked me.

And I answered with vehemence, "Never! They are my stock in trade." I love and have faith in them but do not always understand them.

As for politics—they are people.

Politics was a real shock to me, but a gradual one. I had been introduced to the inside workings by Quezon. The most shocking revelation came in 1953, when I returned to Manila and found myself a candidate for the presidency. I learned then the meaning of the smiling face and the knife in the back.

Again the sacrifice—I yielded the race in favor of Magsaysay and became his national campaign manager. He won and I decided once more that I could best serve my country on an international scale.

Then I was back in Washington as a peso-a-year special envoy of Magsaysay's. I had wished to resume normal life and remain in Manila. There were several offers from firms there that tempted me. Powerful interests in Manila asked me to remain. Magsaysay knew this and begged me not to give up, not to desert him, as he expressed it.

If I had thought only of myself and my future I would have refused my reappointment as ambassador and returned to the Philippines. But again, no one knew better than I that the Philippines was facing crucial years, and the relationship between my country and America was all-important.

I returned to Manila to resign as President Magsaysay's personal and Special Envoy to the United States. My wife and I had agreed that after resigning I would return to Washington with her during the winter, fulfill some commitments that I had made to write articles and a book, and then travel in Europe for three months.

But Magsaysay would not hear of my leaving the government. Early one morning he came to "Kasiyahan" unannounced. We discussed Philippine-American relations and his fears about the future of our country. He felt that what he called "some wise men" were misleading the people and whipping up resentment against the United States. He foresaw how such "wise men" could, by their actions, misrepresent the true feelings of the Filipinos and be misunderstood in Washington.

"We cannot allow this to happen, General," he said with feeling. "You must continue as our ambassador. The Americans believe in you. Our people have faith in you. I need you in Washington."

Magsaysay was a bundle of nerves. He could not remain seated for long. He stood up and pulled some folded sheets from his hip pocket. (He was wearing the Barong Tagalog, the Filipino national costume, which is an embroidered shirt without pockets, made of pineapple fiber and worn with the tail out.)

"General, I have your appointment as Philippine Ambassador to the United States." He placed the sheets of paper on the breakfast table in front of me. "And your oath of office. I am administering your oath right now."

I became ambassador to Washington for the second time.

The day before my departure for the United States a military review was held at Camp Murphy in my honor. After the review President Magsaysay conferred on me the Golden Heart, the presidential decoration that he had originated. He was awarding it for the first time to a public official.

The Philippine Trade Act had to be extended. It was to expire on December 31, 1955, according to its provisions. The Philippine government wanted some corrections made, to rectify the inequalities, to change some of the onerous provisions. A panel was to be sent to Washington from the Philippines to discuss with an American committee the changes that the Philippines wanted. In order to be able to negotiate such changes the act had to be extended for one year, and for this, congressional action was necessary. President Magsaysay entrusted this job to me. Against many obstacles I succeeded in getting the extension.

The Filipino and American negotiators then went to work. The Philippine mission, headed by Dr. José P. Laurel, succeeded in having some of the injustices in the trade act corrected. The American group had James Langley, a New Hampshire publisher, as its chairman. The new measure was called the Philippine Trade Agreement (see appendix). Congressional action was again necessary to have it enacted into law.

My ambassadorship went on under President Garcia. He and Magsaysay were both good men, and good friends of the United States. It has been my honor to work with the Philippines' six presidents in turn, and from Quezon to Garcia each has had some special contribution to make to our country.

A man dreams all his life and is fortunate if a handful of what he has dreamed comes true. I have seen these of my innermost dreams come into being: first the Southeast Asia Conference in Baguio in 1950, then SEATO, Bandung, and the Pacific Charter.

When in 1950 I tried to organize the Southeast Asia Conference I went from door to door in Washington and was cold-shouldered everywhere. The State Department would have nothing to do with my suggestion. Then in 1954 John Foster Dulles decided to organize a somewhat similar group and asked the American Embassy in Manila to secure information on Magsaysay's views. Magsaysay referred Dulles to me. I had had a plan and a charter for such an organization drawn up since my escape from Bataan. I could not resist saying: "Mr. Secretary, can't you see this has come full cycle? Four years ago, in your role here as the special adviser of Secretary Acheson, I begged you to help organize such a conference and you gave me the cold shoulder. Now you are asking me what I asked you then. If you had agreed with me then much that has happened since might have been prevented."

He said, "Don't rub it in."

Now warships of the member nations of SEATO patrol the Pacific, representing the united power of the United States, Britain, Australia, New Zealand, France, Thailand, Pakistan, and the Philippines.

Then came Bandung. I have written a book on Bandung but I did not tell there of the political maneuvering that went on in advance of that historic conference. Suffice it to say that I was on the ground early, and by rallying forces and laying plans was able to cut the earth from under the feet of my Red enemies as they advanced. The wiles learned in many international conferences paid off at Bandung, and never to better advantage.

The value of Bandung? Let Americans ponder these statistics: There are 9.5 Africans and Asians to 1 North American, or 1.19 Africans to 1 North American and 8 Asians to 1 North American. If these preponderant masses rise, the earth will tremble.

In Africa and Asia today is the spirit of revolution. During my lifetime the dark curve has moved upward. It is inevitable, the sharing of the light. Youth is on the march in every land, and in the fever of their advance they want to tear down that they may build anew, but often the good dies in the destruction. It is a cliché that the shrinking of our world will enable us to understand one another better. This is not always true. Close neighbors do not always make for better understanding. Families harbor resentments. As the countries are brought closer we must take extra pains to be understood and to erase the tensions that lead to misunderstanding.

Our world is constantly in change and the great change is always toward freedom. When we speak of freedom we speak of equality. Nations will rise and fall but equality remains the ideal.

I am a molecule adrift in a mighty ocean, but I see in my life the molecule struggling for its full place. I have seen my struggle duplicated a billionfold, not only in the Philippines, but in Asia and Africa, yes, and even here in America. The universal aim is to achieve respect for the entire human race, not for the dominant few.

Our fight in the Philippines to gain special recognition in the military bases is more important to us than military aid. This is a serious charge I have made and it shocks Americans. They need shocking—many of them. *The Ugly American* has not been read by millions of Asia's unlettered peoples, but they know the term. The colonel's lady has been jolted out of her important base in many an alien land within the past ten years, and it is up to her to remember that she is that country's guest, not its empress.

I have wonderful, wonderful friends in the United States, which has been my refuge in war and my second home. Honors and attention and affection have been heaped upon me. I know this is neither because I am a Filipino nor despite the fact that I am a Filipino, but because I came here at the peak of war wearing on my lapel the four-star insignia of a MacArthur aide. I was not a person in my own right. I was the living emblem of Bataan.

America gave our world the traditions by which it lives.

Valley Forge, Lexington, Bunker Hill—who in America speaks
of these today? But in the depressed areas of the world the
names of America's great are remembered with honor.

Ten years ago America was the most respected and loved
country in the world. Today it is the lightning rod that attracts
ire, envy, jealousy, criticism. Once it was an international pas-
time to blame England for all wrongs, to "twist the lion's tail."
Now the game is to yank the eagle's feathers, and as we all
know, the American eagle is bald.

Still the American belief in fair play and justice for all has
been established and remains the working creed for the future
world.

I have been given much of the kindness of America and of
most of the world. It opened its full heart when word reached
us of the death of our oldest son, Carlos, Jr.

A painting of Mike—this was Carlos' name during the war—
hangs on our embassy wall in Washington. It pictures a young
man with the face of a boy.

Carlos Llamas Romulo, Junior, died on October 11, 1957, in
a plane crash on Luzon. No life can be lived without tragedy or
without regret. Whenever I look on that dignified young face
I feel the deepest grief which is based upon regret. Mike's life
was short, but he had undergone much other boys never know.
As a schoolboy he had been trapped by war and trained to hate
and hunt and kill. Then there was peace and a few years of
school in Manila. I was in Washington. He came to Washington
to complete his education; I was with the United Nations in
New York, London, Geneva, Rome, New Delhi, flying to and
fro between Manila and New York.

I wrote to a friend: "Four months in Paris, four days in Washington, and now off to New Delhi!"

That tells the tragic story. Four months against four days
with my growing sons. What time did I have for them? How
much did I know of this boy I so deeply loved? I saw so little
of him. Always I was looking forward to the day when there

would be time to relax together and enjoy one another. Then Mike was grown, he was married to Mariles, he was the father of two darling little boys who are with us now. And still I kept looking forward to the day I could drop the burdens of the world and share life with Mike and Greg and Dick and Bobby.

Four days before the crash I had a letter from him. "Don't you think it's time you rest, leave public life, take time to know and enjoy your grandchildren—and us?"

I give time to those grandchildren now, his sons. No words ever hurt as deeply as those, the last he wrote me.

He was just beginning to enjoy life.

If I had any doubt that what little I have been doing for my people is appreciated by them such doubt was dispelled the morning my wife and I arrived in Manila to attend our son's funeral. Our plane landed at 5:45 in the morning and at that dreary hour I was surprised, as our plane taxied on the runway, to be met by a huge crowd, a crowd larger than that which welcomed me as president of the United Nations several years before. It was a silent crowd and I am sure they knew I could not recognize them individually, but they took the trouble to come to the terminal before sunrise to show me and my wife that they were with us in our darkest hour.

Messages of love and sympathy poured in from every province of the Philippines and from all over the world. I have always found letters of condolence difficult to write. I know now how much more difficult they are to read.

I was sixty on my last birthday and the 1960's are also on their way. I think the world and I feel the same about this milepost, that we are just on the verge of an exciting new beginning. Because it will be either that or inundation.

That birthday was the first celebrated in our "Kasiyahan" home in Manila, which we built ten years before. That year we had also spent our first Christmas there, and celebrated the marriage of our third son, Dick, to Tessie Romero, a charming girl educated in London. Several years before Greg had married a lovable young lady, Chloe Cruz, of Bacolod, Negros Occidental. They have two children, Virginia Caridad and Rodrigo Luis. Now only Bobby, our youngest, remains unmarried.

Flying with my wife and our winsome daughter-in-law Mariles, Mike's widow, across the Pacific, I brought Mike's two little sons, Carlitos and Miguel Antonio to this family reunion. As a baby sitter I have shown what I believe to be rare talents, but I have crossed the Pacific many times and never had such a strenuous trip. There were moments I thought I was more than sixty.

But most of the time, when I think at all about the subject, it is with a breathless sense of starting again. Life has never seemed more of an adventure.

I have no thought of retiring. I may leave public service soon, but I will continue working. There is too much to be done. The world and its inhabitants are far too interesting to think of leaving them, and every day starts out anew with its measure of eagerness and youth. Every morning I awaken as a young man.

There are indications that this is a matter of the morning only. I no longer care about dancing the night hours through, and a walk is far more satisfactory than a game of ping-pong. And it has come to my mind several times that I should have two pairs of reading glasses. My one pair is always upstairs or down or at any rate away from the place I am and wish them to be.

"Lolo, you are always losing your glasses," my grandson Carlitos said the other day. "Are you getting to be a very old man?"

I assured him indignantly that I was not.

Recently I was asked to participate in a radio panel with Senator Clinton Anderson and seven others for a national broadcast originating from Madison Square Garden.

I left the Waldorf with my timed-to-the-split-second script

in hand, found myself before the mike with my time coming up, and reached into my pocket for my reading glasses. They were not there! I squinted at the typed page and was helpless. Here, I thought, is a time for any powers of concentration I have to come to my aid, and somehow I carried out the gist of the speech and wound up on the dot.

This made me realize that no man is immortal. But there are satisfactions that have come with my years. I have had the pleasure of seeing each of my sons grow into manhood and find a place in the world where he can develop and be content.

It has also been my privilege to help train a group of young men and start them along their way. As Resident Commissioner I had two able assistants, José Imperial and Manuel Adeva. One is now our ambassador to Australia and the other our ambassador to Japan.

My chief adviser in the United Nations was Salvador P. Lopez, now ambassador to France; there was never a more competent counselor or a more loyal friend. José D. Ingles, ambassador to Germany, and Mauro Mendez, now minister to France, will always be remembered with gratitude. In Washington my executive assistant was Leonides S. Virata, and my undersecretary in Manila was Felino Neri. Both are now business tycoons in the Philippines, and more will be heard from them in the future.

Lopez I selected from the classroom at the University of the Philippines, where I first taught English. He was bright, studious, and a good writer, and I saw in him possibilities of development. Mendez was our class poet in the Manila High School, a brilliant writer, who was one of my city editors on the *Tribune* and an editor of the *Herald*. I never had a more devoted friend.

And there were others I picked up along the way. Narciso C. Reyes, whom I brought from Manila, is now our minister to Burma. Juan C. Dionisio, our consul general in Honolulu, I plucked from Stockton, California, where he was a free-lance writer. Filemon Rodriguez, my assistant on the Far Eastern

Commission, had been chairman of our National Economic Council and one of our leading business executives.

I had no special method of selection. The potential for development was in them all, but beyond that the quality of loyalty.

Now when I travel, the young men I helped train and encourage welcome me all over the world. They are still my boys.

I see them, and lads like them, entering the Army and Navy Club in Manila and the Baguio Country Club, freely entering as is their right, and I wonder if they can possibly understand how long and how hard we fought to get them there.

What have we gained—we Filipinos—in the past sixty years? Today we have a sense of country. We were an unknown people before the war in the Pacific. Now we are known.

American history has been for so long taken for granted that American children are often ignorant of it. The Filipino is not blasé. The wonder of what has happened to us is still upon us.

We have had many problems. Recovery has been slow. There has been corruption and communism to fight, and we fought it. The Filipino has always fought corruption—Spanish, American, and his own.

Our government is now stable. We are on the rise economically. But we must have time.

From the very beginning Quezon warned us there would be disadvantages to freedom. We have found this to be true. Gradually the difficulties are being surmounted.

We thought Quezon's death would bring havoc to our country. We feared freedom would die with him. This has not happened.

We feared havoc when Magsaysay died. The country carried on.

The suspicions of sixty years ago have perished. It is not suspicion and distrust the Filipino feels now, although these have been handed him in large doses from Moscow. He does not take to their bitter medicine. He is resentful of the American largess poured on Japan; still the Filipinos showed their trust in

America in the reception given to Eisenhower. That display showed the true emotion in Filipino hearts.

We are certainly not anti-American in the Philippines, but we do feel the relationship between the two countries needs updating. We are no longer the little brown brothers of America. We are America's friends, sovereign equals.

The underlying passion of all men is for freedom. We can only move forward as sharers in this great enterprise of civilization. The century is half-gone. The battle for freedom is half-won.

Evolution is always moving toward equality. Each time a country signs a treaty with another it whittles away some of its national sovereignty. Gradually matters of domestic concern take on international importance, as these barriers fall.

There are spots of evil on our world. There are hideous incidents and beings that are human cancers. But in the main our world is made up of people of potential good will, willing, if the path before them is outlined, to become sharers of the light. Sometimes a glimmer of understanding can show the way.

During this first Christmas season spent in Manila I was driven home from an evening party by our family driver, who lives in "Kasiyahan" with my married sons. Like all Filipino help he is respectful and dignified. The grandchildren call him "Gigi," a name we have all adopted.

On this night, as I was leaving the car, he stopped me. "Sir, may I ask you a question? You know we drivers talk while we are waiting for our employers at parties. Tonight we talked of you. We know you are a good friend to America. Tell me, is it true that Americans are so bad that for $1.95 they will execute a man because he is a Negro?"

"Where did you hear such a thing?" I demanded.

"It is common talk among us drivers."

By this time I had recognized the source of the story: the Negro in the South who stole $1.95 from a woman and was sentenced to be executed. The Communists had made a great copy of this throughout Asia, distorting the facts in a way calculated to inflame all races of color. It had seeped through the masses.

I told him, "It isn't true. The man was found guilty and sentenced to die, but the sentence was never carried out."

He persisted. The propaganda had sunk deep. "It is true colored people are insulted everywhere in America?"

"What do you mean, insulted?"

"Not treated like human beings."

"That is not true. When I first went to Washington as a student, Negroes were not admitted to theaters or restaurants. Now they go everywhere."

Then I said, "You must try to understand. You did not attend the party I attended tonight, did you? You were not invited?"

"No, I waited outside for you."

"Were you insulted at not being asked inside?"

He saw the light. But he said again, "But why are they against colored people in America?"

"They are also against whites," I told him, and tried to explain the cancer spots of hatred—religion against religion, strata against strata—that exist even in America. I did not tell him of the time I had shared a suite with a Jewish friend at a fashionable mountain resort in New York and was told by the assistant manager, out of hearing of my guest, that my guest would be obliged to have his meals in our suite since the hotel was "restricted."

"Cancel my reservation," I ordered, and the hotel man, who knew the important personage I was to meet in his hotel, hastily rescinded his ban and gave my Jewish friend the freedom of the place.

It is difficult to explain such incidents to an uneducated man of Asia. The hotel incident took place ten years ago in New

York State. It could not happen there today. The world advances in humanism, retreats, and goes forward again.

We inch forward like worms dragging in the dust. But the spark is within us all. I have seen it everywhere in our world and I have seen its recognition increase. The worth of the human soul is undergoing a new evaluation, and not by color or creed. Within my sixty years the debasement of humanity and its triumph has been demonstrated. I have known heroes old and young, I have seen them live and die. I know more are in the process of growing, and their young, brave faces are lifted in hope. When the world looks dark we must remember them, for we have need of them always, and by their lives they make the rest of our human race worth-while.

My personal life continues under the storm and stress of life on Capitol Hill. As ambassador my duties press as heavily as ever, and as intermittent chairman of the Philippine delegation and former president of the United Nations I keep in close contact with that institution and find myself summoned into action in key moments, such as during the crisis in the Middle East. Otherwise Washington encompasses most of my days.

The proudest moment of my entire life was not when I was elected to the presidency of the United Nations. It came ten years later, in 1959, when the Freedoms Foundation of America in Valley Forge, through its Board of Judges, chose me for the special Freedom Leadership Award heretofore presented only to heads of state. This was the acme of all I had fought for my life long.

The Norwegian Nobel Peace Prize is for those who labor for peace. This American award is for those who have fought for freedom.

My election as president of the United Nations was the culmination of my diplomatic career and my fight for world peace.

The winning of the award in Valley Forge marked my rec-

ognition as a man from the Philippines, who had fought for
freedom both in war and in peace.

After a long day's work at the office, the steady rush of meeting people and discussing Philippine-American problems and
world issues, I take little interest in the cocktail parties and teas
which end the days in Washington. If I can possibly delegate
my wife to such missions I ask her to attend them alone. Society is an important part of a diplomat's life. Mrs. Herbert
May, Mrs. Perle Mesta, Mrs. Gwen Cafritz, Mrs. Polly Gug-
genheim entertain their friends, and we enjoy being invited. But
one has to be selective and it is impossible to attend all the parties
given daily along the "cocktail route."

My ideal evening is to come home and know I need not
leave the house again until morning. These nights I cherish.

I play with my grandchildren and tell them a few bedtime
stories. My literary career has never encompassed fairy tales,
but now I find myself an expert in them, as every evening the
story must be new and any effort to ring in a before-used tale
is met with indignant cries of, "You told us that one!"

So I indulge in legends both scary and moral, with local
settings such as Sheridan Circle, where we live, and which point
up the advantages of eating all one's cereal or not quarreling
with one's brother.

After the children are asleep and the house is quiet, with
Virginia perhaps out doing the social rounds for us both, I
relax in pajamas in my room and read through the morning
papers which I only found time to skim before. I read the New
York *Times* and *Herald Tribune*, the Washington *Post* and
Evening Star, and the magazines I like, such as *Newsweek*,
Saturday Review, *Foreign Affairs*, *Fortune*, *The Atlantic*, and
Harper's. Then I read a chapter or so of the current book of the
month and perhaps a few pages of heavier material, such as my
present interest, J. B. Priestley's *Literature and Western Man*.

Perhaps I dictate a few letters or notes or outline a speech or article to the dictaphone machine by my pillow.

Then, these intellectual pursuits attended to, I relax over my secret vice, a good mystery, until I am half-asleep.

I dream of the future at such times, always of going home to the Philippines, seeing my sons' families grow up around me in our "Kasiyahan," and giving what I can to the younger generation of my country of the undying dream of freedom.

There are more immediate pleasures to look forward to in the inevitable pressures of the day. Luncheon at one of the Washington clubs, the Metropolitan, Cosmos, or Army and Navy, where I will meet with Washington in action and catch up with the news of the hour.

There are trips to delight in; among them is my favorite, a visit to the Bohemian Grove in California where one rests under the giant redwoods, sans telephone or troubles, surrounded by old friends.

There is always promise of the interesting tomorrow.

A car stops at our door and Virginia is home; the day is over. The personal world of home closes around us.

All in all, it is a good life we are living, in a good world filled with good friends.

Appendix

BECAUSE it shows the work that had to be done and the uphill fight that was waged to get the agreement passed by both Houses of Congress, and it is typical of the laborious effort exerted behind the scenes whenever any Philippine legislation has to go through Congress, I reproduce below the news dispatch reporting the passage of the Philippine Trade Agreement, as written by Herb Gordon, chief of the Far Eastern bureau of the International News Service, and datelined from Washington, published by the newspapers in 1955.

"General Romulo did it again!"

That is what Majority Floor Leader John W. McCormack said when informed that the U.S. Senate had passed the Philippine trade agreement bill. It was approved by the U.S. House two weeks before and on the floor Congressman McCormack paid tribute to the work of President Magsaysay's personal and special envoy in the Bandung conference in April and in San Francisco last month.

To all those who like your correspondent know the uphill fight that the trade agreement had to surmount, the Massachusetts congressman was saying nothing new. For it was Carlos P. Romulo who called all the shots, who told us correspondents what would happen next, who correctly predicted when the committee on ways and means would call a hearing, how many votes would be in favor and how many against, when a rule could be obtained from the rules committee, when it would be programmed by the house leadership, what would happen on the floor.

And Romulo knew all this because he was in the thick of the fight and was moving in Capitol Hill with the same deliberation and the same thoroughness that he used when single-handedly last year he fought for and succeeded in getting the extension of the trade act with all odds against him.

This year he had to surmount many obstacles. In the first place the agreement was negotiated by the Republican administration and the chairman of the American panel is a Republican. With a Democratic majority in both houses there was already one strike against the bill. The first decision to be made was crucial. Should it be an administration bill, a "must" bill with White House imprimatur, or just one of the hundreds of other bills?

When the first public hearing was called, the antagonism of the committee members against the bill was evident. Not only the Democrats but also the Republicans joined in a severe cross-examination of the witnesses for the bill. After the hearing the congressmen were outspoken in their condemnation of the proposed measure. Congressman Wilbur Mills of Arkansas, one of the most highly respected in the House who many believe is being groomed for the Speakership, said to the reporters that he was not satisfied with the explanation given in the hearing, and that he was not speaking only for himself.

Romulo conferred with Congressman Mills not once but several times. He buttonholed every "doubtful" committee member one by one to give him the necessary information or to furnish the needed rebuttal.

Then came the opposition of the U.S. tobacco interests. When the Philippine panel was in Washington, Romulo arranged a luncheon at which he invited the representatives of the tobacco interests and Senator Puyat and other Filipino leaders. Their differences were ironed out. But when the panel returned to Manila, the Philippine Congress enacted into law Act 698 which aroused the ire of the U.S. tobacco interests. And the opposition of the tobacco lobby cannot be underestimated. Out of 15 chairmanships in the House, the South has 11. The chairman of the Ways and Means Committee comes from the South. That was strike two against the bill.

Romulo held a series of conferences with the leaders of the tobacco industry. He conferred with the Southern congressmen. When he thought he had placated them, came Senator Puyat's speech on the floor of the Senate showing that the trade agreement was all in favor of the Philippines. This was just what the tobacco interests were looking for to bolster their case. They had it inserted in full in the Congressional Record with the statement that in the trade agreement "the Filipinos got all the marbles." Then Senator Puyat made another speech: The Filipinos should trade with Red China. Four members of the committee asked: "Are the Filipinos now threatening the U.S. Congress?"

The outlook was very dark. The varnish and paint interests took umbrage at certain restrictions placed on their products in the Philippines. The agricultural commodities interests were alarmed by a new act creating a new government corporation. Philippine sugar interests stirred a hornet's nest when they made representations to get a share of domestic sugar. A hullabaloo was raised in Manila on supposed purchase of surplus tobacco and charges were made that the U.S. tobacco interests demanded this as price for withdrawal of their opposition to the trade bill. The tobacco leaders resented the insinuations because there was "absolutely no truth in them."

Romulo kept on working. Each congressman and senator got an autographed copy of his book, "Crusade in Asia" in which Magsaysay's successful fight against communism is described in detail. The majority floor leader and the minority floor leader inserted in the Record Romulo's interventions in Bandung and spoke on the floor about his work there. He continued his man to man canvas in the House. He was in constant touch with James Langley, the chairman of the American panel and worked closely with him. Langley must also be given credit for his testimony in the executive session of the committee and his heart-to-heart talks with some committee members.

The bill was reported out by the committee. The vote was exactly as predicted by Romulo two weeks before. After a rule had been obtained and the bill programmed by the floor leadership, when the bill was to be taken up on the floor, a number of congressmen from tobacco districts wanted to make statements on the floor to answer charges made in Manila to the effect that the purchase of U.S. surplus tobacco was demanded by U.S. tobacco interests. Such statements would have started an uproar. Romulo again went to work, held a luncheon conference with them in the House cafeteria and succeeded in preventing them from making their statements.

When Romulo thought there would be no trouble in the Senate, Majority Floor Leader Johnson with whom he had discussed the bill several times, was suddenly taken ill. The man to take Johnson's place is the senator from Kentucky, Earl Clements, a tobacco producer. More work. More convincing to do. Congress was on the home stretch. The legislative mill was jammed. Important "must" legislation had to be given priority. Romulo parked himself on Capitol Hill.

Whoever doubts that it was Romulo who "did it again" should read the Congressional Record reporting the discussion of the trade act in both houses. The speeches on the floor echo Congressman McCormack's statement.

Index

Index

335

Index